CW00971762

FLIGHT FOR FREEDOM

A. J. de Nahlik

*To an enthusiast
from an enthusiast*

Andew de Nahlik

MINERVA PRESS

ATLANTA LONDON SYDNEY

FLIGHT FOR FREEDOM
Copyright © A. J. de Nahlik 1999

All Rights Reserved

No part of this book may be reproduced in any form
by photocopying or by any electronic or mechanical means,
including information storage or retrieval systems,
without permission in writing from both the copyright
owner and the publisher of this book.

ISBN 0 75410 780 9

First Published 1999 by
MINERVA PRESS
315–317 Regent Street
London W1R 7YB

Printed in Great Britain for Minerva Press

FLIGHT FOR FREEDOM

By the Same Author

Wild Deer, Faber and Faber, 1958
Deer Management, David and Charles, 1974
Wild Deer Expanded and Revised, Ashford Press, 1988
Management of Deer and Their Habitat, Wilson Hunt, 1992

This book is dedicated to my wife Anne who not only spent hours correcting this and other books before adding an artistic touch to them, but who for fifty-five years put up with my (Polish?) idiosyncrasies. I owe her a debt of gratitude which I can never repay.

I would also like to thank Nick Shreeve Esq. who has worked hard to improve the quality of the first draft of this book.

The last but not least is my gratitude to Mrs Elizabeth Grant, our son's mother-in-law, family friend and an English scholar, for stepping in with help by reading, correcting the final edit, and suggesting valuable improvements after I suffered a stroke and was not able to continue.

Acknowledgements

I have three heroes in my life to whom I have to pay tribute in this work. It is impossible to place them in order of precedence so I will handle them chronologically.

The first was Charles Lindbergh, whose flight across the Atlantic in the days of my boyhood fired my imagination and enthusiasm to be a flyer, an enthusiasm which over the years had become an addiction.

The second was D.F. Chipping, at the time I knew him, flying officer, DFM, Battle of Britain Hurricane pilot. He was my RAF flying instructor at Montrose. He complemented my enthusiasm for flying with the flying skill which he taught me. Not only did he give me the skill, but it was through him that I gained my RAF and Polish Air Force pilots wings with an assessment of Exceptional, the assessment which figured in my pilot's logbook several times during my flying career, but which did not make up for my defective vision which limited my flying at a later date.

The third Air Vice Marshal 'Johnny' J.E. Johnson, CB CBE DSO DFC, the flying legend among the fighter pilots of the Royal Air Force. From his early wartime days he was the image of what I would aim for; alas my defective vision proved an insurmountable obstacle.

I was privileged to serve under his command when he commanded Middle East Air Force and I was stationed at RAF Eastleigh (Nairobi). He visited Eastleigh on occasions and joined me on a few safaris. During one of these, I had one of the greatest thrills of my life. We were joined by the hero of my boyhood days, Charles Lindbergh. We sat round the campfire that evening – there was I, in the company of two of my heroes, chatting about flying when, in the clear starlit sky, Lindbergh spotted an American satellite – 'our eyes and our future,' he said.

★

Johnny has very kindly agreed to write the introductory note to this book. I am most grateful to him for this privilege.

November 1998

Foreword
by
Air Vice-Marshal J.E. Johnson CB, CBE, DSO, DFC

In 1963 I was appointed Air Officer Commanding, Air Force Middle East and this large parish stretched from Kenya, in East Africa, to Aden on the Red Sea and included the then High Commission Territories of Basutoland, Bechuanaland and Swaziland in southern Africa. There would, I reflected, be ample opportunities for big game expeditions and soon after I arrived in Aden I flew to Nairobi to inspect the squadrons based there and to make discreet inquiries about my first safari. Thus I was introduced to Squadron Leader Andrew de Nahlik who apart from his RAF duties was an Honorary Game Warden of East Africa and so it was arranged that we should make our first safari to the great mountain of Kilimanjaro, where an old friend and old fighting comrade Group Captain 'Dutch' Hugo DSO DFC grew his coffee and sisal at about 7,000 feet.

On another occasion we established our camp on the Amboseli Plain and Denis Zaphiro, the District Game Warden said that a distinguished American would be joining our party and would share my tent. The following morning the camp boy brought our tea and a tall, lean American sat up, shook my hand and said, 'Good morning, I'm Charles Lindbergh! My friends call me "Slim".'

This book, however, is not about our adventures in East Africa, but about Andrew's escape from Poland after the

German invasion in 1939. It is an odyssey of courage, fortitude and resolution of how he and other good men made their way across Europe to England where Polish fighter pilots in the Battle of Britain made up one-fifth of our numbers and without whom we would have been sorely pressed indeed.

21st October, 1998

Contents

Part Two

England and Onwards

List of Illustrations and Photographs

Preliminary pages:

Map of the Polish State
Map of Western France

Part One photo section:

My parents' wedding
Myself, a day or two after my birth, with parents
Father supervising in the field
Family in the country
Cousin Mary, Christine, *Fräulein* Friede
My father and his brother on the steps at the rear of the house
The family
The front of our house in southern Poland
Slawsko
Worochta

Part Two photo section

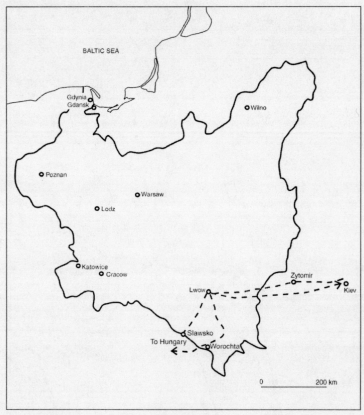

Poland 1939. Reconnaissance route to Slawsko, deportation to and escape from Kiev, and final escape from Poland are shown with a dotted line.

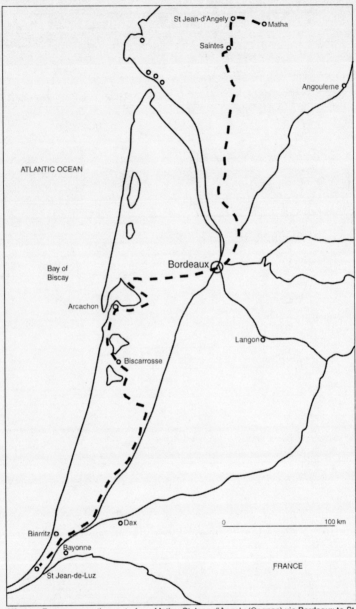

Western France evacuation route from Matha, St Jean d'Angely (Cognac) via Bordeaux to St Jean-de-Luz and Biarritz on the Atlantic coast.

Introduction

Poles in uniform have not been strangers in Western Europe. Polish Lancers who served under Napoleon are justly famous. At the end of World War I, the great Polish patriot General Josef Haller raised invaluable units of Polish Army in France and brought them to Poland in 1919 to back Pilsudski's effort to sustain the newly gained independence.

Twenty-odd years later, a new Polish Army and units of the Polish Air Force were being formed and reformed in France, and the Navy made for the British ports this time under the leadership of General Sikorski, to serve with the Allies against the Hitlerite Germany. The recruits flooded in to serve under his banner after the collapse of Poland in the tragic Polish War of September 1939. They came mainly from the Polish Forces who had been evacuated to Romania. They came from Polish families living abroad, and many were servicemen and civilians who escaped from occupied Poland, often under hazardous conditions and by various routes, specifically to enlist. That is how I found myself in France at the age of twenty.

This book grew out of recounting episodes of my life to my English wife, then to my sons, their children and sometimes to friends and acquaintances, in response to understandable questions such as: 'How did you get to England?' or 'What was your life like in the old Poland?' The incidents, told and retold over the decades, have grown, the edges of recall have become blurred and distorted, facts and people have become idealised and fantasised and indeed some dramatic licence has crept in, some purposely, some unwittingly.

Most of the individuals in the book existed, their Christian names are, as far as I recall, the actual ones but in a few cases they have been changed; most surnames have been changed; some because I could not recall the real ones, others because the people concerned or their children, could still be alive, and I should have needed their permission to write about them – an impossible task if one has no idea where in the world to look for them. The same applies to some locations in the 1939 Russia, by now in the Ukraine where an indication of a person's occupation and name linked with the location might lead to the identification of the individual which even now could prove risky.

Since Gorbachov's *glasnost* and *perestroika*, which emerged unexpectedly like a meteor, the demolition of the Berlin Wall and all that followed, brought about remarkable changes in the countries of Europe. Observations suggest however, that the life in parts of Eastern Europe tends to remain overshadowed by a fear and suspicion of years under the watchful omnipresence of the various security services. These feelings have become paranoiac, and will take a long time to abate; even longer to be erased from minds and personalities of the people affected. Until that day comes, prudence is called for however ridiculous it may seem today. Caution has saved many, indiscretion has condemned more. I do not want any bad feelings, even less, lives weighing unnecessarily on my conscience.

A.J. de Nahlik
August/September 1998

Part One

My Fatherland – Poland

I was brought up to believe that there was no such thing as a good Ukrainian. At school, when I became friendly with one, my family were aghast. The reasons for this were part of the then recent past. Certain other aspects of Polish history are little known in the West.

Antipathy towards the Ukrainians and the reasons for this, were a vital ingredient in my upbringing and education, formal and informal. This background needs to be understood if my experiences are also to be fully appreciated.

*

Up to the seventeenth century, Poland was a major central European power, whose borders stretched from the Baltic almost to the Black Sea, and from Berlin to Moscow and Kiev. The famous Jan Sobieski, elected King of Poland, defeated the apparently unstoppable Turks, first in Poland and then before the walls of Vienna, thereby saving Western civilisation from subjection to Islam.

One hundred years or so later, when Catherine the Great ruled over Russia, Poland had declined in importance and power and, in spite of desperate last-minute political and military resistance, she was overwhelmed and partitioned between Prussia, Russia, and the Habsburg (Austro-Hungarian) Empire.

Imperial Russia occupied central and north eastern Poland, ruling by repression. Dissidents and political activists were beaten, imprisoned and consigned to servitude in Siberia if not shot or hanged. The Russians' dislike of the Poles went much deeper than mere neighbourly contention. Poland was, as it still is, Roman Catholic, with cultural links to Rome and the West. Russia received her Christianity from Byzantium and with it, the Cyrillic alphabet, Gregorian calendar and Eastern thought and culture. The divide between the Roman Church, which is above the State, and the Orthodox Church, which is part of and subject to the State, has been for centuries not only theological, but also political. The missionary zeal of the Poles (who brought the Catholic faith to the duchy of Lithuania at the time a large country, at the end of the thirteenth century, and brought about her subsequent union within the Polish Crown, which already included Ruthenia – now Bielorussia and Ukraine) was seen by the Russians as a military and political threat. The Russians also feared the superior, more advanced culture and intelligence of the Poles. Until the partitions in the eighteenth century, the Russians remembered how much of Russia had once been under Polish rule, especially in the Ukraine.

Under the Prussians, who occupied north western Poland, the regime was also harsh, but with more understanding. This did not mean that the Prussians did not dislike and denigrate the Poles; for centuries, they were accustomed to call them *'Die Verfluchte Polacken'* (the accursed Poles). It was not for *Lebensraum* alone that Hitler marched against Poland in 1939.

The Habsburgs, however, showed themselves to be generally more tolerant. Under their rule, many Poles were appointed to senior positions in the government, many made good careers in the army and the civil service, and some were even to be found at the Imperial Court. So long as the Habsburg Empire prospered, most of its constituent peoples were content.

My narrative is particularly concerned with the city of Lwow and that part of south-eastern Poland known as Malopolska Wschodnia (Eastern Little Poland) which, in the partitions, was annexed to Austro-Hungary. On account of its geographical position, Lwow itself was literally at the crossroads of trade routes between north and south, from the Baltic to the Black sea, and between west and east, from Central Europe to southern Russia and Asia. Such was its commercial importance, that the Austro-Hungarian government gave serious consideration to linking the Baltic, and therefore the North Sea with the Black Sea by a canal between the river systems, and developing Lwow as a main port and commercial centre. It is not surprising that the intense commercial activities and opportunities to be found at Lwow resulted in concentrated business communities of Jews and Armenians, together with Germans and Austrians, as well as Poles.

Malopolska Wschodnia, like Lwow, was historically home to an ethnic mix of peoples. The land, divided into large and small estates, remained largely in Polish hands, owned by the aristocracy and landed gentry. The professions were filled by Poles and other nationalities. The countryside, however, was almost exclusively inhabited by Ruthenians, basically agricultural peasants, kin to the Russian Ukrainians. Only rarely did they scale the social or professional ladder, and then mainly to become Orthodox priests or monks, or skilled craftsmen. Through all the vagaries of changing frontiers and overlordship, the Ruthenians remained a friendly mass of country dwellers, who cherished few nationalistic aspirations. This changed as the Habsburg Empire weakened. At the beginning of the twentieth century, in order to counter the rising movement for Polish independence, the Austrians fostered and supported the concept of Ukrainian independence, which reflected the nationally independent Russian Ukraine. The Ukrainians began to dream of a separate Ukraine, with Kiev as its capital.

The importance of this concept and its impact on Polish society was considerable. The land, which was almost entirely owned by Poles, was populated by a mass of increasingly hostile Ruthenian Ukrainians upon whom depended the working of the Polish-owned estates. The incidence of political crime began to climb steadily.

There was uneasy tension between the two disparate groups. Incidents of Poles being murdered and their property burned were not uncommon, while the Ukrainians were watched as subversive elements and frequently arrested and sentenced. The Poles kept small arms handy, 'just in case', ground floor windows were fitted with steel bars, and guard dogs were set to prowl as a precaution.

When World War I came, Poland was devastated. To quote just one British Historian, H.A.L. Fisher, in *History of Europe*:

Few people had suffered so grievously as the Poles. Their country had been the principal battlefield of the eastern campaigns. It had been drenched in blood and blasted by explosives. It had been the scene of butcheries such as no pen can describe, of butcheries inflicted and endured by subject peoples. Some Poles had fought in the Russian, others in the Austrian, and others again in the Prussian armies. All had fought under compulsion. Then by an extraordinary turn of chance, the partitioning Empires were suddenly overthrown, and the Poles, war wracked and impoverished, found themselves after more than a century of subjection, masterless and free, but with severe problems.

The Ukrainian desire for independence was further fuelled by the revolution in neighbouring Russia, whilst the retreating Austrian armies, towards the end of the war, handed over quantities of their no longer wanted arms and military stores to the Ukrainians. Thus, at the end of the war, when Poland emerged as an independent state, the Polish Army was newly formed on a proverbial shoestring and patriotism was often poorly armed and equipped; this was certainly true where the Poles were faced by the Ukrainians.

Not all Ruthenians, by now universally referred to as Ukrainians, wished to renounce their Polish inheritance. Families were split down the middle, as happens so often in tragedies of this nature. One famous example is that of the Szeptycki brothers, one of whom was a committed Pole, a general, who became the first chief of staff to Pilsudski, Head of the newly created Polish Army, while the other, equally committed to the Ukrainian cause, was the Greek Orthodox archbishop of Lwow, and an ardent Ukrainian nationalist.

In the exhilaration of gaining independence, no attempt was made to reach any understanding with the Ruthenian-Ukrainians. The consequence was that the withdrawal of the occupying Austro-Hungarian forces was marked by an insurrection of the exceedingly well armed Ukrainian activist peasantry. At the same time, the bands of the sovietised Russian army unexpectedly and unofficially penetrated the country in scattered groups, seeking to subvert the demoralised German soldiers and to sovietise the remains of the retreating German army. The young Polish army was unable to cope with the situation and simultaneously to contain the retreating Germans, the infiltrating Russians and the Ukrainian revolt.

In October 1918, the Ukrainian rebels besieged Lwow with a well armed force of over one hundred thousand men. The Polish army was unable to help. Lwow was left to defend itself. Everyone who could bear arms manned the defences. Schoolboys and schoolgirls fought alongside their fathers and grandfathers, mothers and grandmothers, and many made the ultimate sacrifice. My own family, on both sides, was heavily involved; some lost their lives, including a lad of only sixteen. The siege lasted for nearly two months. Lwow was eventually relieved on 22nd November, but it was many months before some sort of uneasy peace was finally established.

It was at this time that my parents met and subsequently married.

In the meantime, argument over where the eastern frontier with Russia should be established, raged unresolved. It was this uncertainty that led to the Polish-Russian War of 1920. Contrary to the advice and wishes of the League of Nations, but with the tacit understanding of the French and British (who had yet to abandon active support of the White Russians), the Polish army invaded Russia and reached and occupied Kiev in early 1920. Their intention was to establish a Ukrainian province embracing both Polish Ruthenians and Russian Ukrainians under the governance of the Poles.

This was too much for the Russians to stomach, and they launched a massive counter-attack under the Cossack Marshal Budyenny, which drove back the Polish forces. By mid-May, the Russians were well into Poland and soon at the outskirts of Warsaw. Taking French and British advice, Poland sought an armistice and opened negotiations. The first Russian condition was that the Polish Army should be sovietised; this was rejected outright. Events now overtook talk. The Polish commander-in-chief, General Pilsudski, in concert with the French General Weygand, devised a two-pronged attack (a precursor of the classic pincer movement made famous in the Second World War). The Russian army was decisively defeated before Warsaw itself. This victory, known as the Miracle of the Vistula, was won on 15th August, 1920.

The end to fighting was soon followed by the settlement of the Russo-Polish frontier question. The western part of old Ruthenia, including Lwow, remained part of Poland, much against the wishes of the Ukrainians; the eastern part, the Ukraine, with Kiev as its capital, became part of the Soviet Union.

Such was the state of affairs when I came into the world.

Childhood Memories

My family on both sides followed professional occupations. They shared the social and intellectual pursuits and pleasures of townsfolk and considered themselves 'county' gentry. My father did not follow the family pattern and chose to live in the country, where I, my brother and sisters spent the greater part of our early life. I was the eldest, being born in 1920.

Perhaps my father's preference for the outdoor life was a reflection of his mild eccentricity. As we grew up, we extracted a story from him which he enjoyed telling, but out of my mother's hearing. Having graduated as an engineer, he had a violent quarrel with my grandfather, and ran away from home. His travels took him to Spain, where his inability to speak the language made it difficult for him to find employment. He did have one skill, however, which was greatly appreciated: he was an accomplished horseman. This led to his finding a job as a picador. His career as a bullfighter came to an end one afternoon when he came to his senses laid out in a chapel on a marble slab with rows of candles on either side, a cross at his head, and a chorus of local beauties in black mantillas bewailing his untimely end and chanting prayers for his soul.

My mother had also travelled abroad, and spoke more freely of her experiences. She had gone to London before the First World War to study the new science and art of photography at the London Polytechnic. Her stories were illustrated by photographs from her albums and constant reference to her magnificent tripod-mounted teak and brass camera, which had a ground glass focusing screen and a large rubber pneumatic ball to operate the lens shutter.

Home, from my earliest recollections, was a long, squat, single-storied timber manor house with a high, pitched roof. This concealed what was really a second storey, a long and lofty attic at one end of which was a large playroom. At the other, kitchen-end, were rooms for the domestic staff and in between, an assortment of store and spare rooms.

I can only remember one of the domestic staff. Konstanty, senior among the servants, was something of a Jack of all trades. At home he served at table, and organised the delivery of vegetables and fruit from the garden and meat from the farm. When my parents went to town or were away visiting for more than one day, Konstanty would drive the carriage and look after them. Sometimes he would act as head beater during a shoot. He was also a keen amateur fisherman and beekeeper, and would fish the river when fish was needed, he also kept the house supplied with honey.

Fishing provided one of my most vivid memories of Konstanty. Fish was needed in a hurry, and Konstanty was despatched to land a pike or a carp, for which he set out with a net in a small boat. Within a short time of his leaving the house, there was a general commotion and my parents were called to the river. I rushed down to the bank after them. By the time I arrived, Konstanty and another man were already out of the boat and on the bank. Before them was the fishing net and in it an enormous pike. The fish was killed and brought to the kitchen. I remember vividly its vast and splendid silver belly, brown back and gaping cruel mouth, full of sharp and ugly teeth. Konstanty picked up a long sharp knife and began to gut it. As he slit it, an amazing number of smaller fish spilled out, some of edible size, some still alive and wriggling. That monster pike weighed twenty-five kilograms. Its head was mounted and hung for many years on the wall among my father's hunting trophies.

My other main memory of Konstanty, is of his carving. I doubt whether he could read or write but he was a natural wood carver. This was his only indoor pastime; when he had nothing else to do he was always carving. His tools were simple – sharp knives, a small mallet and an assortment of nails. The house was full of his handiwork: breadboards, bowls for salad and fruit, salad servers, figures and other ornaments – and table napkin rings. He had a store of the latter and when we had visitors, he would carve their names on them, and they would be used as place cards on the dinner table. He must have had to work hard at it, for in those days we had many visitors, often from abroad, who would come to shoot with my father or perhaps just to spend a few days in the country. All this was in Northern Poland near the East Prussian frontier.

Then my maternal grandparents came to stay with us for a few days. They came by motor car, and this made a considerable impression, for it was the first time I can remember seeing a car at close quarters, let alone being driven in one. When my grandparents left to return to Lwow in the south-east, they took me with them. I shall never forget that journey. It took two days and I was car-sick the whole time. I did not see our northern home again for many years, because the reason for that journey was that my parents were moving south to a new estate near Lwow. Many years later, just before the war, we were going for a holiday at the seaside and made a special detour to look at the old house. What I saw was not what I remembered. The house, the farm, the distillery had all shrunk, everything seemed to have become shabby, small and run down. Now it is no more, for it was razed to the ground during the war.

Our new house was different in every respect. It was

larger, two-storied and pale cream in colour. The interior was spacious with large rooms, including a ballroom, which was big enough to allow sixteen couples to dance a full mazurka without cramping their style. Furthermore, there was a guest house in the grounds, so that we could offer frequent hospitality to friends and relatives without any overcrowding. In front of the house was a large round lawn bordered with flowers, with a drive running round it. In its centre was an enormous lime tree which towered over the house. There was an avenue of trees on either side of the house, limes on one side and beeches on the other. The grounds at the back sloped down in a series of terraces with formal flower beds, then a tennis court, and at the bottom a fruit and vegetable garden. Beyond that stretched seemingly endless acres of marshes and meadows.

With us came two familiar retainers, who served to provide me with a sense of continuity between our two homes. First was the indispensable Konstanty, with whom I had developed a close rapport. To me he was a miracle man, who could charm me both with his carving and, as I grew older, with a seemingly inexhaustible fund of stories. He also became our refuge when we, as children, were in trouble – and we seemed to be in trouble with increasing frequency: being too late for meals, breaking irreplaceable pieces of glass and china when playing with a ball in the house (an activity which was strictly forbidden outside the nursery) and for every other form of childish mischief. Konstanty was the peacekeeper between us and our parents, and we loved him for it. He was as conservative in his outlook as any countryman can be. When my father acquired a car and learned to drive, he wanted to teach Konstanty too. Konstanty was deeply offended. 'Are horses no longer good enough for you, sir?' he demanded indignantly. I remember that he refused to speak to my father for days after such effrontery…

The other retainer was Jerka. Jerka had been the farm foreman in the north and came down to do the same job. Like Konstanty, Jerka was a man for horses. It was Jerka who taught us how to ride, who made sure that the mounts we were given matched our size and capability to manage them, and who let us use our parents' horses when they were away. Alas, Jerka did not take kindly to the ways of the south and could not settle down. Eventually, he returned to where he belonged.

The move coincided with the start of my education, and this provides a strong recollection. I did not go to school: the nearest school was in Lwow, some twelve kilometres away, an hour's drive each way in a horse buggy, so schooling came to me at home under a series of pedagogues. The first of these was already installed when my grandparents delivered me to our new home. This was Miss Mary, my mentor – or tormentor as she appeared to me. A small schoolroom separated her room from mine, and every morning was devoted to lessons. My wings having been so suddenly clipped, it is not surprising that Miss Mary and I did not get on. To my eyes, and as I still remember her, she was elderly, exceedingly ugly and had long yellow teeth, small piggy eyes and a mass of very dark brown wavy hair. Miss Mary was responsible for my general education. She was however aided by a succession of young lady colleagues responsible for languages, all of whom I considered to be in league against me. Some of these ladies came for a few months, vanished and then returned again. It was only later that I appreciated that they constituted what can best be described as a peripatetic language staff circulating between the larger houses to reinforce or enlarge the basic tuition of the resident tutor.

Among these language wizards there was, for example, the petite middle-aged American Miss Cathy, who taught us English. Then there was the pretty and gay *Fräulein* Friede. Her stay was short because she was making eyes at my father, not to mention the other men who came to visit us! Another, Mademoiselle – she never appeared to have any other name – was large and well built; her only redeeming feature was that she was an excellent horsewoman. *Señora* Carmelita, on the other hand, was exceedingly good-looking and a wonderful dancer. I think she suffered the same fate as Friede, and for the same reason. She was never replaced. Perhaps Spanish was not considered so important as German, but Friede was followed by *Fräulein* Irma. These young ladies seemed to be endlessly coming for a few months, then going away, only to return for a 'refresher'. Miss Cathy however, became a family friend and lasted till the war started. The young ladies also doubled as additional babysitters and childminders, for I had a younger sister, and then a twin brother and sister who arrived when I was nine. Apart from all this language tuition, there was a continual stream of foreign visitors to the house, which thus became a multilingual establishment with the emphasis on English and German.

My father was occupied in looking after the estate, which supplied the family factory in Lwow, where the fruit, vegetables and meat were canned, and where bacon was smoked, hams cured and sausages manufactured. To meet this demand, production was on a large scale, vegetables and fruit were harvested by the ton. There were acres of asparagus and hundreds of pigs. To assist him in the work this involved, my father employed young agricultural students and recent graduates who sought experience both of farming and of social life. Most of them were young ladies, who not only worked hard, but played hard as well especially when there were guests in the house. How I envied my older cousins who found favour with these attractive young beauties while I, although the son of the house, was only regarded as the baby, or at best, a young boy!

As already explained, my parents had travelled widely, and continued to find pleasure travelling in their married life. Much of this was achieved by car. My father was proud of his prowess behind the wheel, and drove tirelessly. I was allowed to accompany them on the shorter pleasure trips but seldom on the many journeys undertaken to promote the family business.

Life was never dull, but became especially lively during the holidays, when uncles, aunts and cousins descended upon us in droves. They were mainly town dwellers, and not all of them were at home in the country. Those who enjoyed it were popular with us, the others we despised. Perhaps we made our feelings too apparent, for our parents were always insisting that we looked after them properly, whichever category they fell into. 'They are the family, even if some are only remotely so,' they explained, 'and even more important, they are guests, and it is your duty to look after them.'

However, although they were very strict about the way in which we looked after their, and consequently our, guests, our parents sought to ensure that we enjoyed our life, especially those aspects which they themselves enjoyed and could share with us. We were taught national and ballroom dancing, the appreciation of good food and wine, horsemanship and riding from very early age, and were encouraged to develop an interest in all aspects of country life. We were also expected to learn about the domestic side of life, and to help in the house, cleaning glass, china and silver, looking after our own rooms, grooming the horses and cleaning the guns. Konstanty did not appear to approve of these activities – probably because our help disrupted his routine and gave him even more work to do.

We were excused chores during high days and holidays, when there were guests in the house and we, the children, had to look after and entertain the younger visitors. This was especially so during Christmas.

In our family, Christmas festivities started nearly a month beforehand. They opened with the celebration of my name-day, that of the patron saint, St Andrew, whose feast is on 30th November. Apart from the fact that, in Poland, such feasts are celebrated with more emphasis than birthdays, St Andrew's night had a special significance. According to folklore, if one melts beeswax and pours it on to cold water on St Andrew's night, one can foretell the future from the shadows formed by the solidified wax when projected on a screen. For days before the event we searched for beeswax – and the search generally ended in the hut of the beekeeper, who had prudently hoarded wax for the purpose, and could be cajoled into parting with his treasure, especially when Mother's name was invoked. Then a sheet had to be acquired and ironed absolutely flat with no creases. The flat sheet was stretched over a wooden frame to form the screen, on which shadows could be cast and seen from either side. Finally, a large tub had to be found and scrubbed scrupulously clean so that it would be allowed into the hall.

When the time for the ceremony arrived, wax would be melted in a long-handled pan over the fire in the hall fireplace, and when it was liquefied it would be poured into the water. Everyone had their own technique for doing this, in their effort to produce a good 'future'. Some would pour it gently, as if trying to control the shape which formed, others would do so in a single jerk producing a 'whoosh' of vapour and steam. Every member of the family was allowed at least one turn. The shadow images of the cast wax would be interpreted by my mother, with frequent interjections from others with alternative suggestions, all accompanied by much joy, hilarity and leg-pulling. The shadows never predicted anything like the future that was to await me! When the interpretations were over, mulled wine and ginger cake were served to everyone, marking the end of the evening.

Six days later Saint Nicholas (whose feast day is 6th December) would arrive. Saint Nicholas is the same as Santa Claus or Father Christmas in Britain, but in Poland, Santa Claus filled our stockings during the night of his feast day – the Christmas presents followed eighteen days later.

On Christmas Eve, the Christmas tree and the presents were delivered by the 'Angel'. The Angel had to arrive between the moment when the first evening star appeared in the sky (a link with the Star of Bethlehem) and before the end of the Christmas Eve dinner, called *wigilia*, which marked the vigil of the anniversary of the Birth of the Christ Child. Traditionally, it consisted of twelve courses, one for each month of the year or, as some said, one for each of the Apostles. In some parts of Poland, all the main courses were meatless, except for the soup and the sweet, cheese and fruit. Elsewhere, meat was grudgingly also allowed, generally fowl or game. There were many unswerving traditions for *wigilia*. The soup was always *barszcz*, a beetroot soup with either cream or *uszka* (small ravioli), which are meat or mushroom-filled pasta ears. Hot, freshly killed carp had to be found a place in the menu, as did also freshly killed pike in aspic. At the end came *kutia*, a Lithuanian pudding dish made of cream, honey, and poppy seed, mixed with brandy-soaked dried fruit, nuts and barley. The climax came when the head of the household threw a spoonful of *kutia* at the ceiling. If it stuck there, it would bring luck in the coming year.

When we were small we would be taken for a long walk on the pretext of looking for the evening star. While we were away, the Angel brought in the tree, decorated it and laid out the presents. Setting up the tree was no mean feat, for it was always placed in the ballroom and reached right up to the ceiling, at least four metres high. When we were very young, this walk took place early in the evening, allowing us to open and play with our new gifts before *wigilia* and then, overfed and overtired, we would fall into bed while the grown-ups went to Midnight Mass. As we grew older, the Angel would arrive as soon as the food was finished. Of course, someone had to be deputed to leave the table 'to see if the Angel had by any chance arrived'. His arrival was then signalled by the sounding of the bell and the playing of carols on the gramophone. Whether he arrived early or late, it was difficult for us children to contain our excitement.

Eventually the secret of the Angel was revealed to me, and I was given the honour of lighting the candles on the tree, ringing the bell and then putting on an appropriate record of carols on the gramophone. Once or twice I was very tempted to switch the record for something quite different, but I was too afraid of the consequences to do so.

Between Christmas and New Year's Eve, my Father would organise a shoot. House guests, neighbours and friends would assemble early in the morning and there would be a few drives, usually for hares. As children we would attend the shoot luncheon somewhere in the woods. Tradition demanded that we eat *bigos*, a stew of sauerkraut, pork sausages and vegetables, with baked potatoes washed down by generous helpings of vodka. Needless to say, we did not share in the vodka until we were almost grown up.

The season's festivities ended with a New Year's Eve party, Sylvester's Night, with dancing, drinking and eating which often lasted until breakfast time, after which those who wished, could go off shooting. Most went to bed to sleep it off!

Thus we grew up and developed, surrounded by care,

love and attention. The family fortunes fluctuated over the years, but we children were blissfully unaware of these ups and downs until much later. My education advanced steadily, both formally and informally. Only later did I come to appreciate that I was a poor pupil and a mediocre student, shielded from scholastic disaster (and later, expulsions) by luck, family charm and personal contacts. On many occasions what really counted was not what I myself knew, but who my parents knew.

Towards Adolescence

Hunting, it is said, is the 'Sport of Kings'. It was certainly my father's greatest pleasure. He sought to share it with me from the earliest days, first by taking me out with him, then by giving me instruction in the variety of skills required. I found that I had a natural ability in fieldcraft from a very early age, and could creep up, unexpected and unnoticed, on a variety of animals. I had an innate understanding and sense of wind and the peculiarities of wind eddies, and it was not often that my quarry, stalked for real, with a weapon or camera, or practice, would pick up my scent once I knew of its presence. Indeed, I could get closer to the quarry than my father but it was of little avail, for my skill with rifle and shotgun was poor. Even after I had been presented with a shotgun and later, a rifle, I was unable to shoot straight. My father was as fine a marksman as he was a horseman; alas, he was short-tempered, and consequently incapable of instructing in either. The more exasperated he grew with my shortcomings, the worse I became!

I was in despair until a chance came to unburden myself to a distant cousin, with whom I was walking round the estate in the absence of my father. I was probably ten at the time, maybe a little younger. This cousin was a shot of repute, a man who killed game birds and ducks on the wing with a .22 rifle, disdaining the shotgun of lesser mortals. On hearing of my plight, he took me in hand. For two days we were shooting at targets with a small rifle and a shotgun. Tree stumps became pock-marked, rubber balls holed and earthenware plates, thrown up in the air, to be smashed either by being hit or crashing back to the ground. Eventually we started on magpies, rooks and other vermin. When he had finished with me, he declared me to be a tolerable shot – at the cost to me of a very sore shoulder.

My lessons in hunting and stalking, in woodcraft and fieldcraft, as well as marksmanship were to stand me in good stead, but the improved marksmanship gave them a new meaning. Not surprisingly, this passion of my father's was increasingly shared with me. I can still wax idyllic on the sport in which I have since participated in many parts of the world, and described in my books[1] and in various articles. I retain many vivid memories of those days with my father, and especially of his great pride in my success when against all expectations I shot my first hare at the age of seven.

The year 1929 stands out in my memory. The winter was one of the hardest ever. The snow fell thick before Christmas. For us children, it was like paradise. We were out on skis from breakfast till dusk, well protected against the very hard frost, revelling in the fresh fall of snow at night and brilliant sunshine during the day. When Christmas came, our visitors from Lwow were hard pressed to complete the twelve-kilometre journey. It was bad enough when they arrived; on their return a horse-driven snow plough had to be sent to clear the road ahead of them.

If it had not been for a houseful of relatives, my father would have spent Christmas in bed. As it was, his ill health threw a shadow over the festivities and the traditional Boxing Day shoot brought a significant turn for the worse.

---

[1] *Wild Deer,* Faber & Faber, 1958; *Deer Management,* David & Charles, 1978; *Wild Deer 2,* revised edition Ashford Press, 1988; *Management Of Deer and Their Habitat,* Wilson Hunt, 1992.

Our guests left hurriedly, fearful lest they be trapped by the snow and knowing that as long as they were about, my father would not retire to bed to recover. A few days after Christmas, my father's health not improving, mother summoned a local family doctor who was also a friend. He lived some ten kilometres away and agreed to come if we provided transport. So a sleigh, pulled by four horses, was sent to fetch him. The round trip took some six hours, most of it over open fields, for the road was quite invisible under the thick blanket of snow. A severe attack of pneumonia was diagnosed. My father really should have been sent to hospital, but under the circumstances this was out of the question. Fortunately a retired nurse who lived near the doctor, was persuaded by him, in a long telephone call, to come out of her retirement to look after Father. The sleigh which took the doctor home brought her back, with a suitable supply of the drugs and medicines prescribed. Once she had thawed out from 'the worst experience in my life', as she described the journey, the good nurse devoted herself wholly to tending my father.

My sister, Christine, and I were not told how critical father's condition was. We continued to enjoy the snow, which by mid January reached the windows of the upper floor so that we could only get out of the house by the upstairs door on to the veranda. Our allotted task was to feed wild life and game.

Each day we would pack rucksacks with corn or cooked vegetables to take to the fields and the woods, where we would be greeted by starving hares, partridges and deer among other wild life. Alas, we would find many dead in the fields and woods. While skiing in the woods we were startled, if not frightened, by the noise of explosions which we could not understand. Our fear vanished when we were told that the noises came from tree branches and trunks cracking open in the fierce frost. Our efforts proved to be a losing battle as we found more and more dead birds and animals in the snow. When the snow formed a hard enough crust, our deliveries were supplemented by a sleigh loaded with supplies which were shovelled out. Christine and I would ski out to watch the starving creatures really eat. It was not long, however, before predators realised that they too could benefit from this largesse, and the gatherings of hungry small animals eating our supplies became food for hungry foxes and birds of prey. Then the wolves, hitherto unknown in our part of the country, had also appeared, not only feasting on the bigger animals, but also putting a stop to our youthful outings. Even the workmen, with food in sleighs and horses had to be armed or accompanied by armed foresters.

February came and Father seemed to be losing his struggle for life. We suddenly discovered quite how bad he had become when my mother included in our morning and evening prayers special ones, not just for his recovery but for his life. The combination of our prayers, his indomitable will to live and assiduous care did the trick, and at last he began to mend. Then the telephone lines broke and we were completely cut off from the outside world save for the radio and the infrequent visits of the doctor, for whom we sent the sleigh – not knowing whether he would come or not. Needless to say, he never failed us.

Not until Easter, which that year fell at the end of March, did we see any visitors. The first were our grandparents, who came to stay in the country with us, so that my parents could go away to the sunshine of southern Europe to speed Father's recovery.

For several years after that it became my parents' practice to spend the worst part of winter and early spring in the sun. One year, having suffered a heavy attack of influenza during the winter, I was taken with them to spend a month in Dubrovnik.

My young eyes gazed in wonderment when I first saw the coaches of the International Wagon Lits Express gleaming in the evening light. But the outside was nothing compared to the sumptuous luxury of the interior, with its deep carpets, polished rich woodwork and cut-glass lampshades. The immaculately uniformed attendants vied with each other to be helpful. We occupied two first-class compartments linked by a communicating door. These, and the restaurant car, would be our home till we reached Trieste.

It was the first time I had travelled abroad, and my parents must have decided it was a good opportunity to further my education. I was given the task of searching out the attendant to ask him to help clear customs, to organise our breakfast in the morning and to look after the luggage we did not need on the train. As I was given the passports and tickets, my mother, who must have had some misgivings, stressed the importance of not losing the travel documents. I, accordingly, passed on these strictures to the attendant. If he found this amusing, he did not let on, but played his part with absolute seriousness and promised to take special care of the important documents.

Soon after the train left Lwow, we were ushered into the dining car. The staff, in starched shirts, black bow ties and green monkey jackets, were very attentive. My parents spoke to them in German, it being an international train, and I tried to show that I also knew at least some German. I was especially impressed when the wine waiter enquired if I would like to take wine with my food. I glanced surreptitiously at my father, who gave a little nod of approval, so I chose a white wine and asked for it to be served very cold. The waiter gave a deep bow and with a smile on his face, acknowledged me with 'Jawohl, mein Herr' (Yes, sir).

I thought the wine tasted delicious, and, encouraged by my father, told the wine waiter so as we left the dining car some two hours later.

My mother woke me early soon after the train had passed through Vienna. 'Better to look out the window than sleep,' she said. 'We shall be going through some interesting country and anyway, breakfast will soon be here. We will have it in your compartment, so that Father can have a bit more rest.'

Although I jumped out of bed and dressed at once, I was scarcely ready before the attendant came in to rearrange the compartment for us to breakfast in comfort. I sat by the window spellbound by the spectacular scenery. The railway line ran alongside a large river and in the distance, snow-capped mountains gleamed in the morning sunshine. It was unforgettable.

We stayed in Trieste for a day, putting up in a smart hotel, which had a very international atmosphere about it. So did the town, which we toured in the morning in a horse-drawn cab. All manner of strange languages were to be heard. The harbour, one of the largest in southern Europe, was crammed with ships of all shapes and sizes, from small fishing boats to great passenger liners, bedecked with flags displaying every colour of the rainbow. It was like a fairy story, and my constant exclamations of excitement and joy gave my parents great pleasure.

As we continued our journey, there was a marked change in the landscape. The rich and fertile soils of Austria and northern Italy changed into poor, rugged, and often stony soil. An hour or so north of Dubrovnik, there was yet another change. Now there were citrus and olive groves in profusion, interspersed with orchards and vineyards. The hedges consisted of cacti, I suppose, the prickly pear, which also yields an exotic fruit.

When the train pulled into Dubrovnik, the platform was crowded with people waiting to greet the new arrivals. Hotel staff, bearing a board with the name of their hotel, sought their customers and vied for the attention of the uncommitted. We were booked into the Hotel Victoria – whose name board was immediately opposite our carriage when the train finally stopped. Father beckoned. Uniformed hotel staff immediately set about collecting our baggage. The senior hotel representative, more formally dressed in a suit, ushered us into a taxi; the luggage would follow. The Hotel Victoria had only recently been built and was located in the new part of the town. We had large, bright rooms, each with a veranda overlooking the old town and the medieval fortified harbour. The view was breathtaking but my anxiety to explore everything immediately had to compete with the attraction of the beach and the sea. The hotel had its own private beach, a sandy cove seemingly carved out of the rocks with a flight of hundreds of steps leading down to it. The sea looked calm, blue and warm in the sunshine. We were warned by the hotel staff that it was still cold. Undeterred, my mother and I ventured down to the sand, while my father took a rest. We soon discovered the accuracy of the warning. Although we both loved swimming, the water was so cold we could scarcely bear to paddle. What a terrible disappointment!

This setback was soon forgotten however, the following day, when we took a short walk from the hotel to the old town of Dubrovnik. It was an entrancing place. Roman, Greek, Turkish and Arab influences were all intermingled. Every narrow-sided street was crammed full of tiny shops and workshops where leather-workers, silversmiths and lace makers produced and displayed their wares. In the main streets, larger shops and hotels provided for the luxuries sought by tourists and visitors. On this visit, there were two unexpected attractions for my anglophile parents.

The first was George Bernard Shaw, who was also staying in Dubrovnik. He was regularly to be seen taking his daily walks, surrounded by a horde of admirers. Once I had been told he was a very great man, I managed to take a couple of photographs of him. One of these came out very well. My father decided that we should have lunch at Shaw's hotel and, if he was there, I should ask him to autograph it. And so it happened. We were sitting eating when in walked the grey-haired, moustached and bearded GBS, together with some friends. When his party had nearly finished their lunch, my father sent me over. Quite unabashed (after all, I dare say I did not know just how famous he was), I went to his table and stood quietly for a few moments until he noticed me. Then I asked if he would kindly sign my photograph. He roared with laughter.

'You speak good English,' he said, 'Where are you from?'

'Lwow, sir,' I replied.

'Lwow?' he exploded, 'and what is this Lwow?'

'A city in Poland,' I said, reddening with embarrassment. He looked at my photograph.

'A good photograph,' he said, 'I like it. May I keep it? I will give you another in its place.' He thereupon pulled out a photograph of himself from his breast pocket, signed it, and gave it to me. 'Compliment your parents on your English,' he added, 'and have a good holiday.'

When I returned to our table, he smiled and waved at my parents. They were delighted.

The second attraction was the yacht *Nahlin*. On board were the Prince of Wales and Mrs Wallace Simpson. It was anchored in the harbour, and my mother used to scan it through her binoculars. She had a soft spot for the prince, proudly excusing her avid interest: 'He was born on the same day I was; a very fine man, this future king of England.'

Despite its attractions, we did not stay long in Dubrovnik, for the wind blowing was detrimental to my father's health. We moved south to a place called Kupari, which had a large bay and was sheltered from the winds. The bay was dominated by the Hotel Kupari, which seemed enormous. Around the bay were numerous smaller hotels and private houses, and the resort was packed. My parents were pleased with the move. In the evenings, after supper, we played bridge. My father was an experienced and good bridge player; my mother played more as a duty than a pleasure, and they were both teaching me how. On our second or third evening, a man of about my father's age came over and introduced himself, in German. He and his family were also staying in the hotel and were also bridge players. He invited my parents to join the adult game, and I could join the younger members of his family and play with them. His name was Bata. He came from Prague, where his father had just opened a shoe factory. My father spent happy evenings playing bridge, my mother gossiped with the ladies of the party, and I found companions of my own age. The Batas were regular visitors to Kupari and kept two sailing boats in the bay. One was a large sea-going vessel, in which the grown-ups sailed to the nearby islands and the other was a small boat, for the youngsters. It was at Kupari that I learned to sail and it was also at Kupari that my parents decided that sailing was not for them.

All three of us had a very happy holiday there. My father's health improved and by the time we were due to return, he looked very much fitter.

On our way home, we stopped off in Vienna, staying at the fashionable, old-fashioned Hammerand Hotel. I remember that there was a huge fish tank in the lobby stocked with live trout. One could select a trout which would be lifted out by a member of the staff with a net, and then served as the meal. I think I had trout with every meal, so as to be able to watch the catching of it.

My parents had intended to stay in Vienna for several days, to visit relatives and to go sightseeing. However, it was not to be. There came a cryptic telegram followed by a telephone call from Lwow. My father's brother had died from a severe attack of pneumonia, after an illness lasting only four days. We returned at once, arriving only just in time for the funeral.

If I Only Had Wings...

Although not written until World War II, the popular song *If I Only Had Wings...* could have been written expressly to mirror my greatest ambition, from the age of ten. For me, these words were not just a sentimental hope but a consuming ambition. It all started with a present. My father was accustomed to bring back presents for the family whenever he went abroad. After one such visit to England, he presented me with two rubber-band-powered, propeller-driven model aircraft and a book which, as far as I can recall, was entitled *Every Boy And His Own Mechanics.*

Those model aircraft fired my imagination. The book told me how to fly them, but not why they flew. I watched the birds in search of clues. But the birds flapped their wings, and aircraft did not. Clearly, the propeller pulled my models through the air like a ship's propeller pushed the ship through water. But even without the propeller, my models could glide. So how did the wings keep them up? My engineer father talked about feathers floating gently in the air, but was unable to unravel the mystery of aerodynamics, which I do not think he understood. So he gave me books. But these were too technical and, for the moment, flying remained a fascinating mystery which I could not comprehend.

My enthusiasm unabated, however, I played endlessly with my models until one of them crashed and broke its tail. I sought help to repair the damage and my father passed me on to Dabrowski, the estate carpenter. I soon discovered that I was not the only one whose imagination was fired by model aircraft. Dabrowski repaired the damaged tail, using split cane from a discarded fishing rod. He then borrowed both models and made copies of them, not just for me but for his son as well. Some years later, Dabrowski junior, who was older than I, joined the air force. Sadly, he was killed early in the war.

One thing Dabrowski could not do was to make a propeller. 'That needs carving,' he said. I immediately thought of Konstanty and rushed off to enlist his help. He refused point blank. Perhaps I should have known better of a man who refused to learn to drive a motor car.

'It's a part of your flying machine,' he fulminated. 'It's the devil's own invention and I want no part in it.'

I had now reached the age when I was required to attend school. No longer would the authorities be satisfied by the ministrations of Miss Mary, so long as I passed the examinations at the end of the school year. Despite my scientific aspirations, I was sent to the classical secondary school where my grandfather and my uncle had been educated. Latin featured in the curriculum from the first year and Greek, from the third.

The Miss Cathies, *Fräulein* Friedes and Mademoiselles had taught us languages by ear without inculcating even a modicum of grammar, so learning the dead languages became a nightmare. Declensions and conjugations, past-present and past-perfect, were beyond my imagination let alone comprehension, and addled my brain.

My most eloquent pleas failed to persuade my parents to send me to a science school. 'Look at your cousins,' they would say, 'they can converse in Latin and Greek, and look at you...' The fact that these cousins were nearly as inept at mathematics and physics as I at Latin and Greek mattered nothing. It might have influenced my father, but not my mother and her father, and it was Mother who made the decisions on matters scholastic. I scraped through Latin for two years, painfully aware that I was heading for my first confrontation with my mother. The crisis came when I was thirteen, and in my first year of Greek. My mother was asked to call on the headmaster, who had been a friend of my uncle from their school and university days. He told her bluntly that it would be impossible to make me into a Latin scholar and that in Greek, I could only be considered a disaster. I was not much good at history or literature, either. My only good subjects were mathematics and physics. Having identified my weaknesses and strengths, he then said that he had spoken to the head of a science school and found a place for me there.

Mother returned shamed, crestfallen and angry. Saying nothing of the suggestions made by the headmaster, she summoned me to a stormy interview. My indignation overcame my respect.

'Much ado about nothing,' I blurted out, 'it is stupid forcing me to learn things in which I have no interest, no ability and no understanding, instead of letting me learn the subjects I am good at, and which I do like.' Mother was speechless with rage and stormed out, slamming the door behind her. I had never seen her so angry. Had I over-stepped the mark? I knew that she could be stubborn and strong-willed. Even Father did not argue with her. She was accustomed to having her own way.

My father, who would have understood me, was away. We had family visitors – my maternal grandparents and her brother, the 'classical side' of the family. I feared a family confrontation – me against the rest. I was saved that; instead, I was banished from the supper table and sent to my room with a tray. I could only wonder if my future was under discussion and what was being said about me. After supper, my tray was taken away and, feeling rejected, I started to undress to go to bed when Mother came up.

'Sit down,' she ordered, 'we had better have a talk.'

I sat on the bed, leaving the chair for Mother, but she paced up and down my small room without saying a word.

'I ought to beat you into obedience,' she said eventually, 'but you are too big for that now and your father is not here, therefore, you will listen to me.'

I was subjected to a long tirade of accusations. I was accused of being lazy, stupid, stubborn, apathetic and without any ambition whatsoever. My indignation rose till I could stand no more. I considered her accusations so hurtful and unjust that my fear was overcome. The words burst out of me spontaneously.

'I suppose, I suppose that even if I manage to get through this Latin and Greek gibberish and end up at the bottom of the class, you will still want to send me to university to study law or medicine, because that is what your father and your generation did. Well, I won't. I don't have the slightest interest in them or any of the arts subjects. If you want me to get on, then let me go to a science school and then I can go to a technical university.'

My mother turned as white as a sheet and sat down. I thought she was going to faint. She was not accustomed to any one standing up to her, and coming from her child to his mother, it was as unthinkable as it was unexpected. The atmosphere was tense and forbidding. At last she spoke.

'I am deeply hurt,' she announced. 'I will have to think about it.' With that she swept out of the room, leaving me in fearful suspense.

However, there was a long family conference that evening on the subject of my future. It was finally resolved to accept the advice and the arrangements which had been proffered by my headmaster. To my joy and astonishment, I was told before breakfast the following morning that I would be transferred to a science school.

At last I found myself in congenial company. Instead of

the old poetry, literary and musical circles, I found and joined groups where we were taught carpentry and metal work, an electromagnetic club and an internal combustion engine club. The masters who supervised these clubs encouraged our hobbies. Here also the unresolved mystery of flying was explained to me, clearly and simply. Now I wanted not just to fly models but to design and build my own. Even the approach to physical education was different. The normal activities in the gymnasium were supplemented by a wide variety of active sports, including athletics and winter sports. I had already developed into a good skier and the sports master encouraged me to take it up competitively.

At fifteen, I joined the school cadet force and this gained me entry into the Air League, which concentrated on the air force, and it encouraged the building of model aircraft. It also taught gliding as an introduction to flying, but to be accepted for gliding one had to be eighteen, or to have parental permission to start sooner. I continued to be fascinated by the building of model aircraft. But above all, I became consumed by the desire to fly. I had already read every book on the subject, within my span of knowledge, on which I could lay my hands. However, I dreaded the moment when I would have to ask my parents for the necessary permission.

I now received the greatest shock of my early life. I had been encouraged by the art master, a retired soldier who was also an engineer, to enter the winter art competition. I spent hours creating a painting of a bantam cock in full plumage. I was summoned to his study to discuss my entry.

'I think that as an idea it is excellent,' he said. 'Its execution is faultless and the picture could have got you a high place in the competition. But you have been too dramatic with your colours. If it was meant to be a joke, it was one in very bad taste.'

I was astounded and deeply hurt. I had put my life and soul into that picture. He took it out of his big folder and continued:

'I know that some feathers in the sunlight shimmer in all colours, but the neck and tail are basically red, though they shimmer into blues and blacks. You have made them a strange green which does not exist in nature.'

He looked at the picture and then at me, and saw how uncomfortable I was feeling. 'Surely you must see how unreal this looks…' He broke off as understanding dawned, concern showing on his face.

'My dear boy, my very dear friend, tell me is there any evidence of defective colour vision in your family?'

I could feel the blood draining from my face and started to shiver. My mother's father was almost totally colour blind. I told him so; could it be hereditary? Could I also…

'Defective colour vision can be inherited. Strangely enough, it seems to pass from father through daughter to son; women don't seem to be affected.' He looked at me again. He knew of my ambitions and became even more concerned. 'But you want to fly. Is not colour vision indispensable?'

Of course it was. The colour-vision test was part of the medical. I was nearly in tears.

'Please don't tell anybody, sir,' I begged. 'Please!'

'Do not worry,' he reassured me, 'it will remain a secret between us. I will do all I can to help you, but I'm afraid that I cannot teach you how to distinguish between different colours and you will not be able to learn how to do so.'

It took me a very long time to recover from the shock of this devastating discovery. I spent long hours seeking to improve my colour perception and studying how it was tested. Although I found that colour testing was not part of the medical for gliding, it was an essential part of the examination for a full pilot's licence. And I learned why.

When I reached my sixteenth birthday, I decided that I had to broach the question of flying with my family. Summoning all my courage, I sought out my mother. Her reaction was as I had feared. She was totally opposed to the idea.

'If we had not agreed that you should change school, this would never have happened,' she complained. 'It is they who encourage you in this madness…'

I argued, pleaded and begged till I began to wear down her resistance. Eventually, reluctantly and with bad grace, she conceded.

'I want to have nothing to do with this. I don't understand this flying nonsense. Go and talk to your father. He will have to decide.'

With some trepidation, I did. He must have discussed it at great length with my mother, but to my delight, he decided in my favour. He had reservations. His permission had strings attached. It was conditional upon my progress at school. Of course, I had not dared to tell them about my colour-blindness. If they had any inkling, my parents did not mention it. I had a suspicion that my mother did know and had given her reluctant consent in the belief that it would prove to be an insurmountable obstacle to my flying. Nonetheless, I had been less than completely honest and my conscience troubled me. I unburdened myself to my art master.

'Thank you for telling me,' he advised, 'but you know that you must be completely honest with your parents, and it is your responsibility to tell them.'

I knew well enough that he was right. But the time was not yet ripe, and I continued to keep it to myself.

Armed with my father's written consent, I enrolled in the basic gliding course. This started early in the spring, as soon as the snow had cleared. The course was held about an hour's train journey from Lwow. Instruction took place on Saturday afternoons and Sundays, so as not to interfere with work, and lasted some ten weeks. My ambition was to complete the basic training successfully before the summer holidays and to qualify for the advanced course in the summer.

My dreams of flying were beginning to come true, and this realisation made me work hard at school. I spent all my spare time reading about flying and going to theoretical classes on the subject to prepare myself for the spring course. As the time approached, the snow vanished and skiing was no longer possible, I became over-excited. I spent sleepless hours thinking about gliding; very hopeful and also a little frightened.

At last the great day came, and I remember how chilly it was. I travelled by tram to the station, still in school uniform. I scanned the passengers on the train, wondering who were my fellow-pupils, without recognising a single face. I found out, when we got down from the train at a small station and joined a waiting lorry bearing the Aeroclub insignia. All the other students were 'young adults', the youngest, three or four years older than I. They looked somewhat askance at the schoolboy in their midst. The driver, who was to be our instructor, introduced himself. His name was Szleg.

The gliding school consisted of an office, a crew room and a dormitory where we would sleep, all in one basic hut, and an even more basic hangar, outside which five primitive gliders were neatly lined up.

I was deeply disappointed that we spent the entire weekend in the crew room, being taught theory. It had not occurred to me that I would be the only one who had already mastered it. The nearest we got to the gliders was walking among them during the breaks. It was difficult to conceal my real feelings, especially on my return home, that first Sunday evening. But the course progressed as we worked through the necessary but unexciting process of initial training: ground slides, low hops and high hops, slowly moving the take-off point higher and higher up the hill, so that flight duration was increased from five seconds, then ten seconds, twenty seconds to half a minute. Flights were first straight and level, and there followed gingerly executed turns to the left and the right.

After weeks of this elementary induction, the day finally arrived when we were taken to the top of the hill for a real flight. Strapped in my seat, I was choked with excitement when Szleg gave me my final instructions.

'A turn to the right, then turn left about 180 degrees away from the hill. Level off. Check the take-off point, look to your right for the landing meadow at the bottom. Turn right to land and don't forget the two haystacks and the glider already there. Good luck!'

The rubber catapult party took the strain. Szleg gave the command, and they started pulling for all they were worth. 'Let go!' he shouted, and I was off.

I concentrated all my thoughts on flying, while tears poured from my eyes and my hair streamed as a result of the rushing air. I made a smooth turn to the right and levelled off. Then a tighter and longer turn to the left, and right round. A check showed the take-off point slightly above me on the left, and over on the right the meadow with the two haystacks, and a white glider being pulled away by a horse. It was time to land. The ground rushed towards me at an alarming rate as I levelled off for landing. I could hear the grass brushing against the landing skid for a long time, then came a thump, and then another thump, and we were down, the speed dropping, the wing tipping to the ground. Then all was quiet. I had flown, really flown, even if it took probably less than a minute! I got out and looked back. The other glider was halfway up the hill. I would have a long wait before the horse came back for mine.

I sat down on the grass, immersed in thought. After all that excitement, I shivered, although it was a warm day. I relived the sixty airborne seconds in a rush of confused recollections. Had my performance been good enough? That was the dominant question. It seemed that all my life had been a preparation for this. I had no way of judging Szleg's assessment of my performance, on which it seemed to me my whole future now hung.

I was so engrossed in these reflections that I did not even hear the horse and groom, until I was brought back into the world by the clanking noise as the glider was hitched up. The next glider had been sent off, and Szleg was coming down the hill to meet me.

'That was a good flight,' he said, 'maybe a little too fast, but too much speed is better than not enough. If your eyes are streaming hard, it usually means that you are too fast. You will fly again right away, and just remember the speed.'

Relieved by his approval, I took once more to the air. This time, I was more relaxed and more aware of what was happening around me. I suddenly realised that my first flight had been made in a state of semi-consciousness. This time I was in a state of euphoria, enjoying every moment, at one with the glider and the air. As I was completing the long about turn, there was a barely perceptible pressure on my seat as the glider rose very slightly in a wind current. Taking advantage of this uplift, I managed another about turn and flew along the hill before turning into land. I underestimated the position of the haystacks and missed one of them by a hair's breadth.

'Quite good,' observed my instructor. 'That puff of wind gave you a bit of extra lift. You were airborne about seventy-five seconds. But were you not a bit close to the left-hand haystack?'

I could only blush in reply, and he smiled and did not labour the point.

Szleg had little time to spare for summing up that day, there was too much to do. He gathered us together just before it was time to return and addressed us: 'There is too little time to discuss today's flying. All I have to say is that two of you have earned the second proficiency certificate and badge.' He paused for effect, leaving us all wondering who were the lucky ones, and then continued, 'Zofia and Andrew, you owe the school ten zlotys each, for the certificate and badge. Well done!'

I returned home in cloud-cuckoo-land, imagining myself in a fighter looping the loop, rolling and spinning, revelling in the imagined freedom of the air. And as I approached my grandparents' house in Lwow, I wondered how my news would be received by my parents. I had to wait till the following week, when Father collected me from school. He cross-questioned me about gliding and my success as he drove us home. Some fifteen minutes from home he pulled up by the roadside.

'I have bottled up my feelings for, what, a couple of years, I suppose,' he said, 'but now I need to talk to you.' He took out his cigarette case and lit a cigarette. I wondered what was coming.

'I want to talk to you about your problem with your mother: the problem at the time when you had difficulties with Latin and Greek, and finally you were transferred to your present school. Your mother was very upset by your obstinacy and unbelievable lack of manners. No – don't interrupt me,' he warned, when I drew a deep breath with just that intention. 'I think you owe your mother a very profound apology. I know it seems a long time ago to you, but she is still hurt. Now that you have got your way, that you are at the school of your choice and you have been allowed to glide, and have made good progress at both, it is an opportune moment. And don't tell her that I have spoken to you. Make it seem that it comes spontaneously from you and you alone; make her feel that you have come to your senses and at last appreciate how appallingly you behaved on that occasion.' Without another word, he started up the engine and drove on in silence. I did not feel like defending myself.

It was a lovely warm May afternoon. My mother was sitting on the veranda with her embroidery. The tea table had been laid, but my father went on to his office, ostensibly to catch up with some work. We were alone. Having given an enthusiastic account of my gliding, and paraded my badge and certificate before her, I ate my humble pie.

'Oh, I forgot all about that a long time ago,' she said. However, I noticed that there was a blush of pleasure on her face. 'All the same, I appreciate and accept your apology. I am delighted about your flying success, even if I do have kittens every weekend, knowing that you are sticking your neck out.'

I could not think of anything appropriate to reply.

Cupid Strikes

As a family, we were susceptible to bronchial complaints, especially my father since his attack of pneumonia. As a result, he spent as much time as possible in the sun and in the mountains. When school permitted, I would accompany my parents in their excursions to southern Europe in the spring and to the mountains in the winter. Thus, a pattern developed in my holidays – gliding in spring, summer and autumn, and skiing in the winter. We often spent weekends in the mountains, there were many opportunities to ski, and I became proficient. During the summer and autumn I was able, on many an early morning and evening, to follow that other passion, inherited from and instilled in me by my father, of game shooting and deer stalking. As my accuracy in shooting improved, I became my father's frequent companion. How fortunate I was to be able to follow the three pursuits I loved so much, and to become skilled in all of them.

In the mid-thirties when it became necessary to count the pennies, my parents' visits abroad became less frequent. In spite of these difficulties, Christine and I were sent away to a youth camp on the island of Solta, which is in the Adriatic, off Split, on the Yugoslavian coast. This did not suit me at all, because it interfered with my plans for gliding in the summer. But my parents were adamant: my sister and I would benefit from the sunshine, after a hard winter. I was given an ultimatum: 'Either you go to Solta for six weeks or you can forget flying.' Since my parents paid for my flying, it was an offer I could not refuse.

Our parents, who were going on to the Tatra mountains, took us as far as Krakow, where they handed us over
to the camp organiser, the headmaster of a private school,
yet another friend of my parents. The party consisted of
some thirty youngsters. Those of us who were over sixteen
were made prefects and given different responsibilities. We
were shepherded on to a train, the boys separated from the
girls, and travelled on to Vienna where we were scheduled
to spend twenty-four hours staying at a youth hostel. While
our luggage was being unloaded, I caught sight of Christine
talking to a strikingly beautiful girl. I only saw her for a
moment or so, but it was enough to set my heart racing.

Who could she be?

When we had settled into the youth hostel and discharged our responsibilities, we prefects were told we could
explore the city on our own while the head and his wife
took the younger members of the party sightseeing. Having
been to Vienna before with my parents, I offered to show
the sights to two other boys with whom I had made friends.
We had three objectives – to buy the fashionable Tyrolean
hats, to look round the Hofburg and visit the famous
Spanish Riding School – and then to spend the evening at
the funfair in the Prater. Having purchased our hats, we
strutted proudly to the Hofburg. Because of the hats, we
were not recognised as students and forfeited the right of
free entrance. We did not begrudge the fee! All three of us
loved horses, and were entranced by the performance. Late
in the afternoon, we took a tram to the Prater. We had to go
on the Great Wheel, made so familiar after the war to
cinema-goers all over the world by the film *The Third Man*.
Each swivelling boxcar held some ten people. From the top,
one could see the whole city spread out below. It was dark
when we went on it, and Vienna with all its lights was a
breathtaking sight. By the time we got off, we were hungry,

so we feasted on sausages with sauerkraut and beer. We returned to the hostel in high spirits, which were instantly dampened by the head. We should have been back by eight thirty and it was already gone ten!

As we left the hostel next morning, I saw my beautiful girl again – talking to Christine. So I went over to wish my sister 'Good morning'. I was introduced… Her name was Hala. I blushed, and Christine looked at me in silence with raised eyebrows.

Our next destination was Split. It was not till the prefects were discharging their duty of wheeling the luggage to the harbour that I realised that I had been there before. On the launch which ferried us, we were allowed to meet and talk to the girls for the first time. I was delighted when Christine invited me to sit with her, because her companion was Hala. I tried not to let my interest become too obvious, but could not take my eyes off her. She had auburn hair, a high forehead, blue eyes, a pretty nose and a well-shaped mouth. When she stood up to leave us for a few moments, I saw she also had a marvellous figure, elegant legs and small feet, and was a very graceful mover.

'She's a good-looker,' noted Christine. She was overheard by one of my two fellow adventurers in Vienna, who was sitting nearby with another girl. He looked at Christine, recognised her as my sister, and observed dryly: 'I have known Hala for years. She is a sport and has a very good sense of humour, but watch it!'

I did not know what he meant by this, and reacted by blushing again. Christine noticed and started teasing. At least she kept her voice low enough not to embarrass me publicly.

Soon we entered Solta Bay, admiring the magnificent scenery, and disembarked. At the camp we found accommodation and placings allotted by name. After the evening meal, the prefects were summoned by the headmaster for a lecture on routine and responsibilities, and the importance of setting a good example. On the way up I was joined by Hala, who was also a prefect, and who slipped her hand into mine. We went along holding hands but saying nothing.

Hitherto, I had only thought of girls as indispensable for dancing, and, if they were any good at it, perhaps as pleasant companions on skiing excursions. Maybe I was a little jealous when older boys attracted their attention in preference to me. But gliding and skiing had my undivided attention. Until now.

For the next six weeks, Hala and I were inseparable. The youngsters giggled and nudged, our contemporaries teased – and the head and his wife thought it necessary to talk to us about it, albeit tactfully and separately. Our mutual affections deepened and our relationship grew ever more serious. But in those days, morality was different. Sex was never mentioned, nor was lovemaking considered, but we discovered the meaning of desire and the difficulty of restraining it.

There was plenty to occupy our time. But I have always felt, indeed, I still do, that dawn and the early morning is the loveliest time of the day. I used to get up before sunrise and go for a solitary walk. One clear morning, I heard footsteps behind me. Turning, I was surprised and delighted to discover Hala coming after me. There was a chill in the air, the bay was as smooth as a mirror and blue with it, to the east the sky was golden pink, or so it seemed to my colour-blind eyes, and it was still dark overhead.

'What a heathen idea getting up at this hour!' murmured Hala when she caught up with me. 'But it is rather lovely.'

'I think this is the best part of the day.'

She looked at me inquiringly.

'Even better, when you are here,' I added quickly. Hala laughed, sounding almost embarrassed.

'You are strange,' she ventured, 'a bit of a loner, a bit of a romantic. What really makes you tick?'

'I wish I really knew. I think I am a little confused.'

'Why?' she pressed home her advantage.

I had left myself unguarded against this question. Even had I known the answer, I certainly did not feel inclined to share it with her. We walked quietly along the path above the beach to its highest point, whence we could see the mainland of Yugoslavia in the distance, and below us, the whole of the bay with our camp at the far end. We sat on a big stone and daydreamed in silence. Hala took my hand.

'Penny for your thoughts,' she said, looking into my eyes. I ignored the question.

After a while I suggested, 'Let's run down to the beach and have a swim. I've often done it on mornings like this. The water is quite warm and it's very refreshing. Then we can walk back along the beach.'

Hala was a good swimmer, so I was surprised when she declined; however, she agreed to walk back along the beach.

'But there's no reason you shouldn't swim if you want to!' she said. We ran down to the beach, where I stripped down to my swimming trunks, plunged into the water and swam out into the bay. When I turned back, I could see my white shorts, but Hala had vanished. I returned to the beach, picked up my things and called her. I heard her answer some way down the beach but could not see her. As I walked towards her voice, she suddenly emerged from the bushes; her hair was dripping, her face was wet, her blouse and skirt were patched with damp.

'Sorry,' she said, 'I didn't bring my swimsuit with me. But the water looked very inviting. You didn't see me, did you?'

'I'm sorry I missed the sight,' I laughed.

'You... you weren't meant to see,' she stammered, blushing.

Later that day, after a sightseeing expedition to Split, Hala and I separated for a while to do some shopping, agreeing to meet again and walk back to the harbour. I took the opportunity to buy for her, from one of the many Arab silver workers, a little filigree bracelet.

'I bought you this as a memento of our first expedition to Split,' I said when we met and gave her the little box.

She opened the box. 'It's lovely! Thank you very much.' She put on the bracelet and admired it on her sun-tanned arm. With a look of pleasure, she turned towards me and kissed me lightly on the lips. Then she blushed in the prettiest possible way.

'Thank you,' she said again.

The bracelet drew comment.

Christine, Hala and I started taking out a boat on shell-collecting expeditions. We soon discovered that it was necessary to row to deep water to find shells of any worthwhile size, and this meant taking stones as weights to drag us down to the bottom. One morning, instead of my customary dawn walk, I decided I would go shell-collecting. The water was so clear and unruffled it would be easy to see the bottom even without getting out of the boat. As I was putting out from the jetty, I saw Hala walking down and called out, inviting her to join me. We were halfway across the bay when Hala snorted in annoyance. She had no swimsuit.

'Well, you'll either have to stay in the boat or swim in whatever you are wearing under your clothes,' I remarked. She looked at me severely.

'That's not funny,' she said.

When we reached a suitable spot, I stripped to my swimming trunks, picked up the bag of stones I had prepared and was about to drop over the side when Hala complained.

'But what about me?'

'Well, what about you? What do you expect me to do?' I retorted. She looked doubtful, so I suggested that she work out a solution while I made my first dive. The stones took me down effortlessly, and I collected a few good shells and began the swim back up – much more difficult since I brought the bag of stones back up as well.

I was out of breath when I surfaced. I grabbed the rudder and heaved the bag over the side. I was about to ask Hala to help haul me aboard when I realised that she was not there. Lying in the bottom of the boat were her clothes. The temptation was irresistible. I let go and dived back down. I saw her. She was going down with a stone in her arms, wearing what looked like my shirt. It was too short to cover her. Her long shapely legs propelled her slim graceful body and below the shirt she was bare. It was absolutely entrancing. Alas, I was out of breath and had to go up for air. I climbed on board and Hala surfaced in her turn, bearing several large shells. Her eyes were shining.

'Good shells,' she exclaimed, dropping them over the side, 'but I left the stone on the bottom.'

My very thin shirt proved to be very revealing, and clung transparently to her breasts. She asked for my bag of stones, intending to dive again. I suggested that she had collected enough, but she had seen some really big shells, and insisted. There was enough weight in my bag to take us both down, so I suggested we went down together. I jumped in and, each holding one handle of the bag, we sank to the bottom. My shirt only covered the upper part of her body and it was not till we were busy collecting shells that she glanced down and realised her predicament. A look of horror came over her face. She let go of the bag and tried to pull down the shirt with her hand; without the bag, she shot up to the surface like a balloon while I followed more slowly. She tried to get into the boat before I surfaced, but seeing me come up next to her, dived under the boat to the other side. I heaved the bag on board and started to laugh.

'I think you are a horrid pig!' she screeched.

'And I think you are the most charming and beautiful thing I have ever seen,' I retorted. With that, I pulled myself aboard.

'What are we going to do?' she pleaded. She asked me to pass her clothes to her so that she could dress in the water.

'You're crazy,' I said, 'I think I've seen as much of you as I am likely to, but I'll do the decent thing and turn my back so that you can get back on board and put your clothes on.'

The expression on Hala's face showed that she did not altogether trust me. She took a long time thinking about it.

'Mind you do as you promised or I will never speak to you again,' she said. I did as I had promised and turned my back, till Hala invited me to face her. She was holding my flimsy shirt in front of her. It barely came below her waist.

'I didn't realise it was so short,' she blurted out. 'What must you think of me?'

'I think you have a very beautiful body and I love it.'

'Well, you must promise me you won't tell anyone what happened, or I shall be the laughing stock of the whole camp.'

So I promised, and she rewarded me with a kiss, given with a singular lack of reluctance.

'I tell you what I shall do, my dear Hala. I shall always keep this shirt, and in future whenever I am lonely I shall hug it and think of you inside it.'

Hala did not quite know how to take this. I, on the other hand, meant every word of it. I kept that shirt for a very long time.

It was still early when we returned to camp, which was only just beginning to show signs of life. We were famished. Hala went into the kitchen and returned with coffee, hunks of bread and plum jam.

'Do you know,' she said, avoiding my eyes while she was

talking, 'I'm ashamed to admit it, but... you know, er... you know, I am not embarrassed by you seeing me liked that.'

This episode brought us even closer together. We found a private trysting place where we explored the delights of proximity, of cuddling and passionate kissing. Just once I was allowed to fondle Hala's breasts, but nothing more. Perhaps it was as well that our holiday came to an end. When we said goodbye to each other, and to Solta, it was in the knowledge that something very important had happened to us both; something that we would remember for the rest of our lives.

Flying High

Hala still filled my mind when I got home. In a way, I was quite relieved when my mother questioned me about her. She had found out from Christine, who I could hardly have expected to keep quiet on the subject. She had also sought and received reassurances from the headmaster. My sadness at being separated from Hala was offset by the marvellous news which awaited me on return. I had been accepted for the advanced gliding course, which was to start in a few days and continue almost to the end of the school holidays.

The gliding centre at Bezmiechowa, run by the Aero-club of Lwow, was one of the best known in Europe. I arrived to find the course had already assembled, for my instructions were a day out. The ridge on which Bez-miechowa was situated was several miles long, which allowed several gliders to soar simultaneously in safety. There was no shortage of gliders, from the most basic to the high-performance Eaglets designed for the newly introduced gliding competition in the Olympic Games. However, even advanced pupils had to start at the begin-ning, and we started with the simple Magpie. Four pupils and an instructor were allocated to each machine. My instructor was called Miet.

He explained the cockpit layout – not that there was much to explain: the only instruments were an air-speed indicator, climb and descend indicators and an altimeter. His instructions were exact.

'Take off, turn to soar along the ridge. If you cannot get

lift, fly away from the ridge and land uphill from the bottom of the valley. Horses will come to pull your glider back, and you must walk alongside, holding up the wing.'

Miet already knew that I had managed to soar for eleven minutes, when few had managed more than three at the basic gliding school and referred to this when explaining why he was sending me off first. I climbed into the cockpit, strapped myself in and was catapulted off by the rest of the team. There was a moderate wind blowing, and I could see several gliders happily soaring above. The slope was steep, and the ground fell away sharply. I turned to the left and felt myself being lifted up and up, till the top of the ridge was well below me on my left. Filled with a sense of exaltation, I flew right to the end of the ridge, turned and flew back, still with plenty of height. I could see my group watching me from the launch site as I flew over them to the other end of the ridge and back again. We were not supposed to do more than one length of the course, so I broke away from the ridge, losing height, and went into a shallow dive to land uphill. I did not take into proper account my own speed or that of the wind and as a result I did not touch down at the bottom of the valley as instructed, but halfway up the hill. The glider finally came to a halt near the take-off point. Miet, rightly, greeted me with a sharp rebuke: 'When you have more experience you will be able to land high up on the ridge, but from now, on you will do as I tell you and land at the bottom.'

We each had two flights that day. We were judged to have performed sufficiently well to be promoted to the higher performance Mosquito the next day. The days were not long enough for us. We flew incessantly, the weather being kind. Every day I flew, I learned something new. The exhilaration of being like a bird and, in this splendid isolation being free, made me at once proud, pleased, humble and inadequate. From the air, everything looked different; the earth and earthly life appeared in a different perspective. These feelings gave me a sort of moral uplift. It was not that there was anything wrong with my morale, but I felt that something new was being born and reborn within me every time I was in the air. One manifestation of this feeling was audible; once airborne, I hummed and sang to myself. I did not realise that the voice carries downwards through the still air further than on the ground. Down below, I could be heard quite clearly. My leg was pulled mercilessly and I was asked to sing something different because people were getting bored by the same old tune! I tried hard to stop this extraordinary habit, especially when it became an obsession which I could not control. It came subconsciously and remained with me for many years and many thousands of flying hours throughout my flying career.

By the time the three-week course had come to an end we had all achieved the first leg of the Silver Badge – five hours' soaring after take-off. Three of us managed the second leg – achieving a height of a thousand metres above take-off. None of us managed the last leg of fifty kilometres' flight. The most I managed was forty-seven kilometres, before thermals forced me down. It was galling to have got so very close to the hat trick.

Then it was back home and back to school. Hala and I had been exchanging short letters since we had parted, but when I got home I found a long letter awaiting me, and I responded in kind. She was regaled with minute descriptions of my flying experiences. So were my family. Both my time with Hala and my flying had wrought changes in my character. I had acquired a greater degree of assurance and self-discipline, and a more adult and mature attitude, which showed itself in more thoughtfulness, more anticipation of other people's thoughts and actions, and a greater ability to react to them. On the other hand, I was becoming more and more of a loner, happiest in my own company, and missing the isolation of flying and skiing. Whether Hala's company would have made any difference I do not know. (I was in Lwow and she was miles away in Warsaw.) What I do know is that I missed her.

I began to think about my future, and turned to my art master for advice. He invited me to his home for tea, the following Saturday. Afterwards we went into his study.

'I know an air force doctor,' he said, after a few opening exchanges, 'and I have spoken to him. My friend tells me that colour vision is important, but that there are people who have flown in spite of it being defective.' My heart leapt at this welcome news. 'He even told me how colour vision is tested.' He opened a drawer in his desk and drew out a black book. He opened it at random. There was page covered with coloured dots, and suddenly I realised that some of the dots formed a pattern of the figure 82.

'What can you see?' he enquired.

'Eighty-two,' I answered.

He looked at me and opened the book at another page. We went through the entire book. On some pages I could see nothing. But as we turned the pages, I noticed tiny numbers at the top and bottom of each page indicating the sequence of the pages.

'You can distinguish some numbers but not others,' commented my mentor. 'You are obviously not fully colour-blind, but I don't think you are up to the required standard. I am prepared to help you on one condition – and I want you to give me your word that you will adhere to this condition for the rest of your life.'

Not knowing the condition, I was reluctant to promise the unknown.

'The condition is', he explained patiently, 'that you first learn to fly as a civilian. If you don't find that your colour perception places you into any danger and if your flying, in the opinion of others, is very good – and I mean very good – you may go on and apply to join the air force. You realise that not only am I helping you to risk your neck, but I am aiding and abetting you to cheat. And, by the way, I do not want your parents to know about this.'

I was very surprised that he felt strongly enough to be prepared to go to such lengths to help me.

'Take the book. You can keep it for two days and learn the charts by heart. The key to the pages is at the back. I want it back on Tuesday morning. 'Incidentally,' he added, 'these books are used all over the world, so you can cheat any ophthalmologist, wherever you may be. But remember the condition on which I do this.'

I was rendered nearly speechless. I was so moved by his kindness that I found my eyes filling with tears as I tried to thank him. I discovered what thanking someone from the bottom of one's heart really meant. It could not be translated into words.

By Sunday night, I knew those charts by heart. Then I applied for a medical. For this, I had to go to Warsaw, and that meant I was also able to spend two days with Hala. Absence, we found, had made both our hearts grow fonder. I called at her house, in the Old City. Hala was alone; her parents were out, but I would be expected to stay for dinner. In the meantime, I had her to myself. We squeezed tight into a large armchair and exchanged news… After half an hour her parents arrived.

'Hala has told us a lot about you, of course,' said Hala's mother, once we had been introduced, 'and you are very welcome. From the constant flow of letters, we gather that you are keeping in close touch.'

I was not quite sure how to answer; I feared I detected a touch of sarcasm, and was not sure how to react. Hala's father came to my rescue.

'You're keen on flying?' he enquired. 'I would love to fly

myself, but I suppose I am too old. Do you intend to make flying your career?'

'I love flying,' I replied, feeling that I was being interrogated, 'but I am not sure whether I would prefer the air force, or to go to university and read aerodynamics. The truth is, sir, I'm not yet quite sure which way my future will develop.'

The conversation then turned to other matters. After dinner, Hala suggested that we should go dancing, but I wanted to introduce her to my father, who happened to be passing through Warsaw at the same time. So we went to his hotel, the Europejski, where we had a drink together.

'I'm delighted to meet you, Hala,' he said. 'We have heard so much about you but I did not suspect that my son had such good taste.' He was in his element. Father liked good-looking girls. 'So what are you two planning to do tonight?'

'We're going dancing,' I replied.

'We thought of going to the Cafe Club,' added Hala, for I had no idea where to go in Warsaw. 'It's Tuesday and they are broadcasting, so they will have a good band.'

Father looked at me thoughtfully, and then asked if he could have two minutes' conversation in private. So I followed him out nervously, wondering why he needed to speak to me on my own. He put his hand in his pocket and pulled out a wad of notes.

'I don't want to get in your way,' he said. 'Here, take these and have a good time. Congratulations again on your good taste.' With that he left me, and I returned to Hala.

'Where is that charming father of yours?' she asked.

'He's rather tired and has decided to have an early night. He approves of you!'

So we went dancing. Dawn was breaking when we got back to Hala's home.

'Can you imagine what Solta would be looking like at

this time of the morning?' she asked, giving me a kiss. 'Thank you for a wonderful evening.' With that, she went inside.

I passed my medical. On my return, I went to thank my art master. He congratulated me warmly.

'It's not my success, sir,' I protested with humility, 'it's yours, and I shall remember you as long as I live.'

'Well,' he observed, 'I hope you live a long time. I shall be thinking of you often. If you kill yourself flying, I shall have you on my conscience.'

Now, flying absorbed all my attention. But it was expensive and my parents would have found it difficult to support the costs of my ambition. Fortunately, I was awarded a scholarship by the Air League, and was able to enrol in a flying course at the local Aeroclub.

The aeroclub which I joined was the Lwow Aeroclub, where the flying training was entrusted to active, reserve and retired air force officers. Among them were two young lieutenants, with one of whom I became particularly friendly because I admired his skill. They were both experts in aerobatics, in which they gave demonstrations from time to time. After one such exhibition, which left me open-mouthed in admiration, he came up to me for a chat.

'How's flying?' he enquired.

'After what you have just shown us, what I do is not flying,' I answered.

'Your day will come,' he promised. 'But in the meantime you might be able to help me.'

It was a shrewd move. He must have known that, after his aerial stunts, I would be only too anxious to help. I made that clear.

'At your school, there must be several, maybe many, boys of German and Ukrainian origin. In fact, I know that you are friendly with a Ukrainian and also with a German. I also know that you and your family are great patriots, and that your parents and grandparents took an active part in the defence of Lwow. I know too, that you have German cousins living locally. I will be honest with you, and I appeal to your patriotic feelings. We need as much information as we can gather about what is going on in the Ukrainian and German circles. I am not suggesting you spy on them, only that you let me know if you hear anything. I would be very grateful for your help.'

Flattered beyond belief and full of admiration for this fantastic flyer, I did not know then and did not realise for a year or two, that I had been skilfully recruited into a voluntary intelligence network.

I concentrated single-mindedly on powered-flying instruction and gliding, and no one doubted that I would pass all the flying exams with ease. My school studies were sadly neglected. I was confronted with this neglect with brutal frankness, and threatened with unspeakable consequences if I did not take prompt corrective action. In my last year at school, my mid-term results were deplorable and success in matriculation was not predicted. My mother appealed to me to make a real effort; my father gave me a stern lecture.

It was Christine, however, who engineered a change in my outlook. In desperation, she wrote to Hala, who promptly wrote to me pointing out a few home truths. I was livid. I tackled Mother, who denied all responsibility, and quarrelled with Christine, who admitted nothing but told me I got what I deserved. But Hala's letter did the trick. I began to work as I had never worked before. In the end, to everyone's surprise, I not only passed my matriculation but did so with distinction, and then passed the university entrance exam. At the same time, I was progressing so fast in flying and skiing that I had hopes of being selected for the Olympics.

There can be few experiences more exhilarating than flying high-performance sailplanes. One becomes as a bird, soaring high in the air. Only the singing of the air and the faint moaning of the sailplane disturbs the absolute solitudinal silence. At times, the currents were so slight that the lift would be no more than a few centimetres a second and at other times, so strong that one becomes afraid that the wings would not stand the strain, the skin of the wing showing visible signs of stress, the wing-tips bending and twisting. Once height had been achieved, then one could emulate the skill of a hawk or an eagle in aerobatic display. That was life, that was joy!

The hours in my log book mounted and with it, my experience, and it did not pass unnoticed.

Miet had now become deputy chief instructor at Bezmiechowa. One day while I was there, he addressed one of the other instructors, with whom I was by now friendly.

'Karl, the SG28 is now ready after its rebuild. Would you take it up for a test, and if it's all right, we can put it on the line later today.'

So Karl ordered the SG28, one of the most advanced sailplanes, to be brought out. To save time, he was towed up on a winch, and, once he reached some two hundred metres, levelled off and released the wire. It was a good morning for flying; cumulus clouds were building up and there were thermals from the fields of ripening corn. Karl got into an uplift and circled tightly. The machine seemed to be performing well, and he soon reached a thousand metres. He was an expert and never missed an opportunity to gain extra height. But this day, his job was not so much to gain height as to put the machine through its paces, and we anticipated an exhibition of air artistry. We saw his sailplane emerge from the up-current and slowly lose speed, with the nose well up, facing into the wind. Finally, it almost stopped, and we could see the glistening surface of the rudder move to one side: he was going to start with a spin. The wing dropped and the machine spun once, twice, three times as he came out precisely into the wind. He pushed down the nose to gain speed. He was still well up, at about seven hundred metres. We could hear the increasing whine of the glider as it gained speed. Then Karl pulled the nose up sharply and went into a loop, a perfect circle with not a degree of deviation. He was going to loop again. He pushed the nose down and pulled up rather violently. We could almost imagine the joints of the sailplane protesting. Or was it entirely imagination?

Karl's machine was now some six hundred metres up and half a kilometre away. We heard something snap and the next moment saw one of the wings begin to flap, exactly like a bird's wing. We watched, unbelieving. As if in slow motion, bits of the wing began to fall off, at first small bits, then pieces of plywood covering the leading edge of the wing, then strips of the canvas cover, then the whole wing. For a second or two the sailplane appeared to be suspended in mid-air, then it slowly turned on its back and went into a vicious spiral, faster and faster, lower and lower.

'Jump! Jump quickly!' shouted someone behind me, frantically.

Karl, of course, could not hear. But as if in response to the shout, the cockpit canopy fell away. We watched horror-struck, waiting for him to get out and open his parachute. Nothing happened. There was an almighty crash as the machine fell into the tall old pine trees of the forest. We could hear the branches breaking and the sailplane disintegrating among them.

Then, complete silence. No one spoke. From the bottom of the hill, we could hear the whine of the rescue vehicle. At once, we all started running towards the crash. The forest there was thick, making progress slow, and it was easy to become disorientated. My stalking experience gave me confidence. Jumping over fallen branches and old tree stumps, hampered by the undergrowth, I ran for all I was worth. Then I saw a bit of shiny plywood and white canvas in a tree and knew I could not be far away. A bit further on, there was the tail of the machine sticking out from thick undergrowth.

'Here he is!' I bellowed as loudly as my exhausted lungs would allow. I could hear voices behind me, and shouted again. Fearful of what I might discover, I advanced, despite knocking knees. The gaping hole of the cockpit stared at me like a blind eye. All around lay debris. At first I thought that Karl was not there. For some reason I had expected him to be sitting in the cockpit. Then I saw. His harness was undone. His body had been forced by the impact underneath what was left of the instrument panel, and the top of the stick was alongside his neck. One of the mainstays of the fuselage had pierced his body. There was blood everywhere.

I turned away and was violently sick. I knew there was nothing anyone could do for him.

Miet was one of the first on the scene.

'There's nothing we can do. Leave him for the doctor. Back to the starting point, all of you.'

I am sure I was not the only one thankful to leave the scene. Struggling back through the undergrowth was so difficult it was amazing how quickly we had got there. Miet marshalled us and the machines.

'These things happen,' he said, 'but they must not stop us. Karl would want us to go on, and we shall.'

He made every one of us take to the air. We did so without much enthusiasm, keeping well within the limits of safety. It helped us to get to terms with what we had just witnessed.

Down to Earth

When I began my power flying course at the Aeroclub, I found myself under Captain Pawel, the senior instructor, and Stefan, a reserve officer who was also the club's engineering expert. It was Stefan who took me up for the first time. The aeroplane was of an old French make, which had seen service in World War I and subsequently, in the Polish air force. A number of these planes saw their frail life out in aeroclubs up and down the country. The routine which I was to follow for many years began as soon as we climbed into the cockpit.

'Switches off,' shouted the ground crew.

'Switches off,' answered Stefan.

'Fuel on.'

'Fuel on,' acknowledged Stefan.

'Throttle closed.'

'Throttle closed.'

'Suck in,' shouted Stefan, leaning out of the cockpit.

The ground crew swung the propeller. Nothing happened, of course, as the switches were off. He swung the propeller again and again; eventually he called, 'Contact!'

'Contact!' repeated Stefan, throwing the switches. The ground crew gave the propeller a powerful swing and the engine burst into life. There was smoke and the smell of oil.

'Dirty and smelly things, these rotary engines,' shouted Stefan over the intercom. 'Are you ready?'

'Ready,' I answered, nodding my head.

We taxied to the take-off point where the duty starter was in his caravan. Stefan described everything as he did it. My hands and feet rested lightly on the controls, and I could feel his fairly brutal movements of the rudder pedals and the subtler movements of the throttle lever. He turned across wind at the starter's caravan.

'Are you ready?' he asked again. I nodded. The starter waved his flag and Stefan turned into the wind.

'Keep your hands on the controls and your feet on the rudder. I will explain every movement I make.'

We took off and flew for a while. Stefan, talking the whole time, concentrated more on the use of the engine than on flying the aircraft, for the controls were basically the same as those in gliders.

'I want you to make some gentle turns to the right and left,' he told me. 'Remember that you will need less rudder and more aileron than you do when flying a glider. Your nose will tend to drop, so you will have to pull gently on the stick.'

'I would like to get the feel of straight and level flight, first,' I asked. 'Is that all right?'

'You've got the controls,' he answered.

I found that the machine was always slewing to the left, and that to keep it straight, I had to apply the right rudder. I asked Stefan if this was typical.

'That's the effect of engine torque,' he explained, 'pulling the machine in the opposite direction to the rotation of the propeller.'

At length, I learned how to fly straight. Then I applied the rudder as in a glider, but the nose dipped.

'Keep the nose up. You hardly used the ailerons,' corrected Stefan. I got back on to a straight and level course and tried again.

'That's better,' he encouraged. 'Now try turning the other direction.'

I did as instructed and found that the machine behaved differently.

'Did you feel the difference?' asked Stefan. 'That is the effect of engine torque again.'

We flew on for some time and then Stefan asked if I knew where we were. I looked down. Lwow was nowhere to be seen. There were fields below us. I glanced at the altimeter; we were at two thousand metres.

'I didn't realise we were so high.' Stefan laughed. 'You've been climbing steadily all the time. Have you found your bearings yet?'

I looked down again. Suddenly, just behind the lower wing, I saw my home.

'We're about twelve kilometres north of Lwow.'

'That is exactly where we are. How did you know, or did you guess?'

'I live down there,' I replied, pointing down.

'Luck!' exclaimed Stefan, who had not known. 'In future, I shall expect you to know where you are. You have a map, I hope?'

We turned south, and soon found both Lwow and the airfield. Stefan brought the aircraft in to land, explaining the procedures all the time. When he had landed, he suggested that I should try to taxi back. When I tried, I soon had the aircraft rolling much too fast, and was duly corrected.

'That wasn't bad, for a first attempt. We'll have a rest and go up again in half an hour's time.'

In fact, we went up twice more that day, and I was able to start my power flying logbook with three flights totalling two hours. On my way home, I reflected on my experience and how powered flying compared with gliding. How different they were! Like comparing a bicycle with a motorbike, perhaps? I missed the almost silent and graceful sailplane, which contrasted so noticeably with the harsh, stocky, smelly, noisy machine. The powered aircraft handled differently and remained airborne without difficulty. In short, while both were flying machines, there seemed to be a big difference!

I returned the next day, although it was a Sunday. We practised take-offs and landings. By the end of the second weekend I had logged nearly eight hours' dual. I knew that there were those who had flown solo after eight hours, but I did not yet feel ready for it. In the middle of the following week, there was a holiday. At Stefan's suggestion, I went up to the airfield in search of more practice. When I got there, Stefan was in the air with another pupil, and Captain Pawel was on the ground looking bored.

'Come on, Andrew,' he said, 'let's see how you are progressing.'

We climbed into a machine. He told me to start the engine, and then to taxi to the starter's caravan.

'Okay. She's all yours. Take off, make a nice flight round the airfield at precisely three hundred metres, all turns precisely ninety degrees, and come down to land, and I want you to touch down precisely at the starter's caravan.'

'You couldn't have been more precise in your instructions.' I tried to be funny.

'Don't take the piss out of me, young man. I like to be precise, and I like my pupils to know what I expect from them.'

We took off and I did as he wished. However, I touched down a little past the caravan.

'I told you to touch down precisely at the caravan, and you didn't. Go round again.'

I taxied to the caravan, waited for the flag and took off again. He did not say a word till we had landed.

'That was better,' Pawel mumbled as if to himself.

We took off once more. My instructions were as before. However, when we were down wind from the airfield, I saw him put out his hand and place it on the switches. He turned them off and suddenly the engine stopped.

'I want you to carry out a forced landing in the near corner of the field.'

Stefan had taken me through this procedure before, but he had never switched off. He had only throttled back to let the engine idle.

'She's all yours,' boomed the captain over the intercom, 'if you mess it up, we're in trouble. We can't restart the engine now.'

I turned carefully into the wind towards the airfield. We could just reach the near end of it. The eerie silence and the stationary propeller were unnerving and the aircraft was losing height rapidly.

'Just like gliding,' stated Pawel, 'remember, she won't swing with the engine not running.'

We touched down just fifty metres inside the perimeter. A recovery truck was racing over from the club hangar. We handed over the aircraft to the mechanics, threw our parachutes in the truck, and walked back. Captain Pawel analysed my every action from the time we had left the dispersal. Stefan was waiting and looked enquiringly at both of us.

'Not bad,' commented the captain. 'He's all yours.'

Stefan took me to one side. 'How did it go?' he asked.

'I think it was okay,' I answered. 'I hope I didn't let you down.'

'We will fly again as soon as the machine is refuelled.'

We rejoined the aircraft. When it was ready, we climbed in and taxied over to the take off point. Stefan waved to the controller and beckoned him. He came over and the two talked for a few moments.

'Right, one circuit and landing,' ordered Stefan.

We flew round and landed. Stefan got out by the caravan, tied up his safety harness, and stood at my side.

'Off you go, then,' he said. 'One circuit and landing. I will wait for you here.'

'You mean I am to fly solo?'

Stefan nodded. 'Good luck!' was all he said.

I lined up into the wind, opened the throttle, and was off. When I had reached the required height and throttled back for level flight, the engine coughed and spluttered. I felt the power dropping for a quick moment, then it picked up again. Even so, the quick irregularity of the engine sent a shiver up and down my spine. Would the engine fail before I finished my circuit? I suddenly realised how quickly I had come to rely on the engine rather than on my wits, which had to be exercised all the time in gliding. The realisation calmed me down. After all, I had practised forced landings, so even if the engine did fail, I was only back to gliding. Fortunately the engine did not stop; it purred happily on. I finished the circuit and throttled back for the approach to land. My landing was awful. I bounced and bounced, the machine creaked in all its joints every time I hit the ground, and I had to go round again. My second landing was better, and as I taxied back to the take off point and the waiting Stefan, I knew that I was in for a well-deserved ticking off.

'You may call that flying, and you may say that you have flown solo, but I have to tell you that yours was the worst first solo landing I have ever had the misfortune to witness. Come on, we will try together.'

He climbed in and we took off. This time all went well. It was a perfect landing and he said so. Then he sent me up alone once more. I got it right at last…

After that, I never looked back. I got my licence three months later and became the youngest licence holder at the aeroclub.

I suppose this all went to my head. I was bursting with pride, and my only topics of conversation were flying and skiing. I did not appreciate it at the time, but I must have become unbearably cocky and socially impossible, which did not prevent me from showing my certificate of competence, graded 'Very Good' to my art master. He was very pleased. At least I had the grace to acknowledge: 'It's all thanks to you, sir.'

Captain Pawel pulled strings and found me a grant. As a result, I was able to fly a great deal and had soon clocked up one hundred hours. This was quite a lot for a civilian pilot, and it enabled me to qualify for an advanced flying course which included aerobatics. This course was full time, not just consecutive weekends, as hitherto, and I had to wait till enough candidates could be assembled. In the meantime, as well as powered flying, I also went back to gliding.

One such day, when conditions were favourable, there being a lot of cumulus building up, my old instructor and now friend, Miet, was controlling the take off area.

'Take the Five,' he said to me, 'no, not that one, mine. It has a better finish on it and is a little faster. Off you go, and make sure the barograph is calibrated and sealed. Try an out and return flight; aim at 150 km out and 150 km back, say Lublin and back.'

It was a rare privilege to use his machine, and I thanked him accordingly.

Immediately after take off, I got into a powerful uplift; the machine was going up like a lift; the vertical speed indicator showed two metres per second. At three hundred metres, I flew on to where a bigger cumulus also promised good lift, and where four other sailplanes, albeit of a lower performance than mine, were circling. As I got under the cloud, the lift started, but as I was getting closer to the other sailplanes I flew away from them to the edge of the cloud, and in a few seconds I was above all of them

Looking down at the take-off area, I could see the number of my machine and a red arrow next to it, which told me I should set out on my cross-country flight. I set the course north. I had nearly reached two thousand metres and was close to the base of the cumulus. There was lift everywhere. If the day continued like this, I was confident I could get to Lublin and back without trouble. Ten kilometres ahead was a huge cumulus and I made for it. As I reached its shadow, I discovered the meaning of real lift, and the altimeter went crazy. I must have been halfway across the cloud shadow when I was sucked in. In the cloud it was cold, the machine was buffeted by the vertical speed and the altimeter was still climbing. I concentrated on instrument flying: not easy, as I had little previous experience. I tried to fly on a northerly course to get out of the cloud.

Suddenly, there was a complete change in the sailplane's behaviour. From a strong upcurrent, I found myself in a strong down draught. I looked at the altimeter – 3,800 metres and falling. I looked at the airspeed indicator – 125 kilometres, 130 kilometres and increasing. Thought I, what the hell is happening? I knew I was not in control.

The machine was whining and whistling and there were groans from behind me. I saw dust from the bottom of the fuselage fall past my face and land on the canopy. I must be upside down, I thought, though it did not feel like it. The machine was buffeting more and more, the wings were flexing, and I could see the plywood surfaces working. I had a sudden vision of Karl and his sailplane falling to bits in the air and at that moment there was a bang, as if someone had fired a rifle close by my ear. The sound seemed to come from the right and I automatically looked in that direction. The wing looked different, but how? Then I looked at the other wing and knew. I went cold inside, very, very cold. I had lost my right aileron; I knew I was in dire trouble.

Now I saw not only Karl's broken glider, but the whole of my short life flashing through my mind, together with a flurry of my prayers seeking help, deliverance and forgiveness, to an orchestral accompaniment of cracks and bangs, as bits and pieces of the right wing were now visibly breaking off.

I tried to move the controls. In some directions, they were quite limp, in others, stiff and unyielding, and the machine responded to none. There was a gaping hole in the right wing just by the cockpit and the plywood and the fabric on it were slowly peeling off. The instruments were in the same state of confusion as my mind; there was no rhyme or reason in their readings, and being still in the cloud, I was utterly lost.

Wanting to get out, I remembered that the cloud was cold, and that the upcurrents in it would prevent my descending by parachute. With a final crack, the remnants of the right wing flew off, to be immediately followed by the left one. At that moment I saw the ground. I was plummeting almost vertically earthwards with a slight, porpoise-like movement of the fuselage.

I pulled the canopy release and the canopy flew off; I released my harness pin and was forcibly thrown out of the cockpit. Desperately searching for the rip cord, I finally found it and pulled. I felt the chute stream out and open with a clap, arresting my fall and jarring my body. I gave a sigh of relief and said a prayer of thanksgiving. By now the ground was only five hundred metres beneath me. I was swinging under the canopy like a pendulum, and tried to remember what I was supposed to do to control it. I pulled the cords first on one side and then on the other, and eventually succeeded in checking the swing only seconds before hitting the ground. The ground was hard. I hoped I was still in one piece. But there was a light wind blowing which, filling my chute, was dragging me towards a line of trees. By the time I had undone the harness, the parachute was caught in the branches of a big oak.

People were running across the field towards me. I staggered to my feet, feeling bruised but otherwise unhurt, and walked towards them. There was a tall, middle-aged man, a woman and two younger women.

'Are you all right?' asked the man, solicitously. 'We saw you come out of that cloud without wings. One wing has fallen in the park. Let me introduce myself: my name is Tarnowski, this is my wife, the Countess Tarnowska, together with Zosia and Marysia. You had better come with us.'

The Lull

During the last few years before matriculation, and then while at university, I spent most of the academic year at Lwow to save the twelve-kilometre journey from home every day. There were enough members of the family with spare rooms who were more than happy to put me up. My favourite relatives among the senior generation were my grandparents. For a time, I lived with them, when at school. When not lodging there, I visited them whenever I had a spare moment.

My great-grandmother also lived with them and she was also a great friend of mine, in spite of her age. Although over eighty, she had a splendid sense of humour and still spoke several languages fluently, read voraciously and had a sharp enough eye to do fine embroidery and crochet lace. She was tiny, with masses of snow-white hair. We often sat together, while she told me stories of her youth in the mid-nineteenth century. She was a great patriot, and filled my head with stories of Poland's heroic past, some from her own experience, and others told to her by long-past generations. Her stories were mixed with a deep knowledge of writers, poets and composers and all the old and new traditional and patriotic songs. I listened avidly, for they reinforced the high sense of patriotism and national pride with which we were all brought up.

One such occasion, I will never forget. We were talking about my future when she suddenly stopped what she was saying and went absolutely silent.

Then, quite out of context, she said, 'Please promise me faithfully that you will never forget that you are Polish, even when you are serving in foreign armies.'

I was astounded. Then she repeated the sentence, word for word for a second time. I asked her what she meant.

'I don't know why I said it,' she answered. 'I really have no idea. But I know, I can see it.'

After this, she asked me to leave her because she felt very tired. When I asked her about it subsequently from time to time, she would either disown it, or confirm that it was my future. It was to prove an accurate prophecy.

My grandmother was quite excited about my flying, and would, sometimes, slip me a little money to help out with the cost. She often said that she would love to be able to fly herself, but was now too old. She was certainly the only one of my family who whole-heartedly approved and supported it. Of the others, my father seemed the least concerned about the possible danger.

'After all,' he would say philosophically, 'one can have an accident on a bicycle.'

My mother, on the other hand, was genuinely concerned and worried. Knowing the enormous influence my mother exerted over family affairs, I lived in perpetual dread that approval for my flying would be withdrawn, especially once I finally confessed to the problems created by my colour-blindness. In this, I was lucky, for I found strong backing from a friend of the family, a one-eyed pilot; I often flew with him in his aircraft. He took the stand that if he could fly with vision in one eye only, which ruined his judgement of distance, I could fly just as well with my defective colour perception. Because he was well liked and respected, his support carried weight.

My position became even more tenuous after I sustained two further accidents, both of which were judged to have been my own fault. In the first case, I flew a glider into the ground and thereby damaged a leg. It took an operation and a few months' recuperation to mend. No sooner had I recovered from that when, while practising for a flying display being mounted by the aeroclub, I crashed a small aerobatic machine which burst into flames on impact. Apart from being slightly burned on the back, I was fortunate to survive without major damage.

Both accidents were the result of over-confidence in my flying ability. I knew I was good. Maybe I was told I was good too often for my own well-being. As a result, I had been pushing my luck, and familiarity had bred contempt. The time had come to learn a few home truths.

Captain Pawel, who represented the alpha and omega of flying as far as I was concerned, summoned me to his office one evening. He told me that he had just been re-reading the reports on my two accidents and that neither report was very complimentary, for both had been easily avoidable. He looked hard into my eyes.

'We have no spare money to waste on careless pilots,' he stated bluntly. 'I am formally warning you that if there are any more reports of your poor airmanship, and both accidents were the result of this, I will have to suspend you from flying.'

Despite the fact that I knew I deserved it, I was devastated by the warning. I spent hours, no, days, thinking and taking stock. As a result it became clear, even to me at last, that flying was a serious pursuit. Not only was it more dangerous than my other hobbies and pastimes, like skiing for example, but as a pilot, I was in charge of a very expensive piece of equipment which did not belong to me, but which was publicly owned and acquired through the efforts of many people, so that one could learn to fly. I had been fortunate enough to have both the opportunity and ability to fly, and this was something which should not be treated light-heartedly or abused. Taken seriously and responsibly, it might provide me with a career which was close to my heart; squandered by carelessness, it might not only jeopardise my ambitions, but blow me into smithereens and the aircraft with me. Once I had analysed and recognised the problem, I applied myself to rectifying my shortcomings.

At university, I discovered the heady privileges of undergraduate life, mainly, the freedom to organise one's daily life as one chose, for only a few items in the curriculum were compulsory. I devoted much time 'gained' therefore, to flying and skiing. But not all.

So far, I had heard nothing further on the subject of intelligence-gathering. The pilot whom I admired so much, who had sought to recruit me, had not mentioned it further. Now contact came through one of my fellow undergraduates.

There was a need to identify those who had fallen under the influence of Hitler's ideologies, whatever their nationality or ethnic affiliation, and especially to discover their possible contacts with Ukrainian political activists. It was the time when the Nazis were trying to form an underground network, the Fifth Column, later to become so infamous throughout Europe. I was reminded, gently, that I had German family connections, some of whom were not above suspicion, and had an Ukrainian school friend who was, it was suggested, politically active.

I was politely but firmly instructed to keep my eyes and ears open, and to report anything, however trivial it might seem, and to do so in such a way that my interest was not compromised. My patriotism was apparently seen as sufficient for national interest to override loyalty to family and friends. It was, however, made clear that there was no interest in Polish politics, either for or against the government, with the possible exception of the Communists. This presented no problem, for while I was of no party, especially the two main political parties, I could neither stand nor understand the Communists.

By the end of 1938, my generation recognised that there could soon be another war. The German propaganda machine was getting into full stride, and German demands for the Polish Corridor, which separated Germany from East Prussia, increased in frequency and threat. Our elders did not appear to be disconcerted by these warlike noises, having faith in diplomatic solutions and guarantees from the West. All the same, the family factory received increased contracts for tinned food for the armed forces clearly a build-up of war reserves. This background did little to encourage concentration on academic work. I spent even more time flying and gliding.

Then, in early 1939, I was sent to England, to improve my English and to gain work experience in the aircraft industry. After a few weeks and before I had completed the planned programme, I returned home as a result of an irresistible invitation to participate in a gliding competition. Also in early 1939, I heard from Hala that she was being sent to Belgium to improve her French. She was to stay as an au pair with a Polish diplomat and study at the local university. We spoke on the telephone on the eve of her departure, renewing our promises to write regularly and often.

Back in Poland, I spent two weeks of the summer at the gliding centre of Bezmiechowa, prior to the gliding competition. I happily accepted the offer to be there, everything found, in return for linguistic help. There was an unusually large international group – English, French, Hungarian, and a Swede. This group became well integrated right from the start. However, I very soon realised, because I had to help them make telephone connections and frequently overheard part of the their conversations, that some at least had interests other than the gliding activity in which they were all eagerly participating.

I, of course, took every opportunity to glide. In particular, I hoped to gain my 'D' Certificate, for which one of the stipulations was attaining a height of 3,000 metres. One day, I was circling upwards in pursuit of this goal, when I lost lift. I began to search for a new one, since every second cost me height. Then I found a new thermal, and began to climb again. Below me lay Bezmiechowa. I could see the pin-like outlines of white, cream and red sailplanes waiting on the take-off line, and several pinky-brown faces peering upwards. Two machines were soaring over the ridge, others circling in the thermals. Further down the valley the silver ribbon of the river wound its way between the hills, and along it ran the grey-brown line of the road. Several cars marked their presence along that road with heavy plumes of dust lazily drifting in the slight wind. Most of the hills were covered by the clean and fresh looking forests. I wondered what wildlife lay beneath the canopy.

All the time my height was rising, reaching 2,000 metres before the lift petered out. I did not mind. I was happy and singing my head off. A kilometre away, a cumulus cloud was building up fast, and I flew into the shadow. The lift I expected was there, and I rose rapidly. At 2,600 metres, I was still under the cloud, but only just, and in danger of being sucked in. It was not an experience I wished to repeat. I thought that if I straightened out and flew to the edge at a high speed, I would be safe, and soon out of the cloud's shadow where the lift was. All the same, the cloud just sucked me in before I reached the edge.

Inside, as before, it was grey and chilly, and the machine began to buffet slightly. With a sigh of relief, I came out of the cloud into clear sunshine. I was pleased, I reached 2,900 metres in the process. The cloud top was way up above me, but I decided not to risk playing further with the cumulus, and to find a new thermal. Below me I could see three sailplanes circling in clear sunshine, which showed that there were thermals about. I flew with the wind searching for lift, and eventually found a slight upsurge. I only needed a little more height to reach my 3,000, and climbed slowly, aiming for a margin of 200 or 300 to be on the safe side.

At 3,100 metres, I sensed a shadow flicking across the glider. A large bird, or maybe another glider, I surmised, looking upwards. All I could see was the glare of the sun reflected and dispersed by the scratched perspex of the canopy, and beyond that, nothing. Better keep a sharp look out, I thought. A bird will fly away, but another glider or worse, a powered aircraft, might not see me below.

I reached the 3,300 metres which I had set myself. It was now too late for a cross-country flight, and in any case I was not briefed for one, and I needed 300 kilometres, for which insufficient time remained. I had just decided to start descending when the flicker of a shadow passed again.

I looked up. Close to the sun was an aircraft. It was certainly no glider, but in the glare I was unable to determine what it was and what it was doing. I tried to turn under it to get a better look, but the pilot seemed equally determined to stay in the line of the sun. My only hope of finding out was to drop my speed to near stalling. He could not fly as slowly, and would have to reveal himself.

I lifted the nose very slightly and my speed began to drop. There was a slight shudder of the wings as my glider slowed to the stalling point. I knew that in another second the nose would drop. At that moment I saw him, and heard his engine, in front and above me. It was a strange biplane, certainly not of Polish construction – I knew them all too well to be mistaken. It was still too much in the sun for me to see the registration marks. In the meantime, I was struggling to keep control of my own glider, as it wallowed, sank and shook at my very low speed. I imagined that the pilot of the aircraft would have similar but greater difficulty trying to stay in the sun, playing a sort of hide-and-seek, if that was his intention.

And then I saw black crosses on the fuselage and a swastika on the rudder. A German! I could scarcely believe it, but there was no doubt. I now even recognised it as a Henschell military reconnaissance plane.

I kicked the rudder and went into a spin. At about 2,500 metres I came out of it to see what he was doing. There he was, circling gently around me and, as I pulled out of the spin, he came towards me. Goose pimples broke out all over my body. I could see the pilot and his crewman quite clearly. I thought that there was a machine gun mounted in the rear cockpit. Suddenly he waggled his wings and turned away, flying in a southerly direction, in a shallow dive. We were only a short distance from the Czech border.

I spun to lose height, and landed near the take-off area. I wondered how much had been seen and understood by those watching below. The first to reach me was the chief instructor, a captain in the air force reserve. He helped me to take off the canopy.

'You are to speak to no one about this,' he said. 'We will notify the military authorities and then I want you to sit down and write a detailed report.'

I was picking up my parachute and getting the barograph from its compartment when he turned round and asked: 'By the way, did you get your height?'

It was the 16th of August. Little did we know that we were only two weeks from war.

The Storm Breaks

At dawn on 1st September, 1939, the German army marched into Poland. Lwow, where I then was, was astir at a very early hour and the streets were full of people meeting, talking and seeking reassurance. News was scarce, but hopeful. Soon loudspeakers were set up in the streets, and in windows, to be surrounded by eager listeners. General mobilisation had been ordered, and official broadcasts announced courageous resistance to the unprovoked onslaught.

While we Poles were full of hope that our country would be successfully defended, the local Ukrainians dreamed that their hour of independence was at hand. As we listened and talked, steel helmeted soldiers, often in horse-drawn carts, were everywhere in evidence many of them engaged in setting up anti-aircraft defences, and all cheered and encouraged by the onlookers.

Soon the radio was crammed with coded air-raid warnings, which interrupted the constant flow of news, official announcements and martial music. Popular initial fervour began to dampen as the listeners heard of the relentless advance of the German army against desperate opposition, of the bombardment of sea defences and harbour installations by the German navy, and the bombing of cities by the Luftwaffe. Lwow was a long way from the fighting, but any illusion of safety on that score was rapidly dissipated. Shortly after 11 a.m. on that first day, a formation of Heinkels appeared overhead. The sporadic anti-aircraft fire was ineffective and was completely ignored by the attackers. Bombs exploded on the industrial suburbs and around the railway station.

Three days later, the British and French, honouring their treaty obligations, were also at war. This lifted flagging morale, but otherwise it had no material effect on the situation. The news consisted of announcements of tactical withdrawals. The Germans were already half way to Warsaw and masters of the air.

Although a member of the auxiliary forces, I was not called up with the general mobilisation of the reserves. I tried to offer my services in various places but was told to wait: my call-up papers would come. By the time they did, a few days into September, Lwow had been bombed several times. The city centre itself was barely touched but the railways were in chaos, both from bombing and military saturation. My call up ordered me to report to an anti-aircraft training unit in the centre of Poland; it was very doubtful if I could get there. Having packed what I thought I might need, I reported to the local garrison headquarters to find out what I should do.

I arrived to find a state of confused tension. Even when I managed to get past the guards and into the building, I was at first unable to find anyone in authority or willing to take a decision. Finally, I found the garrison duty officer and explained my position. When he found out that I was a pilot, all be it not air force qualified, he made a couple of telephone calls as a result of which my papers were changed. I was to report now to an emergency airfield near Luck, where a useful job might be found for me. What is more, trains were said to be still running in that direction. He amended my papers, exhorting me to take good care of them.

It took a day to reach the airfield at Luck. To my surprise, I was welcomed and felt wanted, for there was a shortage of crews for the small communications aircraft which had been requisitioned from the aeroclubs. I was allocated a machine and given a very quick briefing that evening.

The briefing was simple. Pilots were expected to hedge-hop in order to avoid being spotted by the Luftwaffe; we were warned of our own ground forces opening fire at any aircraft flying over. The main task was to deliver communications, usually despatches and orders, to specified destinations and possibly to bring return reports. Landings would be in fields, probably unmarked. We were to deliver, collect, whatever was given to us and take-off for the next destination as quickly as possible, to avoid attracting enemy attention while on the ground, our aircraft not being painted in camouflage colours. If the unit to which delivery was being made had moved without possibility of ascertaining their destination, the delivery was to be brought back to base; if the base had moved in the meantime, pilots had to use their own initiative, possibly finding another air force unit. The aircraft were not fitted with radio, and all navigation was by map reading.

Finally, I was issued with a pistol and ammunition, ordered never to allow myself to be out of petrol and, in the last resort, to set the aircraft and any papers on fire to prevent their capture.

I tried to reconcile what had happened hitherto and what was going on around me with my ideas of what the war would be like. I do not know what I had imagined, but after the last few days it certainly did not fit in with my expectations. Was this a big game for the 'grown-ups', weird, frightening, challenging and even absorbing? Where did I fit into it? Was I just a pawn?

My first flight took me towards the Russian border, a short one, to a major headquarters. Hedge-hopping as instructed, I could see the roads crowded with people, domestic stock being herded along, carts full of personal possessions including furniture, drawn by horses, bullocks and even cows, pulled by children and the elderly. Here and there, could be seen a car in the mass of people, and rather more cars abandoned, no doubt having run out of petrol. From the air, I could see the uplifted faces very clearly, pale, drawn, tired and above all, angry. Often fists were shaken – gestures of hopelessness if they thought I was a Pole, or of defiance, if a German. At one point, I flew over a small army detachment. As they heard my approach, they turned to face me. Before I realised what they were, I found myself looking down rifle barrels and saw the spurts of blue smoke and flame as they fired. Fortunately for me, they did not understand deflection and missed.

With one exception, all movement on the roads was east and southwards; the exception was a troop of light tanks moving westwards, at speed, across country.

I found the HQ exactly where I had been told, and an unmarked landing strip, close by. A motorcyclist came out of the trees to meet me, and guided me to a point where my aircraft could be pushed under overhanging trees for cover. He took me to the communications centre, where I delivered my sealed package and was told to wait in case there was anything to be taken back. The army captain in charge looked haggard; the blue circles round his eyes suggested that he had had little sleep of late. I asked him if he could supply any petrol, especially if I had to fly anywhere further than return to base.

'We are short ourselves,' he said. 'We have no aircraft fuel, only ordinary car grade. We might spare a can for you, if that is any good?'

'That would do, so long as it is filtered and it isn't diesel.'

He left to organise this, after first detailing a soldier to fetch me a hot drink. It was only then that I appreciated

what was going on around me. Radio and telegraph opera-
tors were transmitting with chattering Morse keys, others
were listening intently and scribbling incoming messages,
but the radio, other than the National Radio announcements, was silent, as was the telephone switchboard. Men
came and went, some dirty and covered with layers of dust,
others looking equally tired but still tidy. A few had ban-
dages over minor wounds. After a while, the captain
returned.

'A can of petrol is on its way to your aircraft,' he announced, 'and we want you to take something to the
Southern army HQ. Whatever happens, this packet must
not fall into enemy hands. Deliver them to the senior
communications officer there, and good luck!' He gave me
the map co-ordinates of my destination and I was taken
back to my aircraft.

I found a truck drawn up alongside, and soldiers removing a camouflage tarpaulin, with which it had been covered
for better concealment. I climbed on to the wing and
poured in the petrol, having torn off my shirt tail for a
filter. We pushed the machine clear of the trees. Luckily,
the truck driver knew a little about swinging the prop. Even
so, he did not follow the drill, or my hasty instructions,
properly and he stumbled just as the engine fired. The
propeller must have missed him by a hair's breadth.

I took off, more or less from where we were. There was
not enough wind to make any difference, and the fact that
soldiers had found it advisable to camouflage my machine
made me feel more vulnerable and added a sense of
urgency to my departure.

Once airborne, I turned south for my next destination,
which was on the other side of Lwow. Something
prompted me to look back to where I had just come from.
Puffs from explosions were rising from among the trees. I
looked up. High above was a formation of German bomb-

ers, and I could see the shower of bombs falling from them. I had got away just in time, and the narrowness of my escape brought home the fearful reality of war. I grew cold and frightened and wondered if those I had just left could still be alive, and whether they lay dying, or seriously wounded, without adequate medical help. Even if I did fly back, what was there I could do to help? My duty was to deliver papers, so I flew on, tears streaming from my eyes.

I spotted Lwow from afar, not only by its familiar landmarks but by columns of smoke rising from the city. I worked out that they came from the airfield and from the railway station and marshalling yards. I decided to skirt the city to the other side rather than fly over it, wondering whether the family factory and the house where all the family were staying, were safe.

The location where the headquarters should have been was easy to find, but of the HQ there was no sign. At the side of the woods were fresh-looking vehicle tracks leading to the road. I followed the road, thinking I might find the headquarters convoy. The road was full of people, and among them was a large military convoy of a variety of vehicles. I hoped that this was Headquarters on the move. Alongside the road, a little ahead, was a long meadow suitable for landing and with a few old trees to give camouflage. I brought the aircraft down and taxied to the trees and ran to the roadside, having left the engine ticking over. I managed to flag down the leading vehicle.

'I'm looking for Southern army HQ,' I shouted to the driver, as he slowed.

'That's us,' he shouted back, and drove on without stopping. I managed to halt another vehicle.

'I have a packet to deliver to the army communications centre,' I explained. An officer in the back offered to take them from me.

'Sorry,' I apologised, 'My orders are to deliver them to

the senior communications officer and no one else.'

'Please yourself,' he replied. 'The communications cen-tre is in a big lorry with aerials sticking out of it, some hundred metres back. I'll take them for you, if you like.'

I declined his offer, and waited, keeping an anxious eye on my aircraft with its engine ticking over. At last, I saw the big lorry with the aerials and managed to flag it down. A major opened the cab window. I asked if he was the com-munications officer.

'That's me,' he replied, so I handed him the packet and got a signature for it.

'You'd better beat it sharpish,' he said, 'your plane is too easily spotted from the air.'

Indeed he was right. My not camouflaged machine stood out in the field like a sore thumb in spite of the nearby trees. As he drove off, I ran back to my aircraft. Above the noise of the road traffic, I suddenly heard the roar of a powerful engine. Looking back, in its direction, there was a fast, low-wing aircraft just skimming tree tops flying towards us. At first, he seemed to be lining up on the road and then he changed direction slightly. People started jumping into the ditches for cover and so did I, being some fifty metres from my plane as he fired his guns. I could see the spurts from the bullets lift from the ground closer and closer to my machine and just missing it. He pulled up and dived back from the opposite direction.

This time he did not miss. There was the bang of an explosion and my aircraft burst into flames. We were suddenly enveloped in a thick black cloud of smoke. The German pulled up again, and, seeing that he had destroyed my plane, lined up on the road and dived again. His ma-chine guns sputtered and then went silent. He roared overhead, presumably out of ammunition.

Once again, all was comparatively quiet. People started scrambling back out of the ditches to continue their journey, swearing at me for having attracted the German's attention. I felt doubtful for my safety.

In spite of the hostility, I had no other alternative but to join them but not until I have walked along the fields in the opposite direction to the throng, waited in a roadside ditch for a while, and shed my flying overalls. When I joined the escapees, they took me for just another unfortunate refugee.

There was no way in which I could contact my base to report my fate. In any case, it would almost certainly have moved somewhere else by now, even if it still existed. I, too, had become a refugee.

I had received my second lesson in the space of an hour or so. Any lingering ideas that war was just a big game of chivalry were finally dispelled.

This was for real. It was a battle for survival.

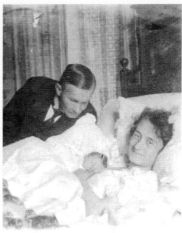

Top left: my parents' wedding. *Top right*: myself, a day or two after my birth, with parents.
Below: Father supervising in the field (cutting the asparagus).

Top: family in the country. (Left to right): my maternal grandfather, the professor's wife, Christine (on the floor), Mother, myself, Miss Cathy (English teacher, on the floor), Miss Mary (general tutor, sitting), Grandmother.
Bottom: Cousin Mary, Christine, *Fräulein* Friede (German tutor).

Top left: my father (front) and his brother on the steps at the rear of
the house.
Top right: the family (left to right): Father, Aunt Nuna, Uncle
Zygmunt, Mother with Christine. (Note my model aircraft hanging
from the ceiling).
Bottom: the front of our house in southern Poland.

Top: Slawsko – the villa of the friends who gave us shelter.
Bottom: Worochta – winter, on our route to Hungary.

Out of the Frying Pan...

At least I was in a part of Poland that I knew reasonably well. What is more, some friends of the family had a country house not so very far away, so I decided to go there. He was a professor at Lwow University, and his wife was a well-known doctor. I had no idea whether they would be there, but it was worth a try.

I became one of the many thousands of confused, bewildered and frightened people fleeing from the enemy, not knowing where they were going, or why.

I only differed from the majority in that I, at least, knew where I wanted to go. In this throng, there was no real news, only gossip and wild rumours. No one could distinguish between the truth and subversive propaganda and, intentionally or not, there was ample of the latter. We comprised a mix of ages and sexes except for an almost complete dearth of men of military age. No one talked about who they were or why they were here. When people did talk, it was mainly of the chances of survival; of the war no one had any real news. Most had their belongings in cases, bags and sacks. The more fortunate led horse-drawn carts piled high with what they owned, and family on top. All were tired, many were hungry and thirsty and everyone was lost – physically, mentally and morally.

A little while after I joined this sorry procession, someone spotted my flying helmet and goggles in my pocket; I was asked whether I had anything to do with the aircraft which the German had shot up. When I acknowledged this, some of those in earshot blamed me for attracting German attention, while others were grateful, saying that if the aircraft had not been there, it was they who would have been the target. I felt uneasy in this company and it was a relief when I could take a turning which would take me to the village where the professor's house was situated.

It was late in the afternoon, and being at last alone, I suddenly realised how tired, hungry and thirsty I really was. I was still a good few hours' march from my destination and I was in need of a rest. The fields were full of ripe cereals, and in a nearby meadow I could see a few cows. At least I knew that I need not stay hungry and thirsty. It was a warm dry night. I spent it sleeping in a dry ditch. I was up and away again at crack of dawn, and reached my destination just before noon.

To my delight, not only was the professor, his wife and some of their family at home, but there I also found my Uncle Zygmunt with his wife and stepson. They had come from Lwow only a day before.

By this time, outside towns, telephones were no longer operating. Papers, even if they were printed in the larger towns, could not reach remote villages. The only source of news and information was the radio. And the news was far from good. The Germans had penetrated deep into Poland. The atmosphere in the house was very tense. Apart from the fact that the war news was depressing and the house was over-full, it was located on the outskirts of a village which was almost entirely inhabited by Ukrainians, who were known to be politically active. This was not unusual in this part of Poland, but the war had stirred up anti-Polish feeling. We were warned never to stray far from the house alone.

Our hosts hoped that, since they had always enjoyed excellent relations with the village, they might be safe. However, in the existing situation nothing could be taken for granted. Thus, we wandered through the garden which surrounded the house in small groups of comparable ages, feeling lost and frustrated, foregathering in the house for meals and news broadcasts. After each such broadcast, we would calculate how long it would take the Germans to reach our part of south-east Poland.

I must have arrived about 9th September. A day or so later, my uncle took me to one side for a very private conversation; it was the day we heard of the Russian invasion from the east.

'I am worried about you,' he said. 'Neither the Germans nor the Ukrainians are good news for you. They must know about your "extra-curricular" activities and have listed your name high in their black book. Even higher than I; they might only hold my role and support in the defence of Lwow nearly twenty years ago against me, and there can't be many here who know of it, a few more in Lwow itself. That was, after all a long time ago.'

It had not previously occurred to me, that my quasi-intelligence gathering might earn a ghastly reward for me and my family. I had scarcely time to come to terms with the Russian news, or the consequences of my personal involvement.

The villagers initiated the action which we all knew in our hearts was inescapable, although we could not conceive what form it might take, it was probably accelerated however, by the news of the Russian incursion. The household had gathered for breakfast when three armed men came to the front door. They were wearing civilian clothes, cloth caps and armbands in the Ukrainian national colours of blue and yellow.

'We want to see the professor and his wife – now,' they demanded.

The maid who had answered the door did not like what she saw, and asked their business.

'Never you mind. Just get the professor and his wife. If you won't, we'll come in and get them ourselves,' they threatened.

The professor, who must have seen or heard what was going on, arrived at this point and intervened. They were all well known to him.

'Jacek, Luna, Juri,' he greeted them each by name. 'Good morning. What can I do for you?'

'We are the local militia,' announced Juri, the spokesman. 'We want any arms and ammunition you have in the house, and we want them now.'

'I don't know if we have any,' retorted the professor, 'and even if there are, what right have you?'

'Don't give us this…!' shouted Juri, interrupting. 'We know there are arms in this house and we have come to search for them.' He signalled his companions, who pushed past rudely, and pointed his pistol at the professor. 'Get everyone out of their rooms. I want them all here in the hall while we search.'

The professor turned to the maid, who stood frozen to the spot on which she was standing, and told her to get everyone into the hall.

And so we were all shepherded into the hall, family, guests and staff. One of the villagers stood watching us with his pistol at the ready, while the other two set off on their search. It did not take long. Some fifteen minutes later, the searchers jubilantly returned with their haul. None of us had made any effort to conceal our weapons. Maybe we should have done so. Had we not been expecting some kind of visitation? But now it was too late.

'We knew you were armed and that you were going to fight us,' announced Juri, seemingly pleased with himself. 'You are all under arrest.'

'You have no right…' the professor started to protest.

'Don't give us that Polish shit. It is you and the likes of

you who "have no right" any longer. The Germans or the Russians will see to that. Right now, we represent the local authority until the occupying powers give us our freedom, which your lot never would.'

For a while, there was complete silence. It seemed as though our captors, after the first flush of success, were as unsure of themselves as we were ignorant of their intentions. Eventually, we were instructed to collect a few personal belongings – quickly, they said – and they would then escort us to the village hall, which was to be our prison. There seemed to be no room for argument or protest. They had our weapons, and opposition would be fruitless. We could only rely on the respect which they still hopefully harboured for the professor and his wife, who had lived among them for many years. They had always seemed quite popular with the villagers, whom they had helped both professionally and financially, and had actually donated the village hall which was to be our prison.

Within half an hour of the intrusion, we were on our way to the village hall, having missed our breakfast. None of us had any experience of such a situation, or what should be one's priorities. Some brought clothing with them, others, jewellery or money. There had been no time to think about it, only the knowledge that one could only take what one could carry one's self.

The village hall turned out to be a sizeable, single roomed, solidly built timber hut. It was simply furnished with chairs and benches and a few tables. Paraffin lamps hung from the ceiling. Juri and his companions followed us in. They must have been very confident that they had found all the arms, for they did not bother to search us, and did not seem interested in anything else we might have brought with us. Juri addressed us.

'We will bring you water. If we find any food in the house, we will bring that as well. We are going to board up the windows and there will be an armed guard posted outside. If anyone tries to break out, they will be shot.'

As if to prove he meant what he said, men outside immediately began to board up the windows. We could see the villagers crowding round outside, the men armed with an astonishing array of axes, scythes and sickles, and a few guns. Then the job was complete, what light got through was in gaps between planking and knot-holes. As a result, we were more or less in darkness, so we lit the lamps.

True to his word, Juri sent in a couple of buckets full of water, and a few old, none too clean, mugs and glasses. With them, came the message: 'Ask for water when you need more, but use it sparingly.'

Judging by the murmurs and sounds outside the padlocked doors, it seemed that more and more people were gathering.

There were some fifteen of us in the hut. The professor and my uncle, as the elders, and the most experienced, automatically assumed the mantle of leadership. They huddled together in a corner of the hut, with their wives, discussing what to do. The rest of us, some in small groups others nervously pacing up and down, were getting on each other's nerves, being tense, worried and dejected.

After deliberating for what seemed at least an hour, the professor motioned us to gather round.

'To be quite frank with you,' he said, 'our situation is not good. Although we have had good, almost amicable, relations with the village, the villagers have been known for years to be Ukrainian activists. Indeed, some of them have been imprisoned as a result. It is not surprising that they are taking advantage of the situation. Maybe I should have foreseen this turn of events, or maybe I was putting too much trust in my good relations with them, especially as we ourselves were never politically involved. That is as maybe. When there is an opportunity, Zygmunt and I will try to reason with them, but we are not very optimistic. They may refuse to listen to us, and even if they do, there is no guarantee that what we have to say will have any effect. We could try to buy our way out; we have money both here and in the house, but if we do, they could just as easily take our money and not let us out, or let us out and then round us up again on another pretext. After all, we are defenceless, and they are armed. And this is not the only village that is anti-Polish. There are many villages between here and Lwow, each one of which represents a threat. We don't know either, whether the Germans or the Russians, whichever get here first, will support them or us. For the time being, therefore, we must sit it out. If anyone comes in we must look as natural as possible and not appear frightened or over-concerned. It won't be easy, but there is little else we can do for the time being.'

We listened carefully, but no one had anything else to say. We settled back into our small groups, discussing what the professor had said and swapping other experiences during and before the war. We spoke quietly in an increasingly tense atmosphere.

In the late afternoon the padlocks were undone and two men and two women brought in some food, some of which was cooked, and all must have come from the house.

'Here, you are,' called one of the men, 'now you can eat. Juri told me to tell you that he will come in to speak to you in about an hour's time.'

Some of us, especially the younger ones, were hungry. We had not eaten since the previous day and the tension had sharpened our appetites. The older ones were less interested in food and ate only as a matter of course, without appetite or relish. I was sitting on the floor next to my uncle's chair.

'What do you think they want to talk to us about?' I enquired.

'How do you expect me to know?' he snapped back.

'Steady on, Zygmunt,' murmured the professor, 'we are all asking ourselves the same question, and he is the first to air those thoughts. After all, you and I have been through war before. We have had dealings with the Ukrainians on both a friendly and a war footing. Have we learned anything from those experiences which we could apply now?'

I was grateful for the professor's intervention. I had a very high respect for my uncle and always considered him a very reasonable man. His reaction, albeit understandable, was unexpected. My uncle himself seemed to regret his outburst.

'This is a new situation,' he remarked after a pause, 'and I simply do not have the slightest idea. I would think that they are counting on the Russians or the Germans, or both, to resolve the problem for them, since neither are on our side.'

His remarks were interrupted by the entrance of several men. Some of them set about removing all the food and utensils; others, including Juri, Luna and Jacek, and who were mostly armed, paced up and down, while the clearing up was completed.

'Sit down on the floor, benches, wherever you like,' instructed one of them, indicating with a sweep of the arm where he wanted us to sit. 'We, the committee, want to talk to you.' Behind them, the door was left open, and we, sitting on the floor, faced the open door. Juri addressed us.

'After many years of suffering under your occupation, the day has come for our freedom. The Russians are going to give us independence. They will soon be here, but in the meantime, we are the local authority.'

Juri sat down astride the end of one of the benches. I hoped he would overbalance it but he did not. His legs were wide apart and between them, I could see through the door. There was a lot of activity out there which I could not understand. It seemed that the villagers, in considerable numbers, were to'ing and fro'ing, carrying sheaves of straw, bundles of wood, logs, chairs and benches. Every now and again, someone would appear with a straw mattress, or with bedding, and some with bundles, which could have been food. I was so absorbed in watching what was going on, that I hardly listened to Juri's voice, except as a sort of background noise, but suddenly his words commanded my full attention.

'Later this evening, we are holding a village meeting to decide what to do with you. Although we have had good relations with the professor and his wife here, we have to regard you all as our enemies, enemies of our cause. We know that you two', he pointed at the professor and Uncle Zygmunt, 'fought against our people at Lwow in 1920. We have suffered from Polish oppression long enough. The village will decide what we should do.' Then he turned to Wladek, my uncle's chauffeur for many years. 'You can go. You are on our side. We know. We will send you back to Lwow and your people.'

Wladek stood up and turned crimson.

'I don't know what you know about me…' he stuttered, 'but I…' He was not allowed to finish.

'Shut up and get out of here. Pick up your belongings and go. You too, go,' he added, pointing at the local domestic staff. Wladek stooped to pick up his bundle and made for the door, followed by two girls. He stopped, and turned towards my uncle.

'I am sorry, sir,' was all he managed to say, and walked out.

Juri did not have anything more to say, so the professor spoke up, 'We would like to have a talk with you. We have a proposition…'

Juri did not allow him to finish what he was saying.

'We will be back after our meeting, probably about seven

o'clock. Save your talking till then.'

I well remember the anger which suffused the professor's face as Juri and his henchmen left us to ourselves. Time started to drag very, very slowly. After some time, my uncle broke the silence.

'They will probably speak to us in Ukrainian. We have to speak in Polish if we are asked any questions. We should say as little as possible, and above all we must not, in any way, implicate ourselves or anyone else. We are refugees from the war, you included,' he turned and looked at me as he spoke, 'and we are not involved in any war activities. The Russians have said that they are coming to help us. While I don't believe them, I may be wrong, but we can turn it to our advantage in talking to the locals. If the Russians are coming to help us, Poland will not be the same again.'

Uncle had just finished speaking when the door opened and Juri came in.

'Right, all of you outside,' he ordered.

Slowly, hiding our emotions with some difficulty, we filed out of the door. The red evening sun was casting long shadows everywhere. We were motioned to stand on the grass under an old tree in front of a table and bench occupied by the 'committee'. The villagers stood in a semi-circle behind us.

'It is the decision of the committee that you will be held in custody here until the Russians arrive. We will hand you over to them.' He turned to the villagers, 'Do you agree with the committee?'

For a time, there was complete silence. From the corner of my eye, I could see the villagers on the ends of the semi-circle. Their faces were tense and unhappy, somewhat confused. They did not seem to know their role in this play, which was new to them. Then a voice from the back shouted, 'If they were in our position, and we in theirs, they would hang us or shoot us. We should do the same.'

There was a murmur of voices; I was not sure whether they supported or opposed the last speaker.

'We should leave it to the Russians to decide. We have done our job in apprehending them,' said Juri. He seemed to be trying to save the situation. 'We should show that we are civilised and know how to behave, even if they would have behaved differently.'

Juri seemed surprised by the hostile reaction to this. Maybe his intentions were genuinely good. Perhaps he preferred to avoid personal responsibility for a definitive solution. Perhaps he expected more personal support from his own people. Behind us, voices were rising in anger.

'Hang them! Kill them! Let them suffer!'

I could feel goose pimples rise on my skin and a cold shiver run down my spine. Juri shouted for attention.

'Quiet! Is that what you really want?'

There was no straight answer, no clear voice in reply, just the noise of murmuring. Juri, who was watching their faces attentively, spoke again.

'Right,' he announced, 'the committee will consider your views, and we will meet again tomorrow morning after the committee have met.'

It seemed he was playing for time, but he avoided meeting our eyes. We were ushered back into the hut and the door was padlocked firmly behind us. The atmosphere was very depressed and solemn. Frankly, I was scared out of my wits.

'Should we try and break out during the night?' proposed Uncle Zygmunt's stepson. 'We might have a chance.'

But the professor and Uncle were both against it. The guards were armed. The noise made trying to break down the windows without tools made a successful escape highly improbable. Even if we did manage to escape, there were many unfriendly villages, and villagers, in the area. With them, as complete strangers, our lot could be even worse. The professor and Uncle Zygmunt got into another whispered conversation. After a while, they attracted our attention.

'We ought to ask them to come and see us. The time has come to try and buy our way out.'

One of them banged on the door. Luna opened it.

'What do you want, Professor? We are busy.'

The professor requested that the whole committee come to the hut to talk.

'We are very busy, as I said. But I will tell them. You had better tell me what it is about, it may help.'

'No, Luna. We would prefer to talk to you all as a committee. All I will say now is that we have a proposition to make to you.'

The professor spoke in a quiet, friendly voice, seeking to win the peasant's confidence. Luna went out, without committing himself, locking the door behind him.

From time to time, we would peer through the gaps between the boards and through the knot holes, trying to see what was going on. It was darker inside than out, and although the sun had gone down, there was still sufficient light to see vaguely. There were a lot of people out there, but they were not talking loudly enough for us to hear what they were saying. From the tone of their voices, it sounded as if there was much fierce argument.

The villagers were building bonfires outside, presumably to provide light rather than warmth for the guards, for it was a warm night even for mid-September. I watched these activities for a while, and then turned to join the elders and their wives, who were once more in deep conversation.

'They seem to be building bonfires round the hut,' I observed, 'maybe to keep the hut well lit during the night. I hope they will keep the bonfires sufficiently far away from the walls not to set them on fire. After all, we've had a very dry summer so far, and the timbers must be as dry as parchment.'

'You don't mean...?' the professor reacted at once. 'They wouldn't dare!' He came to the window to peer through a crack. A worried look spread across his face, lit up by the red glow which suffused through the gaps. We sat very quietly. The benches and floor boards had become very hard, and we fidgeted incessantly in search of greater comfort.

Now Uncle Zygmunt took his turn at the crack.

'We ought to remind them, perhaps, that we still want to talk to the committee, and at the same time point out that some fires seem to have been built too close to the walls,' he suggested, without removing his eyes from the crack.

'You may be right, Zygmunt,' agreed the professor, walking over to the door and banging on it, 'we need to show them that when we asked to talk to them, we meant business.'

Juri's voice came from the outside, in response to the banging. 'We have no time now. We may see you later.'

It seemed to me that his voice was full of anger, and maybe concern.

It was quiet in the hut. It was also stuffy and I found it impossible to sleep. Well into the night, there were sounds of heightened activity outside, and scratching noises against the walls of the hut, as if something was being stacked up against it. It could have been brushwood. I dared not utter my thoughts. Uncle Zygmunt's voice spoke, not far from me.

'What the devil is going on outside? What are they up to now?'

No one answered, but we were all thinking the same thing. They were arranging wood against the hut to set it on fire.

Suddenly there was another noise in the distance. It

sounded like powerful engines with a metallic clatter. At first I could not identify it. Then I realised I was hearing heavy vehicles, maybe tracked vehicles like tanks, on the road. The sound grew louder.

'Listen,' a voice whispered, 'there are vehicles coming towards the village.'

The sound was now very clear; the voices of the villagers died down and in the eerie silence, only the noise of the engines and the crackle of the fires could be heard. Then there was a cry of 'Russkis! Russkis coming.'

A new kind of commotion ensued. Soon, the sharp cold lights of headlamps, or maybe searchlights, penetrated the cracks in the boarded-up windows. There was the soft noise of bare, running feet, the shouts and words of command in Russian, and answering shouts from the Ukrainians.

'We have Polish prisoners in there,' shouted a voice outside the window, as the engines were switched off and their noise died down. 'Shoot the bastards!'

Then we heard a deep Russian voice, full of authority, 'Stand back, all of you. Stand back and douse those fires.'

The Ukrainian voices were suddenly stilled. Then came the noise of heavily shod feet running. We looked towards the door, full of fear. Someone kicked it open. In the opening, stood a huge Russian officer with a machine pistol in his hands.

'Who is here and who are you?' he demanded in passable Polish.

The professor stepped forward and introduced himself in good Russian.

'I am the owner of a house just outside the village, and these are my family and guests who were staying with me. We were arrested by the villagers and kept here since this morning.'

'I commend you on your Russian. I will have you escorted back to your house now. You will stay in the house until I see you in the morning. None of you will leave the house. There will be guards posted outside.'

We were directed to an empty lorry. I looked round at the hut as we left. Along the walls were arranged sheaves of straw, bundles of brushwood and some timber. The embers of the bonfires, which were now close to the straw and brushwood, were being extinguished by the villagers and some soldiers. We had had a narrow escape from being burnt alive. Although we had no idea of what the morrow might bring, we were relieved to the point of happiness to be returning to the professor's house.

The inside was a mess. There had clearly been some looting, perhaps while food was being collected. At least, there was still enough food left to feed us, and we consumed it eagerly.

The big Russian arrived next morning.

'I apologise for the trouble you have had. I am glad we arrived in time and we will deal with the village rabble. I understand that you have cars and that you have some petrol. I would like you to leave here as soon as possible. I will get the necessary papers for you within the next two or three hours; they will see you safely to your destination.'

We were told to pack what we wanted to take with us, and be ready to leave as soon as the papers had been delivered.

On our journey to Lwow we were stopped on numerous occasions by Russian troops, but the papers we were given saw us through without difficulty.

That evening we were back in Lwow.

Into the Fire...

The Polish war was truly a blitzkrieg; it lasted barely two weeks. The Germans and Russians met in the middle of Poland – as allies. The Russians came ostensibly to 'help' – but help came from them no more than it did from Poland's own allies in the West.

The Russians were in control of eastern Poland. Red army convoys drove into and through Lwow. Their might and size was awe-inspiring, yet the vast quantity of powerful modern machinery was still backed up by horse-drawn equipment, such as cart mounted machine-guns. Their police, responsible for internal security, were reinforced by the Ukrainian Militia, but officered by the Russians. The Red army now occupied the old Polish army barracks, with allegedly insufficient officer accommodation, consequently, many officers were billeted in private houses. My grandparents' house, where we now lived, quartered two lieutenant-colonels, one an artilleryman and the other a political officer. They kept very much to themselves, did not appear to speak Polish, and, as we made no attempt to speak Russian, contact was minimal. However, they expected to be provided with meals from time to time, and consequently supplemented our rations. These supplies varied from lavish and luxurious to sparse and poor.

Despite their ignorance of our language, they demanded a constant supply of newspapers, old or new. This puzzled us, till we began to discover damp, wet, smelly and crumpled sheets of newsprint, sometimes with similar strips of linen, discarded under their beds. They used the papers to wrap round their feet! Eventually they were introduced to socks still to be found in shops, and the demand for newsprint declined.

The shops of Lwow were a real Aladdin's Cave for the Russians. Clothes, luxury goods and jewellery sold like hot cakes; as it was not possible to replenish the shelves, the shops were gradually emptied. They had an insatiable appetite for watches, especially ones with oval faces, for which they paid ridiculous prices, regardless of quality.

At the beginning of October, the Soviets celebrate the anniversary of the Revolution. It presented an opportunity to impress the local populace with the irresistible might of the occupying force, and the Red army mounted a mammoth military parade. Our house overlooked one of the marshalling areas, so I was able to watch part of the parade without going out. Clearly, the participating units were specially selected; there was not a horse to be seen. It was all motorised troops, motorised artillery and hundreds and hundreds of tanks. I took photographs surreptitiously, to supplement those I had already begun to take in more routine situations.

General Timoshenko, then the commander in Poland, took the salute. Later that evening, he and his staff, resplendent in full regalia and accompanied by many of their wives, attended a gala performance at the opera. These ladies, not wishing to be outshone by the splendour of their husbands' uniform, acquired long gowns from the local shops. Alas, many of them had not been able to distinguish between an evening gown and a night-dress, and many, innocently sported the latter, though supported by layers of petticoats beneath, as their custom then demanded. Some of the city elders, fearful of giving offence, attended as expected, but not a Polish decoration was to be seen.

We were confronted with the question – what should

we do? There was talk of the university reopening, but few of us students felt like going back under the circumstances. Studies ceased to have a high priority. Speculation about the future was rife. News was scanty. There was little about Poland in news broadcasts from England and France, which only few were able to receive. Local sources were under Russian control, and discounted. However, it gradually became known that a Polish government in exile had formed in France, and that units of the Polish forces were being formed there. Such information, circulated by word of mouth, was frequently coloured by the imagination of the teller. More practically, the nuclei of Underground movements were being formed from the day the Polish war ended, both under the Germans and under the Russians. Some set out to create escape lines and help those who wanted to leave to join the Polish forces or to escape political danger; others, to create communication networks to receive and disseminate news and instructions from the west, and others just to go on fighting.

I, too, became involved in such activities, but we were all young, ambitious and trying to impose our own ideas on what should be done. All wanted to lead; none, to be led. One such project was to locate aircraft allegedly hidden away by the air force and still flyable. I attempted to find them and also to locate people who would be willing to get them out to Romania. We understood that remnants of our air force still existed in Romania, and believed they could use them. What we did not know was that all Polish forces in Romania were interned. It did not occur to us that even if these aircraft existed, they probably had no fuel or oil, both unobtainable commodities, or that, should we succeed, the machines would be promptly confiscated by the Romanian air force. Much time and energy was spent in looking for these mythical aircraft. Not one was found.

I next sought to do something more positive with a

greater chance of success, such as seeking out potential recruits for the Underground or for the forces in France. Although more successful, our early efforts largely failed through aimless lack of co-ordination and careless talk. Luckily for us, the Russians were not yet organised to deal with subversion and resistance outside their own borders. We soon recognised that our failures and mistakes could be dangerous and costly – which was already the case in those parts of Poland under German occupation. At that time, the Germans were far harsher, better organised and more implacable in dealing with the local population than were the Russians; after all, they did have current practice! We set out to investigate every failure and learn from our mistakes.

One aspect of the amateurism of our organisation was a total lack of internal security. We had no system of identification to use in day-to-day work. Anyone could come and claim to be working for, or on behalf of one of our members, and we had no way to demand proof. We needed something small, unusual, easy to make, easy to destroy in an emergency, and difficult to copy. We all racked our brains to find a solution.

One day, for no particular reason, I was browsing through my mother's box of trinkets, when I came upon my father's silver signet ring. With it, was its waxed impression. That was it!

The crest was a little-known one, and one which could not possibly be copied without knowing its secret, for the engraver had erroneously included an incorrect coronet. Duplication from any heraldic dictionary would have been quite impossible. To improve the security, the colour of the wax could be changed as required. The impression was easy to crush in an emergency. By issuing wax impressions to members of the group, it was at last possible to authenticate strangers who had been entrusted with messages.

This lack of overall co-ordination in those early days resulted in competition, risk of exposure and duplication. For example, one might approach a candidate with a proposition and get the cold shoulder, only to discover a little later that the person concerned was already involved in another group or working independently. Slowly, matters improved. French and British broadcasts became better, and couriers began to run between Poland and the Polish authorities operating from Hungary and elsewhere. These couriers not only brought back reliable news, but, more importantly, carried information and instructions for the Underground. There was also a need to improve communications between the two halves of occupied Poland.

Poland was in a mess. We had lost a war; heroic resistance had not sufficed to stem the overwhelming might of Germany in the west, and the equally powerful incursion of Russia in the east. There was hardly a family which was not confronted with severe personal problems. Yet morale and the will to resist were very high. A great many wanted to get out of Poland and join the Polish forces in France; a great many were willing to stay put and fight from within. We did not fully appreciate at that time, the magnitude and power of the problem that the dissident opposition presented to our cause in our part of the country probably more than under the German occupation. Predominantly Ukrainian, but also Austro/German or even Jewish, they not only knew most of us, knew our background, thinking and political allegiances, and have penetrated our private and often family or domestic life for many years, their loyalty tended to be, for a variety of reasons, to the occupying power rather than us. What united us Poles was that for the first time it mattered little what was the political complexion of the Polish government in exile, so long as it enjoyed the full support and backing of the French and

British, for this embodied all our hopes for the future.

I personally was distressed by two things. My father had disappeared in western Poland and we had no contact with him at all. And I could discover nothing about Hala, nor indeed of her family in Warsaw. There was nothing unique about this situation. One heard daily of disappearances. No one knew whether the missing had been killed, wounded, evacuated, arrested or imprisoned. One had to learn to live with it, praying and hoping they were safe and that their fate would become known.

I thought I had enough problems of my own, but soon found others. Increasingly, my associates, even those older than I, were turning to me for advice and help. I had not appreciated it before, but it seemed that crisis had brought out unsuspected qualities of leadership.

Then Stanislaw Zaborski came into my life. Nothing was ever to be the same again.

He called one evening just as the family were preparing for bed and asked to speak to me privately. I was highly suspicious. The Russians, aided by the Ukrainians, were busy seeking out and arresting potential troublemakers. I asked for his credentials. All he could offer were some papers with his name on them.

'I don't blame you for being cautious,' he said. 'I can give you some of your own history over the last two years. I know many of your friends and relatives.' He then reeled off a mass of information about me, including our capture by the Ukrainians and rescue by the Russians.

I found this somewhat disturbing. I excused myself for a moment and then went into another room to make some enquiries over the telephone. Neither Uncle Zygmunt nor the professor had ever heard of Stan Zaborski, although my uncle suggested he might have assumed another name. I returned to my visitor and asked him how he knew so much about me.

'It is my business to know people and about people,' he replied, 'especially those whose help I need in my work. It is also my business that people do not know much about me. If, when you left me alone, you telephoned to get information about me, you failed – no one would know Stan Zaborski.' He must have noticed my discomfort but continued. 'I have come to ask you to help, on behalf of Poland. We need two things: better radio communications with our embassy in Budapest so that we can pass reports and receive instructions more quickly – and the organisation of good escape routes to Hungary. Both are urgent.'

I was most perturbed. Was he genuine, or was he an agent provocateur working for the Russians or even the Germans and trying to trap me? I needed time to think it all out.

'I am not sure that I can help you, or even whether I want to help you. Right now, I would be obliged if you left.'

He stood up and apologised for having disturbed me and the family. As he left he said, 'I will keep in touch. We will meet again.'

I found it difficult to find sleep that night. Next day, I made it my business to learn about Zaborski. I visited a lot of people and telephoned some others, all well known to me, all completely reliable and of different age groups. Those I telephoned were understandably cautious; those I visited were more open. What I learned about Zaborski in toto was almost nothing. One of those whom I telephoned, however, was Jurek Buc, who had nearly completed his studies to become a vet. Jurek was an energetic sportsman whose magnetic personality earned him universal respect. His voice suggested that he knew something. Shortly after my conversation with Jurek, I received a call from his brother, Tad, who had been a cadet officer in the Polish Air Force Technical College. He asked me to meet them both at Teliczkowa, a popular delicatessen and bar in the smart part of Lwow. Somehow, nothing was in short supply at Teliczkowa, perhaps because it was also popular amongst the Russian officers.

When I arrived, it was very full. One end of the bar was occupied by Russians, some with their women. There were a few Poles at the other. Beyond I could see the unmistakable blond, curly hair of Jurek. As I worked my way to join him, he turned and waved. With him were two others – Tad and the back of someone I did not recognise. They were deep in conversation, before them a half-empty bottle of vodka and the remains of a plate of snacks. When I got closer, I recognised the third man. Jurek stood up to greet me.

'You have met Stan,' he said with a twinkle in his eye.

'I told you we would meet again,' said Stan, standing up in his turn and extending his hand.

I sat down and they passed over the bottle and food.

'Help yourself,' invited Jurek. 'Alas, there is no more where these came from. It is our ration for the day. By the way, Stan has just been to Tarnopol, where he saw our parents. We had not heard of them since the beginning of the war, so we are celebrating. We've known Stan since we were children. We come from the same neck of the woods.'

It sounded a spontaneous statement, but I couldn't help wondering whether it was a deliberate ploy on the part of Jurek to establish Stan's credentials. I had the same feeling when we were joined by a newcomer, Zbych, the son of a well-known personality in south Poland. Stan greeted him the same way as he had greeted me.

'I told you we would meet again, didn't I?'

Zbych finished off the vodka and Jurek invited us back to his flat, where he had another bottle. We squeezed into Tad's car, for which he somehow continued to acquire petrol. It was a very tight squeeze. Tad drove, and Stan told him to go very slowly. He did not want to go far and he had a lot to say. It was clearly contrived. But at least we could not be overheard. Stan spoke.

'You, Jurek, and you, Andrew, know the Hungarian border areas. You, Jurek often ski at Worochta. You, Andrew, ski at Slawsko and have been deer stalking there as well. We need your knowledge to establish escape routes to Hungary. And you, Andrew,' he turned to me, 'as a student of the technical university, know the students. I would like you to ferret out some reliable students who are radio experts and, together with Tad, work at getting a reliable radio-communication system organised, so we can make direct radio contact with our embassy in Budapest, and if possible, directly with France as well.'

He asked us to think seriously about it, about the people to be involved, and to give him a skeleton outline for both plans. He gave us a telephone number where he could be contacted.

'Don't give this number to anyone else, not even if they suggest that I asked you to give it,' he ordered. 'You will not find it in any telephone directory.'

At least it was easy for me to remember: it was the same as ours, backwards.

Stan asked Tad to stop, and got out, taking Zbych with him. We drove on for a while, and since we were near home, I asked Tad to drop me off. I needed to think about what was happening and another drink of vodka would not help!

I felt the need for advice. Since my father had vanished, I turned to my mother and to Uncle Zygmunt. Both were exceedingly cautious, and feared the security forces. They knew, as indeed I did, that any activity against the occupying powers that in which I was to be involved, exposed them to risk, as well as myself. My own generation tended to be rash and accepted risks. I had a duty to protect the family against any unnecessary exposure, and what was unnecessary, I had to decide for myself. Certainly national interest was paramount.

I decided to tackle one problem at a time and concentrate on communications.

I thought of Andy Barak. He was a senior student at university, whom I knew through the aeroclub, where he was a keen flyer. He was also a well-known radio amateur, and had already designed a lightweight, two-way radio for gliders and light aircraft. He was supposed to have a small workshop at home. That might present a problem. His reputation could already have resulted in his being under surveillance. Anyway, I went to see him.

He too, had been called up. At the end of the war, he was somewhere in northern Poland. He had got back to Lwow with great difficulty. I explained quite openly what was needed; he confirmed it could be done. He thought he already had a lot of the necessary components; that he could find a lot more from the university workshops, and if there was anything else, he hoped I could find it for him.

'However, there are problems,' he continued. 'I'm known as a radio amateur, and if the Russians don't know it yet, they will find out soon enough. If they choose to search here and find parts of a full-blown radio station of the kind you are suggesting, I won't be able to explain it away. And another thing, there's a family of Ukrainians living in this block. I've been friendly with them for years, but as things are today… who knows? They could be on the look out. So I really couldn't do anything here. Then there's a technical problem. It's fairly easy to locate an operating radio transmitter. Irrespective of where it is built, it needs to be easily transportable, so that the location can be frequently changed…' He paused, thinking it over, and then went on, 'But these are problems which, with help and goodwill, can be overcome.'

'If solutions can be found, will you help? We need your help,' I pleaded.

'I might be willing to help, but... well, don't get me wrong, but you are talking about *we* needing this and *we* needing that, and *we* might be able to help with bits and pieces. Who are the *we* on whose behalf you are asking? I don't think I am being unreasonable in asking, am I?'

'I don't think it unreasonable or funny that you should want to know,' I replied, 'but what is perhaps funnier is that I am not sure that I can give you a straight answer, or that I know one to give to you. What I can tell you, without mentioning any names, is how I got involved. When you have heard my story, you can judge for yourself and think about your final answer.'

So I told him how I had been recruited. When I had finished, we sat in silence while he thought it over.

'You know Tad Buc?' he asked.

'Yes, I do.'

'It's a funny thing,' he continued, 'I would have thought that he would have been evacuated with the air force to Romania or somewhere, yet here he is in Lwow and, what is more, he manages to run his car even now.'

I wondered why he had introduced Tad into the conversation. Had Tad already been in contact with him? I nearly asked, but thought better of it. Andy stood up, indicating that it was time for me to leave.

'I will think about it, and get in touch when I decide. Give me a few days.'

I gave him my telephone number. As I was leaving, I said casually, 'You will keep this conversation to yourself, won't you?'

He nodded his agreement.

I sought out another potential recruit, another member of the aeroclub who was a qualified engineer. I discovered that Tad had already been in touch with him. So had Andy, and one or two others. I tackled Tad. Yes, Tad had spoken to Andy but not specifically about the radio project. He had been more specific with the engineer, and we decided that I would stick to Andy and he would concentrate on the other engineer. At this point, we were joined by Jurek, and we switched our conversations to escape routes, and exchanged information about Worochta and Slawsko. Worochta was much bigger and Jurek knew many people there. It had a high proportion of Ukrainians, maybe less militant because it was so remote. Slawsko had an even higher proportion of Ukrainians; few Poles lived there. It was closer to the border and no one lived between Slawsko and the border. Jurek was too well known in Worochta and I, in Slawsko, to pass unrecognised. We had to collect as much information as possible about both areas, military and police presence and activity, ease of access, permanent residents, and who could provide 'safe houses'. Neither of us could do so without raising suspicion so we decided to commission various friends, whom we could brief to do a lot of initial legwork for us.

I beavered away at the radio project. I remembered that the family factory had a workshop – and a number of lorries. It had reopened, producing at a low level – supplies being difficult to come by – for the Russians. I went to Uncle Zygmunt, who lent his support without hesitation. His only proviso was assurance of the reliability of Andy. Andy could use a rigid body lorry, and could use the workshop so long as his activities could be covered by the range of factory work. Andy, who had by now committed himself to help, was very enthusiastic. He was taken on the workforce as a mechanic, which gave him free access to the factory. He asked if he could first have the lorry in one of the university workshops. He would use some of the students, who were beginning to return to resume their studies, to do some preliminary work. It was fascinating to learn from my uncle that he himself had operated a factory vehicle as machine gun carrier during the defence of Lwow at the end of the Great War.

Now we began to collate the reports which came back from the ski resorts. It appeared that there were few problems at either centre, no permits were needed to get there or back. There were no Russian troops and very little police activity. There were, however, border patrols on the Polish side, believed to be Russian. We decided to try Slawsko first. As a precaution, I had wangled a written invitation from friends to visit them there, and my hosts would be happy to put up an extra couple of friends or so. We told Stan, who was well pleased. He suggested we should take Jurek's young cousin Kazio with us. So all was arranged and the die was cast.

We laid devious plans for the excursion, 'just in case'. The tickets were purchased the day before, by a friend. We met up on the platform just as the train was due to leave. Nor did we go direct, but stopped off for in Stryj for a few hours. We would arrive on Friday night, go straight to our friend's house which was very near the station. Ostensibly we were there for a long weekend. We would leave on our recce first thing on Saturday morning, return to Slawsko on Monday, make ourselves fairly conspicuous there on Tuesday and return the following day. It would give us plenty of time. That was the plan.

We reached Slawsko without incident, despite the inspecting activities of the Russians and their Ukrainian militia. It was getting dark, but the sky was still bright and the distant outlines of dark blue mountains were clearly visible. Not more than fifteen people got off the train. There were several militia on the station, who waved cheerily to the locals whom they recognised. Two of them intercepted us.

'Who are you?' We gave our names and no more.

'What are you doing here?' We said we had come for a long weekend, for fresh air and rest after the war.

'So you were in the war?' I nodded my head. The others said nothing.

'Where are you staying?'

I gave the name of our friends, and pointed at their house which could be seen from the station across the track, the train having departed.

'Are your friends in the house?'

'I hope so,' I replied, 'for we are expected.'

'Have you permits to be in this area?'

'No, because we were told in Lwow that permits were not needed.'

'They are needed now.' They looked at us aggressively, expecting a hostile reaction.

'Surely you can understand that, having been told we did not need permits, we made no attempt to get them,' I pleaded.

'We only understand that you have no permits.' There seemed nothing further one could usefully say. After an uncomfortable pause, one of them continued, 'How long are you proposing to stay?'

'We hope to go back to Lwow next Tuesday or Wednesday.'

After another pause, he continued, 'We know your so-called friends. We will escort you there to check your story. If correct, we will leave you for the night and will return for you tomorrow to take a statement. If you are not there, your friends may be in trouble.'

They conducted us to the house. The lights were on. We were told to stay by the gate and wait quietly. The militia-man in charge went up and knocked at the door. It was answered by our hostess, who confirmed that she was expecting three young men from Lwow.

'We have them here, but they have no permits.'

'Hello Pieter,' said our host, who had joined his wife at the door, 'surely permits are not needed to come here?'

'You are wrong. Permits are now needed by anyone who does not live here.'

'Well, you should know. So what now?'

'If you make yourselves personally responsible for these men,' said the militiaman, 'we will leave them with you and come back tomorrow with instructions.'

'Of course we will be responsible for them, but where are they?' The militiaman beckoned us to come forward. Although our host knew only me, he did not hesitate to confirm what he had just undertaken.

'We will be back tomorrow,' repeated the militiaman. 'Just make sure that they don't vanish in the meantime.'

'Surely, Pieter,' protested our host, growing angry at the implied threat, 'you know me better than that.'

The militiaman mumbled an apology and turned to leave, while we were welcomed into the house. The circumstances of our arrival had not been exactly happy, and we were all somewhat subdued. There was a lot to talk about. One thing was clear, we could not start out early next morning as planned or we would endanger our hosts.

Next morning we had barely finished breakfast when the militiamen were back. This time they were armed, and wore the hammer and sickle in their lapels.

'Pack your things and come with us,' they said.

We were led up the village street to a house which had previously been the village council house and post office. They opened up a room which had thick bars in the windows and heavy locks on the doors. The door was slammed and we were locked up.

And Grilled...

None of us could have felt very happy. I had already had one experience at the hands of local militia and did not relish the thought of another one. I also feared that this one might not end as fortunately for us as the previous one had. Kazio was clearly very worried; Jurek was offering him advice.

'Whatever they say, don't forget that we only came here for a few days' rest. The only thing we have with us which could incriminate us is a handful of dollars. They may be an illegal currency, but everyone is using them these days, and if they confiscate them, they will probably use them themselves, which may keep them happy. As long as we don't admit why we really came here, we are safe.'

'Don't worry, you two,' Kazio included me in his reply, since he could see I was listening attentively. 'I won't let you down, whatever happens.'

We were not left to brood on our own for long. The militiamen returned and took us to the railway station, from there, by train to Skole, to their district office. This was located in the pre-war police office and prison. It was a gloomy relic of the Austro-Hungarian Empire. The Russians were very much in command. As soon as we arrived, our particulars were recorded and we were separated.

I was taken to a tiny cell. Apart from me, the only things in it were a chair and a filthy old palliasse. High up, near the ceiling was a heavily barred, glassless window. After a while, a Russian soldier came in and ordered me to pick up my knapsack and follow him. He led me to a large office. Behind the desk sat a Russian officer.

Apart from a basic antipathy to Russians, born of a combination of history and the fact that they had occupied my part of Poland, my impression of Russian officers hitherto had not been unfavourable. After all, I had been rescued from a singularly unpleasant death by one of them. My contact with my grandparents' compulsory lodgers had been correct, if on the cold side. So I was taken aback by the hard unfriendliness of this particular officer, for which I had not been prepared. He looked me up and down, very slowly, with icy hostility.

'Your particulars,' he demanded, when he had finished his inspection.

For the umpteenth time I gave my name, address and date of birth, and told him that I was a student.

'Empty your rucksack.'

As I complied with this terse order, he began to handle every item. When I had finished unpacking, he continued his minute examination and ordered my escort to search me. Just as every item in my knapsack was examined, so was every part of me and of my clothes. When the escort got to my chest, he stopped.

'There is something under his shirt,' he said.

'Get it!' snapped the officer.

Hanging from a silver chain around my neck, I wore a silver gorget engraved with the Polish eagle. Superimposed upon it was a relief engraving of the Black Madonna of Czestochowa. On the officer's instruction, I removed it from my neck and gave it to the soldier who passed it over to his superior, after looking at it. I formed the distinct impression that he made a surreptitious and fleeting sign of the cross as he handled it. The lieutenant roared with laughter.

'Were you hoping that this would stop a bullet?' I said

nothing, but the soldier said quietly, 'It's a holy picture, *Tovarishch* Lieutenant.'

'Don't you dare speak that kind of rubbish to me!' he bellowed. 'And don't talk till you are spoken to!' The soldier came to attention sharply. The lieutenant turned back to me.

'Well, what is it?'

'It's a sort of a medallion with the Polish eagle and an image of the Madonna on it,' I explained.

Again he roared with laughter, 'Neither the Polish eagle nor the image will save you. Neither of them carry much weight here. The only one that can save you round here is me.'

'It has probably been blessed with holy water,' blurted out the soldier.

'I told you to bloody well shut up, you son of a whore,' swore the lieutenant savagely. He placed the gorget on the desk in front of him, apart from my other things.

'Why have you come to Slawsko?' he demanded.

I explained that I, and my friends, needed a rest to re-cover from the effects of the war and the difficult journeys which we had each had to make to return to Lwow. When we had been invited to come and stay with our friends, we had accepted the invitation with alacrity.

'And I,' he said, staring at me hard through his small beady and slightly slanting, black eyes, 'I think that you were running away to Hungary.'

I pointed out that the contents of my rucksack were hardly those of someone contemplating running away from home to another country.

'Then you are a spy.'

'Look sir,' I answered, pointing at my things spread out in front of him, 'what spying could I do with that kind of equipment? I don't even have a map, a camera or binocu-lars.'

'And I say that you are either one or the other.'

'Sir, Lieutenant,' I pleaded as politely as I knew how, 'I cannot prove that I am not a spy. I cannot prove that I was not on my way to Hungary. All I can say is, that if either was the case, I would have brought different equipment and different possessions with me.'

He stood up. In his hand was a long flexible rod not unlike a riding whip. He suddenly hit me hard across the neck with it.

'Which way were you going to Hungary? Who was going to help you? Who told you to go?'

Again I said I was not going to Hungary.

'Don't you play games with me, *tovarishch burzujny student.*' (Bourgeois comrade student.) He had turned purple; he was literally livid with rage. He ordered the soldier to throw my things into the rucksack, except for the medallion which he kept on his desk. 'I will get the truth out of you, you son of a whore. I've got plenty of time to do it. Now take him back and bring me the next bastard.'

As I was marched back to my cell in silence, I wondered if I would ever see my gorget again. To the Russian, it had no value, save the silver and gold of which it was made. To me, it was not just my parents' present for my First Communion; it had now acquired a much deeper significance. I was thrust back into my cell, and the door bolted behind me.

It was now late afternoon, and I was cold and chilly. I was also very frightened. I had heard plenty of stories about the Russian so-called security services, from the dreaded Tsarist Cheka to the even more dreaded Soviet OGPU and NKVD. Now that I was in their clutches, did I have the mental and moral stamina to resist them? It was one thing to resolve to be strong; another to maintain that resolve under interrogation, and maybe torture. I tried to pray. But the prayers which I had learned by heart seemed empty, meaningless and lacking in relevance. I discovered a lack of faith, not just now, but in my life and in my heart.

I tried to make a bed out of my few spare clothes and seek relief from my fears in sleep. But sleep would not come, and I began to shiver. So I set aside my distaste and tried sleeping on the disgusting, dampish, palliasse, using my clothes as cover. In the end, I must have fallen asleep.

It was completely dark when I was awoken by the opening of the cell door and an electric torch shining in my eyes. I do not know how long I had been sleeping.

'Wake up! Get up! The lieutenant wants you!'

I did as I was told. There were dim electric lights in the corridor. My escort was bigger, burlier and tougher looking than the previous one. I wondered whether the lieutenant would be the same.

He was. He was sitting behind the desk, across which lay his flexible rod. There was a big mug of black tea at his elbow. He was smoking a cigarette, and the atmosphere was poisoned by the thick harsh smoke of rough Russian tobacco.

'Well, *tovarishch student*, Polish spy, have you decided to tell me the truth yet?' he asked.

'Sir, Lieutenant, I have told you the truth already. What do you want me to say? Do you want me to invent something?'

'You are a bourgeois subversionist, whether you are a spy or an escapist. I will teach you how to behave.' He nodded to the soldier behind me.

I was struck by something heavy, presumably a rifle butt, between the shoulders. As I staggered forward, gasping, the lieutenant brought his rod down viciously on my shoulder.

'One of your friends already told me that you were on your way to Hungary,' he shouted, 'so I know you are a liar.'

Convinced that both Jurek and Kazio would stick to our story, I was determined to do the same.

'If either of my friends said what you say, then they are lying, maybe to please you, maybe because they are frightened of you. No one likes to be punished the way you have just punished me.'

'You dare talk to me like that, you son of a whore, you Polish pig.'

At a sign to the guard, another blow fell on my back just below the neck. A few centimetres higher and my neck would have been broken.

'Now we will talk. Let us start at the beginning again. Your particulars...?'

I repeated my name, address and date of birth. We went through my schooling, my family and the war. The only thing I did not mention was that Ukrainian barn.

'Who sent you to Slawsko?'

We went through the same things again and again as he sought to find an inconsistency.

'Now, what about this medallion of yours?' he asked.

'What do you mean, sir?'

'What is it made of?'

'I think it's some sort of white and yellow metal.'

'Silver, maybe?'

'Perhaps it is silver.'

'Aah. And what is engraved on the back?'

So I told him that it was a First Communion present from my parents and there was a dedication on the back, to that effect.

'So you believe in all this nonsense?'

'Indeed I do. I am a practising Catholic.'

'More fool you. What do you think this will do for you? Do you think it will get you out of this jam?' He spoke scornfully, his face suffused with angry flushes. 'It's all superstitious nonsense.'

'I don't think it will get me out of this jam,' I replied quietly. 'Not in the way you mean, but I believe it will give me enough strength to tell you the truth and not lie just to please you, or because you or the guard hit me.'

I realised as I was speaking that I had foolishly said too much.

'So now you think you are *kulturny*, do you, you think you can talk to me like an equal?' His nod to the guard warned me to expect another blow, but not where it would land. It was across the back of both knees, and I collapsed on my knees just in front of the desk.

'Stay there,' shouted my interrogator as he saw me struggle to get up, 'stay there kneeling down and start praying – but pray to me.'

'I pray, sir, that you believe me.'

He was somewhat taken aback. He hit me on the top of my head, but there was not much power in the stroke.

'Now pray to your picture.' There was a supercilious smile on his face. I began, 'Hail Mary, full of Grace...' I realised that I was really praying, not just with words, but with my whole being.

'Enough. Enough of this gibberish.' He interrupted violently. His face had turned purple, he was beginning to froth at the mouth and there were drops of saliva dribbling down his chin. He ordered me to get up and stand to attention. There was a prolonged silence. I wondered what effect my words could possibly have had. He gave no clue. Instead he snapped an order to the guard, 'Take him back. Get him water and some bread. Bring in the next pig.'

Once again I was marched back to my cell. This time, I was brought a mug of warm tea and a large hunk of fresh black bread. It tasted marvellous. I was very tired. My body hurt where I had been hit. Aching, I drank and ate, and lay down. Before I knew what was happening, I was asleep.

It was broad daylight outside when I awoke. I was sitting

on the palliasse, back propped against the wall when the Lieutenant and the big guard came to the door.

'Have you prayed?' he enquired, smirking.

'Yes. I gave thanks for the bread and the tea.'

He ordered me to follow. He seemed to be quite calm when he sat down to resume his questioning.

'That medallion of yours. Explain to me what it means.'

'I will try to explain, even though I am not sure if you will understand.' As I looked at him, searching for words, he was watching me attentively. I sensed that he was obsessed with my gorget which lay on the centre of the desk in front of him.

I continued, 'Well, it's like this. You believe in your red flag and the hammer and sickle emblem on it. You believe in the teachings of Lenin and Trotsky, but you say you do not believe in any religion. The Polish eagle is to me what the red star, the hammer and sickle are to you – the emblems of the country that I love. While I dare not compare the Madonna to Lenin and Trotsky, you believe in what they said and what they stand for, and I believe in what the Madonna stands for. She has a meaning for me. When your army came into Poland they said – you said – that you were coming to help us. Now that you are here, are you helping us? Making fun of what we believe does not help you. It makes us into your enemies. If you are here to help, as you claim, allow us our beliefs, even if you don't share them, for our religion is our business and not yours.'

The silence while I was speaking seemed absolute. It continued while he digested what I had just said. He seemed unable to come up with a suitable answer. Eventually he said, 'All this is bourgeois superstition. I do not propose to get involved in discussing it.'

He ordered the guard to take me back. I followed him out of the interrogation room and as I passed through the door something hit me hard in the back as if the lieutenant had thrown something at me. It fell to the floor with a metallic clatter. Without thinking, I bent to pick it up. It was my gorget. Instinctively, I also expected another wallop from the guard. It never came.

Locked up in the cell once again, I was utterly exhausted. After a while, the guard returned with another mug of tea and more bread. I sat on the palliasse, trying to fathom what was happening to me. I was in a kind of dream, and in that dream I thought I heard voices outside, and the door open.

But it was no dream. There were Kazio and Jurek with an escort.

'Pack up and come,' ordered the guard. I threw my belongings into my rucksack. Then we were marched out of the prison, into the street and down to the railway station. We were handed over to a couple of Ukrainian militia.

'Don't release them till you reach Lwow,' ordered the guard.

To Russia

Safely back in Lwow, our failure to achieve the object of our excursion did not deter us from resuming our activities, but only increased our determination. It was naive to expect that our brush with the authorities would be forgotten. Poland was full of informers. The Germans had built up a highly effective Fifth Column before the war. The Ukrainians, in their desperate search for independence, served both Russians and Germans, hoping to gain thereby, and during the German-Russian Alliance there was almost certainly an interchange of information when it suited the two occupying powers.

Despite the upsurge of nationalism among the Ukrainians and their collaboration with the Russians, there were still some among them who honoured their past friendships. Such a one was my friend of long standing, a bright lad from a poor, working-class family, with whom I had shared my lunch box on many occasions. Too proud to admit he had nothing to eat because they could not afford it, he frequently 'forgot to bring his box'. We matriculated together. Because he chose to study political economics, he went to a different university. We still met, although less frequently. It was a friendship which engendered problems. My family did not approve. The dilemma of split loyalty, presented itself when I became involved in gathering intelligence; it was largely resolved by the fact that his membership of a different university meant also that I knew little or nothing of his ongoing activities. In fact, I suspected that he was deeply involved in the Ukrainian cause.

Some weeks after the Slawsko affair, a note was dropped through our letter box inviting me to meet him in a large park where we had often walked together in happier days. It was, stated the note, very urgent. I went, albeit suspiciously.

It was early evening when we met. There were few people about, an old man walking very slowly, a couple of mothers pushing their prams, and a couple of young lovers holding hands, with eyes only for each other. We exchanged a few pleasantries; he was leading me towards a quiet corner of the park and there, out of anyone's earshot he dropped the bombshell that had prompted his note.

'If you keep going on the way you are, you will be arrested,' he said. He could not be persuaded to say more, and was clearly anxious to be away and not to be seen with me. I thanked him for the warning.

'You and your family were good to me for many years,' he said. 'I could not reciprocate in any way up till now, but now we are square. I cannot help you any more. Please be careful. Remember, we have not met since pre-war days.'

With that, he turned and walked briskly away. Next day, I met up with Stan and Jurek and told them what had happened. They were surprised that I had a friend on the other side, but recognised the value of the warning.

Stan decided that I should immediately drop all contact with the communications project. It was of the greatest importance, was progressing well, and must in no way be endangered. Everyone involved would be warned that I was a risk. He suggested that I should think of going to Hungary – and investigate new routes on the way.

'It is not only you who are in danger,' he added. 'You are a potential danger to others, your family, and not the least, myself and Jurek.'

At first I felt somewhat offended, but soon I saw the truth of Stan's comments, and said I would think about going to Hungary.

'You know, if it comes to it, I could order you to go,' was his parting shot.

When I got home, I told the family. I had become a danger to them as well, especially to my grandfather in whose house we were living. As proprietor of the family factory and one who had always been prominent in the social, political and economic life of the region, he was not looked upon with much favour by the commissar now installed in the factory.

My mother was horrified by the warning, and even more horrified by the source. She had never liked my friend, but acknowledged that it was 'good to know that there are some decent people among them (the Ukrainians).'

My grandfather said little other than, 'You must do what you think is best. I will back you.'

Neither favoured escape to Hungary. My mother suggested I move away from home. I pointed out that would only expose others, unless I found somewhere quite independent. My mother would not contemplate the idea. In the end I stayed where I was, curtailing all activities. I did make provision for a quick get away, which included wearing a good-quality belt into which were secreted a few paper and gold dollars.

Life became very quiet. I began to think of returning to university, which was about to reopen.

And then it happened.

It was in the middle of the morning. I was about to go out. The door bell rang, and it was answered by my ten-year-old brother. He ran into my room looking very frightened.

'It's them. They are after you – the NKVD.' Then he ran off to tell everyone else.

I went down. I had no option, I could not leave unseen.

'That's him,' identified a Ukrainian militiaman, pointing at me.

'We are taking you with us,' stated one of the Russians. 'You have two minutes to collect your things and talk to your family.' The Russians did not let me out of their sight. It was fortunate that I was wearing outdoor clothing, and that I had a bag prepared. I grabbed it, and followed by a Russian, went to pay a hurried and tearful farewell to the family. Then I was marched out. There were three other armed Russians waiting on the street, and I wondered if anyone had been watching the back, and whether I could in fact have slipped out. It would have done me no good if there was, and the family, even less, if there was not.

I was hustled into a waiting lorry, in which there were already a bunch of gloomy, frightened people. Two of the armed guards also climbed in. The rest got in a small bus alongside. We drove off at speed and then stopped again. More people were bundled in. Any attempt at conversation was abruptly terminated by one of the guards: 'Absolute silence,' he ordered. 'No talking or whispering, or I shoot.'

The back flap was rolled up and we could watch where we were being taken. It turned out to be the old police headquarters, now the home of the NKVD. The yard was full of armed guards, men of widely differing ethnic origins, looking tough and cruel. Ours was not the only lorry discharging its human cargo, some with familiar faces. We were taken down a long corridor in single file, with flanking guards. Our footsteps rang on the stone floor. Along the corridor were cells. The first ten people were ushered into the first cell and so on, until all were accommodated. The doors were left open, but there were two armed guards by each door and we were forcefully reminded about the 'no talking' rule.

It was eerie and unnerving. From time to time, someone would summon up courage to attempt a whisper, some replied a little louder and the guard threatened with his bayonet, yelling, 'Who spoke? Silence!' and would look into the cell trying to identify the offender.

Eventually we were taken out one at a time, luggage in hand, to be interrogated. When my turn came, I was taken before a big, elderly and unpleasant-looking Russian who bore no badges of rank. Having recorded my particulars, he began:

'We know about your family. We know you are a student. You have already been arrested once, when you tried to escape, and we know who was with you.'

'You are only partly right,' I answered, 'we were not escaping. We went to Slawsko for a few days' rest.'

'Do you think I am stupid?' he bellowed. 'Who told you to go to Slawsko?'

'No one told us to go; we were invited, so we went.'

'But you were the ring leader?'

I explained that it was I who had received the original invitation for the three of us, and so I had organised the trip.

'Where do the others live? Give me their addresses.'

We had given our names and addresses many times when we had been questioned at Skole. Obviously, this man had the reports from Skole, so he also had the addresses we gave. I knew that Kazio had since moved. Maybe the authorities didn't know about it, so I gave him the old addresses. He consulted his papers.

'I believe that one of you has moved. Where is he now?'

'Well, if what you say is true, you know more than I do. I only know the addresses which I have just given you.'

He then questioned me at length about pre-war political activities, in which I had never taken part, and about my flying activities, about which he seemed to be well informed. He was obviously trying to show that he knew a very great deal about me, and therefore had the upper hand.

While we were talking, my bag was searched. There was nothing incriminating there, only basic clothing. Then I was searched. They did not find the money in my belt. My gorget, that had created so much commotion at Skole, was ignored.

I had expected this interrogation to be tougher and more painful than that at Skole. However, despite the appearance of my questioner, it had been mild. After about an hour I was taken to a different cell, where some fifteen others were already held. The silence rule was still imposed, so we waited in silence. Darkness fell and, we were left alone to contemplate our individual apprehensions.

At midnight, we were taken into the yard and loaded on to a waiting lorry. The streets were plunged in darkness, so it was difficult to determine where we were going till we reached our destination, the criminal prison. There we were locked up in dimly lit, overcrowded cells. There was just enough room for each one of us to be able to sleep – some curled up on the floor, others propped up against the wall. In here, one could talk. If talking was forbidden, there was no one to enforce the prohibition. I cannot have been alone in distrusting some of our over-loquacious jail-mates, I felt they were plants. Instead of a babble, the noise was very subdued.

After a frugal breakfast of strong tea and black bread, we were ordered outside and loaded into two waiting lorries. In these, we were escorted to a siding at the main railway station. The train was already loaded with livestock and the engine was under steam. Between two guard vans, there were two empty cattle trucks into which we were unceremoniously hustled. The doors slid shut and we were padlocked in. Our guards travelled in rather greater comfort in the vans. Those I had suspected were plants were no longer with us. For the first time, we felt free to talk.

In the truck, there were small, barred and glassless openings high in the corners, which served as ventilators. We soon discovered that it was possible to lift someone up to see out. We took turns in the lifting and looking. It was soon obvious that we were going east. Was Mother Russia to be our destination?

Although not uncomfortably crowded, our accommodation lacked one essential facility. There was no lavatory. Eventually nature forced us to overcome our civilised decorum. A corner was designated. The natural functions could not be denied. We just did not look. We were forced to endure the degrading experience and try to ignore the disgusting resultant stench which permeated the atmosphere.

It was dark when the train stopped at Rowno, a town close to the Russian border. The station was badly lit and under heavy guard. We were allowed out of the train and provided with shovels and buckets to clean out. It was not a pleasant task, but we managed to 'win' a bucket. This would not offer any greater privacy, but at least it would be more hygienic. We were then allowed to wash in a cattle trough filled with cold but clean water, and finally fed with soup, bread and dry biscuits. It was not much, but it was as welcome as the fresh air. Alas, none of this was accomplished in peace; we were chivvied by the guards the whole time.

Despite the surveillance, two or three managed to slip away. The officer in charge was beside himself with rage. We were interrogated as we climbed into the truck, now of a Russian train; the station was combed, but the escapees had vanished and eventually we steamed off once again.

This incident triggered off discussions on the subject of escape. We envied those who had been so quick off the mark, knowing that the further east we went, the more difficult any chance would become. When day came, we were exhausted through lack of sleep. According to the lookouts, we were now in a vast, cultivated, flat plain. Occasionally we rolled through a station, generally too fast to read the name, and when we could, the names meant nothing. We knew nothing of the area.

We were well into the day when the observers reported that we were approaching a large town. We could feel the wheels clattering over points, and then, suddenly a shout from the lookout:

'We're at Kiev!'

The train slowed down and stopped. Then it was shunted on to a siding. Some of the trucks were uncoupled, we were shunted round some more, and then steamed off rather slowly. Some time later, the train stopped. The doors were unlocked and opened, and we were ordered out.

We found ourselves in a siding among several large buildings which looked like warehouses. Waiting for us were rows of Russian soldiers, long bayonets fixed on their rifles. They looked tough, unfriendly and threatening. We were marched off, in groups of fifteen.

We were ushered through a narrow doorway into a hut. Inside were wooden bunks with straw palliasses, on top of which were a blanket or two, and an old mess tin and spoon. Three or four hurricane lamps dangled from the roof rafters. We were told to get ourselves organised and await instructions. There was a door at each end, two armed guards at each.

While we were sorting ourselves out, there was a shout outside. We were ordered to stand up and a tall, middle-aged Russian with Asiatic features entered. It was impossible to tell whether he was an officer or an NCO.

'You are in Bojarka,' he announced. 'This is a temporary camp where you will stay for a few days. The camp is guarded and surrounded by a high fence. The guards are under orders to shoot anyone making any trouble or trying to escape. There will be a meal provided shortly. For the following days, meals will be at 7 a.m. and 5 p.m. You will be escorted to and from the meals and to and from the wash-house. You will be taken to a permanent camp in a few days. That is all.'

We spent much time in the hut: time to think and time to talk. What would be our future? Would we be consigned to forced labour camps, like the Siberian ones in Tsarist Russia before the First World War? Were conditions as bad as reported? It was said that few ever returned. What about interrogations? So far these had been relatively mild, but how long would that last? Above all, the burning question of escape… Voices were instinctively lowered when this was discussed, in case the guards had been specially chosen because they understood Polish.

Camp routine developed, answering some of our questions. We were marched under escort, a few at a time, a few a day, to be interrogated. On the first day, we were marched to the field kitchens for food. These kitchens must have been relics of the Tsarist age; wood-fired boilers, only capable of producing the simplest food. We were marched to collect it and marched back to eat it. Each group of huts had 'its own', numbered kitchen, which was intended to prevent excessive mingling amongst the occupants. One might see a familiar face, but contact was not possible. One such familiar face belonged to John Chmiel. He was my senior at university, a reserve officer, and quite well known as an able organiser in the underground movement. Our eyes met, he winked, nodded his head and waved.

Then there was the wash-house. This was divided into two. The first section was the wash-house proper, containing troughs which were irrigated with running cold water; the second section housed the latrines, old fashioned 'long-drops' arranged in pairs in doorless cubicles. We soon learned that while we were always escorted to the kitchens, this was only the case with the latrines first thing in the morning and in the evening; it was rare for occasional visits at other times. Sometimes there were guards in the block itself, but more usually the hut guard would watch from the hut door.

We had only been in the camp a for a day or two when I saw John again. Once more, it was near the kitchen, he was in a queue alongside mine. There was no possibility of exchanging words with him. He was talking to his guard in an animated but friendly fashion, but his eyes engaged mine. When he saw that he had got my attention, he took a yellow card out of his pocket, looked at it as if reading it, then rubbed it on his cheek and dropped it. By this time, he had reached the kitchen where the serving staff were getting impatient with him. He stooped down quickly and recovered the card, held out his mess tin to collect his food and walked off, alone and unescorted.

He had clearly built up an excellent relationship with his guard, but what was the meaning of the yellow card? It was only a day later that I found out. That day, I was at the head of my hut queue. I was thus first back to the hut and the guard way back at the rear. I had the mess tin in one hand and bread in the other, and was hungrily looking forward to my meal. As I walked into the hut, I saw a yellow card on the floor, just like the card John had been rubbing so ostentatiously against his cheek. I dropped my piece of bread and picked up both bread and card, and made for my bunk. All I had noted on the card was 'Jedrus' – a diminutive of my Christian name only used by my family and the closest of friends. It was surely addressed to me.

My appetite had suddenly vanished and I was consumed by curiosity to read whatever else there was on the card. I had to be so careful, in case anyone saw, and so picked at my food. After what seemed an age, by which time I thought that no one was looking my way, I slipped the card from under the tin, where I had held it concealed, and read the cryptic message: *'Midnight, latrine, J.'*

It was food for thought. It posed questions which I could not answer except by my own judgement, and made me realise that I now had to stand on my own feet. I had been used to turning to others when I felt the need for advice; but there was no one here in whom I dared confide. John was a serious person. He would not have extended this invitation, if he had not meant me to act on it. But how to get to the latrine at midnight? As I sat on the edge of my bunk deep in my own thoughts, I suddenly became conscious that my neighbour was watching me very closely.

'Don't tell me you received a message?' he asked, 'I thought I saw you pick up a yellowy piece of paper from the floor as you came in from the kitchen.'

I was dumbfounded. I thought I had disguised my actions so cleverly.

'No, it was something I dropped as I walked in.'

I don't think he believed me, but mercifully he did not press the subject. I put my head down, praying for inspiration as to how I could get to the latrine at midnight. My neighbour was watching me all the time. I could see him through half-closed eyes. My worry affected my stomach, and I developed an urgent need to go to the latrine. I got to the door, murmured 'latrine', and the guard nodded me past. I went at speed through necessity. The block was empty as I entered the first cubicle, and sat there for a while. Then I recognised the Hand of Providence. I had to develop diarrhoea. If I could be seen running to the latrines at frequent and irregular intervals, I could equally have the need to go at midnight. I returned to my bunk and lay down holding my stomach.

'Got the squitters?' my neighbour enquired. I nodded my head and shut my eyes. I must have dozed off for a while. Then I woke, knowing I had to make another run to establish my cover. I jumped out of the bunk and raced for the door. The guard barred the way.

'Latrine!' I shouted.

A look of understanding spread across his face and he nodded me out, and I raced on my way. After a suitable interval, I returned. This time I did so slowly, bent and clutching my stomach. When I got back, my neighbour showed concern.

'You all right?' he asked, solicitously. I said I was now, but that I had stomach ache and felt tired.

By the time the evening meal came, I had made the trip five times. The guards thought it was a huge joke. So did some of my fellow prisoners. Although feeling hungry, I had to pretend I was not, and picked at the 'main course' of potatoes and cabbage soup. My neighbour offered to finish it for me, and gave me some of his dark bread in exchange, saying it was good for a loose stomach.

Another dummy run, and it was time to go to meet John. The guard waved me out; he was by now familiar with my 'problem'. As I left, I heard footsteps behind me. It was too dark to see, and I pressed on. Two paraffin lamps were burning in the latrines, seemingly bright in the darkness of the night. As I entered, someone followed me in and yet another from the other end, accompanied by two guards, chatting amicably. It was John, who raised his voice.

'When I shit,' he said to them in near perfect Russian, 'I have to sing. I hope you don't mind.'

The guards burst out laughing. One of them replied, 'Why should we mind, as long as you have a good Russian voice. I like a good sing-song.'

John entered his cubicle and burst into song. The tune might have been Russian; it was quite catchy. At first I could not make out the words. But they were in Polish. John repeated them three times to make sure the words were understood. What he sang was:

Siedze sobe robie gowno
Wymyslam jak isc na Grodno
Rano bedzie chlopski woz
Pojdziem o piatej jak bedzie mroz
wpakujem sie w slome
Pojedziem na druga strone
I bedziemy wolni…

which, freely rendered, means:

I wonder as I sit and shit
The way we can get out of it.
At five, when frost lies on the ground,
A peasant cart will come around.
Then hide in the left over straw;
The cart will then its cargo draw
And we'll be free…

I could hardly believe what I was hearing. When John had finished his song and emerged from his cubicle, he was greeted with applause from his guards, who clapped their hands and complimented him on his voice.

As I returned, I wondered how John had organised all this, and why he had selected me to go with him – and who was the unknown third party who had also come to the latrine, presumably on invitation?

Back in my bunk, I began to think what I needed to do. At five in the morning, I could not possibly take all my belongings. I still had on the tweed jacket I wore to get to the latrines, for it was cold out there. It was the jacket I used for hunting, and had strong capacious pockets. I spent the rest of the night surreptitiously collecting all the bits and pieces I wanted to take and stuffing them in the pockets of the jacket and the waterproof that I had spread over the blankets.

Just before five I got up, put on my clothes including the waterproof, as I had done before, and made for the door.

'Again?' murmured the guard, sleepily.

In my bad Russian, I apologised for disturbing him, blamed it on my stomach and made a dash. At the back of the latrine block I spotted the outline of a large farm cart. At the side, was a mound of straw. I could hear voices talking loudly.

'Pssst!' called a voice, very softly, 'here, quick!'

I recognised John's voice and went towards it. He was not alone. One of the workmen motioned us to jump in. The bottom was still covered with remnants of straw. A Polish voice told us to get under it. Then the tools they had been using were thrown on top. Within seconds, the cart moved off.

After a while it stopped. A Russian voice asked, 'Finished?'

'Yes, comrade. You have a load of good straw there.'

'Here is your receipt, then. You will be paid in the usual way.'

'May God bless you,' said the voice on the cart, and received no response. The carter whipped his horses into a smart trot.

Unbelievably, we were out of the camp.

And Back...

After a while the voice on the cart called to us, 'Keep well down and stay quiet till we stop. We have a long way to go.'

Despite the hard boards, the shaking of the cart and the straw dust, and giving thanks that I did not suffer from hay fever, I dozed off. I was in some kind of semi-conscious stupor.

I began to hear voices talking. It could have been those of the carter and his companion because I could not understand what they were saying; but one voice had the intonation reminding me of my father, and then I heard my mother and Hala. I was shaken out of this by the rattling of the wheels of the cart on a metalled road surface. Still only half awake, I began to be tortured by doubts. Have we really been got out? Why and how had John done this? What now?

I knew roughly where Kiev was, on a map, but had no idea of the scale. So far as I was concerned, it could be fifty or five hundred kilometres from home; even more. And we were here, surrounded by Russians and Russian Ukrainians. My Russian was too poor to deceive anyone. Worrying at the problems rather than thinking clearly only served to heighten my fear. Sleep delivered me.

It was the silence that woke me up. The cart had stopped; it clanked and shook no more. A voice broke the silence, 'You can get out now.'

We found ourselves in a tall, dark barn with hay stacked high on one side and sheaves of corn on the other. As the big gates were closed, they shut out the brightness of a late, sunny autumn afternoon. I felt safe and free to look around. I saw three simple-looking peasants, one older than the others, and five escapees. Two of the peasants busied themselves with unharnessing and leading away the horses, paying no attention to us whatsoever. The third stood to one side, as if waiting. John turned and spoke quietly to the third – a gnarled old peasant who spoke in a peculiar mixture of Russian, Ukrainian and Polish. By listening, we learned that we had been transported by this old man, his son and his unmarried brother. He apologised for not asking us into his house; the less people saw, heard or knew of our existence, the safer for all. We were to bed down in the hay loft, and dig down deep if we heard any unexpected noises or voices. Food would be sent over later.

John, who alone had any idea of what was going on, took undisputed command. He introduced us fellow escapees to each other, using Christian names only. We eyed each other curiously, without saying a word. We climbed into the hay loft and when we were suitably ensconced, John spoke to us at some length.

'Right. We shall stay here till late tonight and then leave. I shall go ahead on my own, and you can form yourselves into two pairs. It would be best if there was at least one Russian speaker in each pair, and since I know that two of you are fluent, that simplifies the division. None of us have any papers, we cannot risk being challenged, so we'll have to travel by night and lay up by day until we can find safe houses, which is not likely to be before we reach Poland. We are now roughly halfway between Kiev and Makarow and it is going to take several days to reach the border; how far exactly, I don't know. You will have no contact with our hosts. I will go and see them when it is dark and thank them for what they have done. They may give us food for our journey; if they do, it is of their own free will, for it is not part of the arrangement. If they don't, you'll have to find food where you can.'

Although John did not invite questions, I could not resist asking what the arrangements were, how they had been made, who had made them and why we had been the ones chosen. John was evasive.

'The less you know, the better,' he parried. 'All I am prepared to say is that it was not I who made the arrangements; they were made for us. Each of us here is connected with some sort of organisation or another, and has been active since the war. All I had to do was to identify names from a list that had been given to me. I took the first four that I recognised, but there were others. You, here, were easy since I already knew you all. First, we have to get back to Poland. From there, I suppose we will go on to Hungary and France.'

We formed our pairs. My companion was to be Tom; tall, slim, with a shock of blond hair and a powerful hand-grip which gave the lie to his fragile appearance. He rapidly established himself as the leader of our pair; he spoke excellent Russian and was a qualified navigator in the air force – both skills we were going to need.

All this being settled, we tried to recharge our strength in sleep, but good restful sleep was hard to come. We were woken by the sound of the barn door being opened and someone climbing the ladder into the hayloft. He whistled when he got to the top, for it was too dark to see anything. Given an answering whistle, a young man came over to where we lay, bringing a bundle and a churn. The bundle held bread, cold meat and cheese, and the churn was full of steaming hot, delicious-smelling onion soup. The bearer was anxious to be off, so John just thanked him for the kindness.

'What we are doing is being done at Father's wish,'

stated the lad. 'Not for you, but for his old mother country. For we are a Polish family. We feel Polish, even if we have almost forgotten how to speak the language.' He turned to speak again, as he was about to descend the ladder, 'Good luck to you – and please don't smoke up here.'

As we tucked into the food, which seemed sumptuous compared with Russian prison fare, John dispensed advice. While there were pockets of Polish people who had been displaced and deported over the centuries, most would by now speak, and probably think and feel 'Russian'. Our present hosts were, perhaps, the exception, not the rule. Then he told us to use what little time there was left, getting to know each other, not saying anything about any underground or similar activities, since what we did not know could not be extracted from us by interrogation.

John left about midnight, wishing us all Godspeed. From the barn door, he called back, 'The food and some clothes are here. Take only what you really need. Remember, turn left at the barn door, through the yard and right when you reach the village road. Good luck. See you one day, maybe.'

The door opened and shut. A little later, a dog barked somewhere in the distance. An hour later, Tom and I left. As Tom reached the ladder, he must have missed the top rung, and nearly fell down. Somehow I managed to grab his outstretched hand and helped him to regain his balance. A broken limb was all we needed! We took what food we could stuff into our pockets, but left the clothing alone. Ours would suffice.

Outside, the night was clear and cold. It was dry underfoot and the road surface was good, although unmetalled. We set out at a brisk pace, intending to put as much distance between us and the camp and village as possible. We felt good, our spirits were high, and once we were well clear of the village, we even managed to whistle and hum a marching song. Our luck held. The road was completely deserted.

As dawn began to break, we spied a likely-looking copse a few hundred metres away from the road and decided to hide there. It would give us cover and also enable us to observe the traffic. We had to find out the pattern of road use, especially by the police and military. We were still all too close to Bojarka, and there might be search parties out. Perhaps it would have been wiser to have taken some local clothing and leave ours behind; we were conscious of our get-up quite unlike what was worn by the local peasants among whom we hope to remain unrecognised. What a hope!

We discussed what we should do – it was something we had not yet considered seriously – if stopped and questioned? Tom, whose Polish had the accent peculiar to Polish Lithuania, spoke perfect Russian, and if it lacked the local accent and idiom, it would pass muster for the Lithuanian or the Finnish border of Russia. My Russian would pass muster for nowhere. We decided to adopt a cover story. We were cousins. I was deaf and dumb and not quite right in the head. I had no close family, and was passed from one member of the family to another. It was now the turn of Tom's family, and he had come to take me to their house near Leningrad. It was hoped that they might find a simple job there for a simple young man. Our clothes were a little odd because they were given us by an Ukrainian family who claimed to be escapees from Poland, and had come to find a better life in Russia. They wanted to exchange clothes so as not to look too conspicuous. We had to pay them a little for the exchange, since their clothes were better. The only problem about this was that we had no papers, because we had forgotten to take them out of the pockets. Although this story might satisfy an average peasant, it was unlikely to fool the police. We foresaw that we might have a need to seek information from peasants. We also wanted to change some of our few dollars into spendable roubles. Perhaps we would find a Jewish shop for that – Jews understood money and might be willing to make a deal. Sooner or later, we were going to need money.

Our location at any given time was a major problem against which we had a bonus: as a navigator, Tom could keep us pointed in the right direction which, generally speaking, was west. Other than that, our combined knowledge about the geography of Russia was abysmal; we did not even know the names of any towns, large or small, on our intended route, let alone on the roads we should have been following for our cover story. For this, we would have to rely on Tom chatting up the locals. Furthermore, we had no idea how far we were going. John had guessed it was seven nights to the border. We did not even know how far we could travel in a night.

In the end, we decided to ignore John's advice, and press on during the day. We had plenty of cover from the small woods; there was also maize still standing in the fields and several feet high – adequate to keep us unseen. When we did eventually plough well into the maize, we picked a few of the dry hard cobs and slipped them into our pockets. Thus, we moved steadily on, occasionally crawling and crouching where the cover was inadequate. After some hours we came to a larger stand of timber. As we approached, we could smell wood smoke, and once we had entered the trees, we could hear voices and the rasping sounds of saws.

'Maybe there's a hut, maybe it's just labourers,' suggested Tom. 'In either case, we'd better lie low here in the bushes till we find out what's what.'

So we holed up in a hollow, on a leafy bed, hidden yet able to observe. As darkness began to fall, we saw a party of workmen leave, carrying their tools. The wood fell quiet, but we could still smell burning wood.

'The fire will still be hot,' I remarked to Tom, 'unless they doused it with water. Why don't we roast our cobs and warm up a little before we start out on the road again?' Tom agreed at once. Feeling safe, we walked towards the smell of the burning fire. The embers were still glowing red when we found the clearing where the foresters had been burning off their rubbish. We buried our cobs in the embers and waited till we could smell them beginning to char. They were still as hard as bullets, but tasted sweet, with the flavour of burnt coffee. Supplemented with bits of cheese from our stock, they provided an adequate meal.

It was quite dark when we set off once more. Returning to the road, we stepped out briskly. Every so often, Tom would stop to check our direction by the stars, for the winding road confused our sense of direction. Occasionally, we passed through hamlets and small villages, which were all in total darkness without a light to be seen. Sometimes a dog barked, sometimes there were animal noises. In the dark, these places could equally have been in eastern Poland, with thatched roofs overhanging tiny windows and small doors. We did not risk passage through the larger villages, but negotiated the outskirts till we rejoined the road.

We were still pushing on, after the sun had risen. Tom decided he had to sit down to inspect his foot, which was beginning to be painful. He took off his boot to see if he had started a blister, or if a nail was the cause of his trouble. We were so absorbed in this that we failed to notice an approaching cart, for the dust on the road deadened the sound. It was too late to do anything but brazen it out. To run for cover would arouse immediate suspicion. So we waited for the cart to draw up, and Tom whispered to me,

'Don't forget; you're deaf and dumb. Leave the talking to me.'

'God be with you,' greeted the peasant.

'And with you,' responded Tom.

'Going far?'

'We're heading for Leningrad. You wouldn't take us with you for a little way, would you? We would be very grateful,' Tom ventured bravely.

'I'm taking a load to Makarow,' said the driver. 'If that's any good, jump in.'

I stood silent, trying to look gormless.

'Excuse my cousin. He's deaf and dumb, and doesn't quite know what is going on.'

The driver motioned us to climb up on the tailboard. The cart was loaded with turnips. The unexpected ride earned us a restful few kilometres. We were able to look at the countryside rather than watch the road for danger all the time. The country was flat as far as the eye could see. The skyline was only broken by occasional clumps and rows of trees. Now and again, one could see people working in the fields, hoeing and harrowing, but there was hardly a tractor to be seen. In some fields, late root crops were being lifted and clamped. The toilers, mostly old women, were dressed in drab garments, with only an odd splash of colour from a headscarf; their faces were weather-beaten and wrinkled. They worked in gangs, singing sad-sounding tunes in high-pitched wailing voices, somewhat reminiscent of Eastern Orthodox church music.

The road itself was quite busy, with military and police vehicles travelling in both directions, and a few civilian lorries. We came to a signpost which showed that Makarow lay back from the road. Tom, spotting it, asked if we could get off, and then asked how far it was to Zytomir, the name on the signpost pointing in the direction we wanted to go.

Our benefactor scratched his head.

'Must be a good distance. Probably a day by horse,' he said.

'God be with you, and thank you for a good deed,' thanked Tom.

'God be with you too,' responded the peasant as he shouted to his horses and whipped them into action.

We were now on a major road in full daylight. We decided to try and hide by some willows we saw, hoping they indicated a stream or river. We also hoped their drooping branches would provide some shelter from the drizzle which had started. We were in luck again. The ground was dry and we were concealed. We stretched out and slept.

By next afternoon we had all but exhausted our food supply. We could still find raw vegetables in the fields, but we felt we needed more. Between us we could muster no more than twenty roubles. We had no idea, however, what they would buy – a loaf of bread or a square meal? We simply did not know. Furthermore, we doubted whether it was worth the risk to try.

The following morning, having walked steadily all through the night, we started looking for a hiding place where we could rest, sleep and decide on our plan. About a kilometre ahead down the road, we could see a bridge. That threatened danger: if Russia was on any sort of war footing, bridges would be guarded whether they were rail, road or river. It seemed sensible to secrete ourselves where we could watch as well as rest. We came to the river sooner than expected, the result of an unforeseen bend which brought it close to the road. We slithered down the bank. It was sheltered and the misty sun was warm. The river did not seem cold, so we took the opportunity to wash, taking it in turn one being on the lookout. As I sat watching the bridge while Tom washed, I thought I saw a sizeable fish in the water.

Tom became quite excited when I told him. He was a keen fisherman, and as a boy, had become adept at tickling. If we could find bait, he reckoned he could catch it. Our search for worms by digging with a penknife proved fruitless. Then we found a few breadcrumbs in our pockets, which we supplemented with the odd fly and spider. Tom got into the river very slowly, and then flicked the bait upstream. Stooping low in intense concentration, he slowly got one arm under the water and waited. Fascinated, I watched him, forgetting all about the bridge. From time to time, he would move his arm, or take a very cautious step. It took between twenty minutes and half an hour – I had lost count of time – when zap! There was a quick flick, and a fair-sized fish flew high out of the water and on to the bank. Tom pounced on it in a flash. By the time I joined him, it was dead.

We gathered some dried twigs and debris and lit a fire, over which the fish, impaled on a green stick, was roasted. Sizzling in its own fat, it smelt delicious; Tom refused to yield to my suggestions. I was compelled to wait until he decided it was cooked. It looked good, and came off the bone with ease. It lacked salt and had a muddy smell, but we were starving and not to be deterred. Indeed, Tom was encouraged to try again, but had no success.

The shared excitement of the chase loosened our tongues a little. Hitherto we had only talked about our plans. Now we swapped experiences, he, of fishing and I, of hunting. Suddenly the euphoria vanished. I began to feel sick, sicker and sicker. Tom too had started to look green. He suggested the fish had been too fat, and that we had eaten too much and too quickly on an empty stomach. Perhaps. The unpleasant fact remained that we soon had very runny tummies and could not even contemplate the thought of food.

Having seen no sign of a guard, we crossed the bridge at

dusk. A little further on, we found ourselves approaching a town – Korostyrzew, according to the signpost. That signpost also told us we had come 100 kilometres from Kiev. We debated going through the town and decided it was too risky. The river appeared to be flowing westwards, so we followed its banks, which were gentle and smooth, at least our stomachs felt better and this made us feel hungry again. Our progress was interrupted by tiny tributaries, some quite deep, but not enough to stop us. We followed the river right through the night and well into the morning. By then, we were so tired that we had to stop and rest. We fell asleep.

We had been too tired to notice that we had stopped only a few metres from a ford. We woke up with a start late in the afternoon, to see a cart coming over the ford. Tom was quick. He told me to take off my boots and stand in the water, as if washing my feet. I did as asked at once.

There were three men in the cart, which drew to a halt as it reached our side of the ford.

'Are you going to Zytomir?' one of them asked.

'Yes,' replied Tom, without hesitation. It sounded like the name on the signpost near Makarow, although he had no idea where it was.

'If your friend has finished washing his feet, we can take you.'

Tom waved me out of the water. I came out slowly, remembering I was supposed to a dim-wit, put on my boots without lacing them up and joined Tom. He looked at the cart driver with raised eyebrows and upturned hands and pointed at my boots.

'My cousin is deaf and dumb and not quite with it,' he said. 'No good talking to him.' He got down on his knees and did up my laces.

I smiled away at the men in the cart and hoped that our charade was convincing. One of the younger men on the cart looked at me with compassion.

'Poor bastard,' he said.

We climbed on the cart. I sat on the tailboard looking backwards. Tom started up a conversation as we left the river and followed a track through the fields.

'No one about today,' said one of the men, 'it's market day in town, that's where everyone is. We're on the way to collect my old woman, who is minding the stall.'

As we got nearer to the centre of the town, there were more and more people, many leaving, having completed their dealings. In the centre, the stall-holders were all packing up. We were dropped at one corner, where three women were also packing up.

'God bless you,' said Tom, and waved.

'Where are you going?' asked one of men.

'Leningrad.'

'That's a long way away,' said one of the women and, digging into her basket, she handed Tom half a loaf of bread and a piece of dry cheese. 'Here, take these. You look hungry.'

'God bless you, mother,' said Tom. I knew that he really meant it; so did I. He put his hand in his pocket and pulled out some money, which was refused and waved away. We walked slowly round a corner and out of their sight and hearing.

'What the hell do we do now?' asked Tom quietly. 'We need to get out of here quickly, before we are spotted by the police or someone.'

We turned down a narrow lane which seemed deserted, hoping that any police would stick to the main roads. Halfway up this lane we encountered the mouth-watering aroma of baking bread and frying onions. Nearby was an open door through which curled a thin wisp of bluish smoke. Approaching cautiously, we could see inside. There were two women working by a big oven. One was taking out loaves of bread, the other was tending a kitchen range. The older woman was short and fat, much older than the other. Both had dark hair, the older had Jewish features.

'Jewish women, baking and cooking,' whispered Tom, 'would they sell us some food for twenty roubles?'

I shrugged my shoulders. How should I know? The younger woman, perhaps sensing that she was being watched, turned her head and saw us.

'Could I buy a loaf of bread from you?' asked Tom, on the spur of the moment.

She straightened up, revealing herself to be a good-looker, in the prime of life. She looked friendly, if startled – which was scarcely surprising since we had not shaved for several days and our clothes were distinctly peculiar.

'Here are two men, *Mutti* (Mother), who want to buy a loaf of bread,' she called.

'I don't know. Ask *Vater*,' replied the older.

The younger woman opened a door to an inner room.

'*Vatti* (Father),' she shouted. An elderly man appeared, tall heavily built with a Jewish countenance. '*Vatti*,' she continued, 'there are two men here and they want to buy a loaf of bread. Can we spare them any?' They spoke in a tongue which was neither German nor Russian; Yiddish, perhaps. Forgetting my cover, I blurted out, 'You are not Russian.'

I had given us away, I could have kicked myself; so could Tom by the look in his eye.

The three in the kitchen looked at each other slowly and then at us, full of suspicion.

'For that matter,' said the old man, now speaking Russian, 'you are not what you seem. At any rate, you are not Russian. Your Russian is not good, is it?'

'Are you Jewish?' asked Tom, bluntly, reading my thoughts.

'Did you want to buy bread?'

'Yes,' answered Tom, adding, 'please,' as an after-thought.

The younger woman looked at us and then at her parents. 'They look tired and hungry,' she said.

'As well as needing a wash,' added her mother.

I was astounded. This time she spoke a mixture of Yiddish and Polish.

'Are you Polish Jews who were resettled from Poland by the Russians at the end of Great War?' I asked.

Concern showed in the old man's face as I went on, 'We are also Polish.' I was taking a grave risk. Jews were not popular in Russia; they could have earned credit from the police if they had denounced us.

'Come – quickly,' said the old man in fair Polish, leading us into the back room. 'You guessed right, young man, we are from Poland even if we have been here for many years now.' He looked at us, as if expecting further explanation from us.

'You had better not ask too many questions. Maybe you know too much already,' started Tom, who then explained he was not being impolite, but feared for their safety as much as ours. 'But yes, we are Polish and we are on our way back.'

'You must be tired and hungry,' said the old man.

'Especially hungry,' we answered together.

He showed us to another room, where there was a wash basin, a pitcher of water, some rough-looking soap and a towel. 'Here,' he said, 'have a quick wash. I will bring you some bread and maybe some cheese and some tea, and when you have washed and eaten something, we can talk. Later you will eat with us.'

This Jewish family showered us with kindness. They talked, without questioning, fed us, gave us a change of clothes, so that we were no longer conspicuous, and, having decided that it was too dangerous for us to stay the night, conducted us through narrow back alleys till we were clear of the town. From there, they told us of the safest route to follow, and provided us with more food and roubles for the journey. How could we thank them? I had in my pocket an old silver watch, a present from my grandfather of many years ago. Even that, the old man wanted to refuse, but I insisted that he keep it as a memento of our visit.

The family made a tremendous impression on us both, especially on Tom, who had seemed much less appreciative while we were there. He was normally taciturn, saying little, but he talked about them for a long time, finally saying:

'I have been anti-Semitic for many years, but never again. They have taught me a lesson I shall never forget.'

As we progressed westwards, we increasingly thought of, and discussed, the possible problems of crossing the Polish border. In search for geographic information we consciously discussed the history of Poland, analysed the popular historic literature of wars of the middle ages, with Cossacks and Turks, and the popular songs of army origin of 1914–18 and 1920 vintage. They all mentioned places and rivers and slowly, from these our thinking developed. They reminded us that the rivers flowed in a southerly direction from about Tarnopol region and south, and easterly one further north, more or less where we hoped to be. Hence we might find a river and from the direction of its current deduce our general location. We also remembered that the border was virtually sealed by both sides, for fear of political penetration. Roads and rail lines were few, for there was no need for east–west transport. Trade was minimal, tourism non-existent. At any rate, we did not think that in the border zone, we could risk being seen by anyone – civilian or military.

We decided that we would have to go cross country, mainly at night, once we thought we were about there.

One afternoon a couple or so days after Zytomierz, we were talking about the kindly Jewish family. The countryside looked less and less inhabited but the enormous fields were all tended. We were following a minor road when we came to a small crossroads. There was obviously an old road, now just a track going west, and a road crossing – north to south. Not a signpost, not a village, not a human being in sight. A few trees broke the line of the horizon several kilometres away to the north-west. It was the desolate look of the countryside that dared us to walk in broad daylight. We decided to turn north.

Just before dusk, a small village appeared along the road; no more than a few small cottages. The trees we had seen before were now not far away.

We walked away from the road along a dry ditch between the fields; there were a few headland bushes and we sat under these, thinking. After a long silence Tom, who was deep in contemplation, stood up and finding a bit of open earth, drew a few lines.

'Look at this,' he said. 'Kiev was there, and we have been walking more or less west, solidly, days and nights. We must have covered 250 kilometres or more. The old border must be somewhere to the west; how far we don't know, but not too far. The countryside being so uninhabited here, confirms my feeling. We will have to risk getting some information somehow, and I have an idea. You stay put, and I will go to the village to see what I can find out. What do you think? It is a risk, but if we blunder into the frontier and it is guarded, we are for it.'

There was enough obvious logic in Tom's suggestion for me to agree. Furthermore his Russian was so good that no one ever queried it. In that respect, I was a hindrance to him.

Tom left me under the bush where we sat, and made for the village. I was left in complete solitude, my mind seemingly gone blank. After a while I started to feel surprisingly lonely: a feeling I have never experienced before, the need of someone to talk to, or at least someone to be physically near to.

It was difficult to gauge how long I have been sitting there, probably dozing. But it was dark when I heard a shrill short whistle.

I stood on the lip of the ditch; there was the silhouette of someone standing not very far away, probably on the road.

'Tom,' I called.

The silhouette waved and came forward.

'I thought I had lost you,' said Tom when he joined me. 'I did not realise we were so far from the village. At night, it seemed miles.'

'Well?' I enquired.

'I found an old couple who were quite willing to talk; that's why it took so long. We are somewhere not too far from Szepetowka and, the trees we saw are on the bank of the river Horyn. I remember the name now. They told me that there is a road that more or less follows it; it was much used recently by the Russian forces. The river itself starts in Poland, so if we follow it up stream, we should be all right. They also sold me a few eggs and a piece of bread.'

With that he produced the goodies from his pocket. The smell of bread made me feel hungry.

While I ate, he continued, 'They know very little about the frontier and it was difficult to ask direct questions. We will have to risk it. We'll make for the trees and the river during the night. Once we reach the river, we will have to plan as we go.'

Rested, refreshed and reassured, we started out cross country in the direction of the trees, invisible in the dark, should be. Tom's navigation did not fail us. It was still very dark when the trees loomed black against the sky, and the river was also there. Here was a place where we could wait till morning. Then we could see what was what.

We were woken up early in the morning by the rumble of traffic and a cloud of dust. A military convoy was moving eastwards. No sooner had it disappeared than another convoy appeared, moving in the opposite direction. This one had a number of tanks of various shapes and sizes which were not on the road itself, but just followed the general direction. Only the lorries kept to the road.

We had to wait for the traffic to dwindle to nothing, before we dared move again. No roads for us!

In silence, Tom led along the river, which flowed lazily, and looked shallow. Along the banks and in the fields nearby, we found wide tracks made by tanks.

It was quiet, so we ventured forward in broad daylight until we found a road bridge crossing the river; from a distance we could see that the bridge was guarded.

'You can swim?' enquired Tom. I assured him I could.

'We will have to swim the river in the dark,' he decided. 'We need to be on the west side.'

So we found a well-concealed corner of a field, with a few bushes out of sight, and slept quietly.

It was just dusk when Tom woke me up.

'We swim from there,' he indicated a clump of bushes near the river bed, 'to the tree.'

We crossed the river that night, crossed the road on the other side and tried to follow the general direction of the road, but across country. There was some traffic to be seen so we had to hide from time to time. On one such occasion, we found a barn where we could lie up; in it, there was a stray chicken which provided a welcome meal when we cooked it over a fire.

Although we were lost, at least we found what we assumed to be the answer to our worries about the frontier crossing. An open, large and uncultivated field had its surface churned up, and there, in a large heap, was a mass of tangled barbed wire.

'Looks as if a tank was entangled in it,' said Tom. He then stopped short, looking at me with an expression of incredulity. 'Do you suppose this was the frontier wire?'

So, could we be in Poland again? But where?

The answer was not forthcoming until we came to a minor road going more or less north; it was only a little more than a field track. 'And now where navigator?' I tried to show humour. Tom looked in the two directions of the fork, then he moved forward and off the road where he saw a plank of timber on the ground. He lifted it, it was broken signpost; it read 'Krzemieniec'. We had made it – we were in Poland!

The Great Escape

'Krzemieniec! – I don't believe it,' shouted Tom. 'I have an uncle or cousin who lives there. He is a local doctor who may help us. What luck?'

Several hours later, we found ourselves knocking at the doctor's door. He was a widower, and had a housekeeper looking after him. She was also his surgery secretary. It was she who opened the door.

'I am Tom Zawadzki,' Tom announced. 'I am the doctor's cousin. Is he in?'

It was the first time I heard Tom's surname mentioned.

'You don't look like Tom,' she pronounced. She was eyeing us suspiciously. Dirty and unkempt, we did not invite trust only open hospitality. After a while, she closed the door, left us outside and went to look for the doctor.

An elderly, frail and tired-looking gentleman came to the door and looked us up and down.

'Are you Tom?' he asked, peering into his face with half-shut eyes. 'These days, one cannot be sure of anything.'

After a while, his face relaxed a bit, 'Yes, of course… sorry, you'd better come in.'

Tom introduced me, but the housekeeper barred the door, 'Back door, for you in those clothes,' she ordered.

When they met us at the back door, she had a couple of old coats over her arm. 'You'd better undress here, and put these on before you go upstairs,' she suggested. 'We will burn your clothes. Lucky for us all that we have hot water today so you can have a good bath and shave. While you do that we will sort out something for you to wear.'

An hour or so later, scrubbed and shaved, and in ill-fitting but clean clothes, we found our way into the doctor's living room.

There was food and coffee waiting and while we ate, we gave them both a brief outline of what had happened, to which they both listened carefully. We then gave them our plan. 'In one,' Tom concluded, 'we need to get to Lwow quickly, and without being caught. We have no papers!'

We were sent to bed to have a rest. Tired as we were we barely noticed the soft beds and clean sheets experienced for the first time in many days. During the time we were catching up on sleep, the good doctor was busy calling on his friends and organising our return to Lwow, helped mainly by the local railwayman.

So it was that, the following day, under the vigilant eye of the rail guard, we chugged into Lwow goods terminal, which whilst working, showed clearly the ravages of the recent war. The guard saw us safely out of the yard, through the Russian guards and local 'Milicia' and wished us good luck. We thanked him profusely.

From a nearby telephone box I called Stan, luckily he was in; I reported our return; asked about my family, he reassured me, and offered to let them know about our whereabouts. Stan was short and to the point. We arranged to meet opposite the technical university.

Tom and I waited for a good few minutes beyond the appointed time. No Stan! We were about to give up when I spotted him on the corner of a side street, watching us, and the people around us. Then he caught my eye and beckoned us to follow. He walked ahead. When he stopped, he scanned the few people about in a quiet side street; only then a big smile came to his face.

'I expected you back a few days ago,' he said. I introduced Tom. They talked about Tom's plans and Stan promised to help to get Tom either to his home, under German occupation, or to Hungary. In the meantime, he memorised the address where Tom could be contacted. That accomplished, he almost rudely dismissed him. Tom and I shook hands, wished each other good luck, and he walked away looking lonely and a bit crestfallen.

Stan turned to me, 'Your people are fine. I told them you are back. They had a bit of trouble after you disappeared; your grandfather was taken by the NKVD, but the "lodgers" managed to help him out. He was back home after a couple of days' interrogation. As for you, go home, pack some clothes, and whatever else you may need and can carry, and you'll be off to Hungary. In the meantime, for a day or two, find yourself a bed, but not at home, and meet me and Jurek outside the George Hotel tomorrow midday. You realise that you are a danger to your family, and to us all, so until you leave for Hungary, keep out of the way.' With that, he walked away.'

★

My mother answered the door, at my grandparents' house.

She went very pale when she saw me; there were tears in her eyes. 'I don't understand what is going on? Where on earth have you been?' she demanded. 'What are those clothes? Why didn't you ring? Your friend telephoned, just to say you were back.' And only then she gave me a great motherly hug.

The joy of my return was short-lived. Luckily the 'lodgers' were not in. During the short reunion, I prudently told them as little as was possible, but made it clear to all that I had to leave to avoid being arrested again. So I packed a rucksack and a small suitcase. In the meantime, I needed a bed in a 'safe house', for at least one night. Mother telephoned a distant aunt, a good friend, and she agreed to put me up. For the two days, I was with her, she never asked any questions, and played my favourite Chopins for me, on her piano.

I was torn in my feelings: there was still no news of my father, my grandfather was elderly, and I thought that I had a duty to stay and look after the family. We discussed it at length. There were many families in a similar position. I had become something of an embarrassment at home, and was no longer safe in Lwow. My first duty now was to my country. Going to France, to join the Polish air force, was the only sensible solution.

By now, the Worochta area had been checked out and was in use as an escape base. Getting there has been occasionally difficult but once there, a number of 'safe' houses had been established, local militia squared, and several alternative routes and border crossing points identified, including a 'special' for emergency evacuation; longer than some but safer.

At the Lwow end of the operation, a 'safe' depot was run by Madame Zofja. She could not accommodate anyone as her house had been requisitioned for use by senior Russian officers. In return, Madame Zofja was allowed to keep a maid to help look after her unwanted guests, and was supplied with ample provisions for their entertainment. By insinuating herself into their good books, she became a mine of information – which could be checked through another contact who was employed as a secretary at the head office of the political police. It was thus that a message came from Madame Zofja, warning that there was to be a round-up of suspected people, on a massive scale.

Stan had a number of people at risk, already waiting. Some were in Lwow, they needed to be got out quickly; he sent out messages, warning those concerned of their impending departure. Some were already waiting in Worochta and its surrounds. I also knew a few who needed 'out' and Stan agreed to take them on. Among these in Lwow was a general wounded and cared for at the ex-military hospital by his old friend, a surgeon, a colonel, the head of surgery at the hospital. The general was in great danger from the Russians on many counts and in spite of his condition it was necessary to get him out. The colonel's stepson, an old friend of mine and very involved politically, was also a candidate for crossing and was alerted by me on Stan's behalf.[2]

A day later, news reached me, through a cousin who worked as announcer at the Lwow Radio station (by then under Russian control), confirming imminent arrest of a number of people, 'within twenty-four hours,' she said, and my name was on the list. When I told Stan, he decided to evacuate at once, using a 'special' procedure.

I only had only time to sneak back home for a tearful farewell. The family passed all sorts of gifts to me, some gold coins, some foreign currency, my grandfather produced a small automatic pistol. Only very much later did I realise that these valuables might have eased their lives more than they did mine! Half an hour later I was off, harrowed and with tears streaming down my face.

I had to meet Kazio near Madame Zofja's to collect provisions, and we were then to join Stan and Jurek in the park at a nearby crossroad. Stan had on loan from his farmer uncle and stabled in Lwow, a horse-drawn cart. This was a part of the 'special' procedure. The general, and some of us would be hidden in the cart, under a heap of hay or farm

---

[2] The general was W. Anders; at the last moment he decided against coming with us on account of his condition. A day after we left, he was arrested and deported. Later in the war he came out of Russia with his army formed and freed by the Russian under a Polish/Russian agreement. He was already a famous general and became a national hero of the Polish army fighting in North Africa and Western Europe.

produce, and we would all be off.

It was Kazio and I who were given the job of collecting food supplies from Madame Zofja's, before joining the others. There should have been plenty of time, but Madame had thoughtfully left us more provisions than we had anticipated. As we were already well loaded, it took us two round trips at the double, to carry the load. We completed the second run but we were a few minutes late, for our 4 a.m. rendezvous. A large cart drawn by two draft horses was waiting, with a peasant and companion on the driving seat. The driver shouted to us, 'Come on! We're late and we haven't got time to waste!' It was Stan.

Then came the first bad news. They went to collect the general. The plot to get him out from the hospital was made very difficult by the Russians who, suspecting something, had doubled the guards. Stan's anger showed in his voice. He and his team penetrated the Russian cordon only to be told in the last minute, that the general decided, he was not up to the hard trip and under the circumstances, would take another route.

That apart we did as planned. Kazio and I were creeping into the hay, trying to avoid the unseen bodies, when Stan cracked his whip and the cart rumbled forward. I seemed to have been here before! It was a long time before Stan called us out, saying it was safe to surface for a while. So we emerged in daylight, brushing off the hay and sneezing from the dust. Stan introduced us all to a stranger, 'Mr Bohdan,' was all he said. 'Mr Bohdan' was somewhat older than we were; but why the 'Mister'? When Stan added tersely, 'Mr Bohdan is coming with us, he has orders for me to take him,' it sounded like a warning saying, 'don't ask me any questions!' I did not take to Bohdan, nor by all appearances did the others so we trundled along, conversation restrained.

'We will arrive at my uncle's farm around mid-morning,' explained Stan. 'The family are expecting us for a very late breakfast. This is their cart and their horses. If a car or a motorbike or groups of people appear on the road, dive for the hay. You'd better also take cover when we pass houses.'

We had to do this several times. In due course, we drove into the yard of a prosperous-looking farm, at the far end of which was a large house. As we stopped, a man came out of a shed and Stan jumped down to greet him.

'Come on in. Breakfast is waiting for you. You'd better leave all your stuff hidden in the cart for the time being.'

We went into the house for more introductions, using only Christian names. Stan's aunt greeted us with the old Polish welcome: 'Guest in the house – God in the home.'

We cleaned up, washed and sat down to a splendid breakfast. We talked about everything under the sun, except the reason that had brought us here. As soon as breakfast was finished, Stan took Jurek and me out into the yard, ostensibly to show us round.

'Who is this fellow Bohdan?' I asked.

'Budapest asked for him,' said Stan, 'I don't like him, and it seems you don't, either. However, orders are orders. All the same, he makes me uneasy and I want him watched. I shall ask Kazio to keep on his tail.'

And then came more bad news. Stan and his uncle decided that there were too many of us for safety, in case of inspection by Russian or worse perhaps, the Ukrainian militia patrol. Furthermore, said Stan, 'The team that travels by train to Nadworna near Stanislawow has no guide to take them to our safe houses for the night, because their guide has gone missing, I know that, but they [meaning the train party] don't; Kazio knows the set-up there his relative is much involved.' He decided that Kazio and I would join the train and provide the necessary cover as we knew enough of the arrangements. One other member of the party would go with us by train to reduce the load on the horses. Stan's uncle was well known and expected he would get us to the nearby railway station in his little delivery lorry in time for the train. Furthermore, he assured us, that starting the journey from a minor station no one would bother about any papers, other than tickets. Our cover story was that we were going to buy mountain hay for his mountain sheep, possibly sheep cheese for which the mountain regions were famous, and the cart, which was going by road, was bringing it back.

As good as his word, Stan's uncle delivered us to the railway station and bought our tickets; our train was due in shortly. The train party was briefed to change at Stanislawow, for a slow train in the afternoon for Nadworna, where they would be taken to a safe address for the night. In the morning we were to follow on by bus to Bitkow and Worochta. All being well we would arrive about the same time as Stan with the cart.

The station was almost deserted when the train arrived carrying a fair number of passengers; a number of familiar, anxious, faces were watching through the window, several friends among them. Some having spotted us, winked or gave other surreptitious signs of recognition. We three boarded the coach, but got ourselves seated at the other end of it and without signs of recognition.

Surprisingly, not even the tickets were checked on the train, and at Stanislawow the check was only superficial, so we left the station, in good spirit and unworried; we had time for a late bite at a small cafeteria I knew which was close by. On the way there we were followed, at a discreet distance, by a couple of friends; we contrived to bump into them at a street corner. Should anyone be watching they feigned a complete surprise, which made it look as if we had not seen each other since before the war; we invited them to join us.

The cafeteria was not only working, but also full; a few

Russians and some official-looking Ukrainians apart from a number of locals; we had to bluff it out. Again no one bothered about us.

The next step, a slow train to Nadworna went smoothly. Here we had to spend a night. The first job: to locate the safe houses. One of these was Kazio's elderly aunt, so he was sent ahead to make contact. Kazio was her favourite; while he was away, we, following Kazio's guidance, took the others to the designated safe houses and arranged the time and place for meeting in the morning for the last lap to Worochta and Bitkow area. Kazio was back soon after we finished lodging our fellow travellers. The aunt would look after four of us, but we could not arrive before late at night.

Dusk had fallen by then. Kazio was told of a small country inn in the township where we would find some supper. We were warned that most likely, the food would have to be prepared and we would have to wait; very fortuitous as we had time to waste. Late that night we made for our lodgings. The aunt bid us to take off our footwear and be very quiet, she had an NKVD officer, her permanent lodger, sleeping upstairs.

'No one would dare check the house in the knowledge of his presence,' she said, seeing our consternation. 'You are safe here, but you will have to be away before he is up. I'll give you hot milk and breakfast as well as some bread and butter for your pocket just in case, there is little else I can spare, until he', her eyes looked at the ceiling above her, 'brings me more food.'

We spent the night on tenterhooks lest by dint of bad luck we should be discovered. But nothing happened; the lodger was asleep and snoring well, when refreshed with hot milk and good breakfast we left before first light. We were on the last stage – a bus to Bitkow and then on foot to Worochta and on to Hungary.

Kazio and I, accompanied by two others, found our safe

house between Bitkow and Worochta. Stan and Jurek arrived just before us; Stan was checking on the assembly of our party, Jurek was tending to the horses and distributing supplies of food that they brought for the safe houses. When Stan and Jurek returned we were given a quick briefing.

'Our friend Bohdan,' Stan started, 'I am not sure of him, no one knows him, he produced a written instruction for me from my boss in Budapest. Kazio will be his shadow. I also want you to take these, and use them if necessary. Keep them ready at all times. They have been checked.'

While he spoke he handed to each of us a parcel wrapped in oiled cloth – each parcel contained a pistol automatic and spare ammunition. He had already allocated two army rifles and ammunition to known marksmen in the party.

'What do you mean by shadowing Bohdan?' asked Kazio after a longish deliberation.

'We are a large party. Most of us have been screened and are reliable. However, a few have been wished on me at the last moment, because they were allegedly in danger and needed to get out fast. I don't know anything about them. I don't like the smell of some of them, I am especially suspicious of Bohdan. We simply cannot take any risks. If there is trouble from Bohdan or any of the others for that matter, we may have to be ruthless, yes, I mean ruthless,' he emphasised. 'If it comes to that, I will have to explain to my bosses in Budapest. I don't like the idea, but I will not endanger the party for the sake of one or two trouble-makers, or even suspects.'

'Have to be ruthless?' demanded Jurek, wanting to have it spelled out for him.

'Well,' said Stan, 'we have firearms. We will use them if the situation demands it. Use your imagination. There are also other ways of disposing of people in the mountains.'

Then Stan asked for him and Kazio to be left alone for a private briefing to Kazio out of our earshot.

'I brought a weapon with me,' I said before leaving him and Kazio and passing mine back. 'You might like to give this to someone else.'

'That was not very clever of you,' he reacted quite tersely, 'had we or you been stopped and searched and the weapon found, no cover story could have saved us. It's too late now, but thank God, luck was on our side.'

I felt rightly admonished. Nodding his head, Stan returned two packets to his grip and started talking to Kazio.

We set out soon after lunch. It was a clear day. The snow-capped mountains, whose lower slopes were still snowless, looked beautiful. Underfoot, the ground was frozen hard. In order not to attract unwanted attention, we left our various houses at irregular intervals, in small groups of two and three, following the tourist trail marked with yellow-red-yellow markers. Some twenty minutes out of Worochta, we all met. Wasio, our guide, was waiting for us, with him was a stranger, introduced as the local commander, with Stan remaining in command of the group with Wasio as our guide. Occasionally I had a feeling that Stan was not enamoured of the 'commander' and to a large extent he seemed to disregard him but it was clear that he knew Wasio well as a friend and a guide, and one could see from the start, had an implicit trust in him.

Wasio spent some time checking that no one was overburdened and that all were suitably clad. He produced and distributed an assortment of white smocks and overalls, to be donned as soon as we reached the snowline. The party was then divided into four groups of ten. Wasio would lead the front group. Jurek, Kazio and I were picked by Stan to join him in the rear group; so was Bohdan!

It was time to go. As we got further and further into the hills, the track grew narrower and less worn. After a while, we left it altogether and strung out in single file following a sheep track. The forest became thicker and thicker, wilder and more overgrown; all manner of obstacles blocked our way with increasing frequency. We were also climbing. It became noticeably colder as the afternoon drew on, and now patches of snow could be seen amongst the trees.

Wasio called a halt after three hours. He had been gradually stepping up the pace, which was beginning to have an effect. Some of the party were clearly getting tired. We had halted in a large clearing, with a vista of the mountains towards which we were heading. The snowy tops of the mountains were glowing in the red of the setting sun. In the shadows, the snow looked blue, and below the snowline stretched the primeval forest, all dark blues, browns and blacks. In quiet and peaceful tranquillity of a happier situation I could have admired it more than now.

We were given a respite of fifteen minutes. Wasio did not rest. He wandered from group to group, encouraging those who were flagging, enquiring about the condition of people's feet. He spoke to each group separately, dispensing advice about night-walking in the forest.

'When it gets dark, you must stay in visual contact; you should be able to see at least two people in front of you. If you lose contact, call, but not too loudly, and stay put. Anyone hearing such a call must pass it forward to me. I will then come back and find you. Remember, if anyone is lost, so is everyone behind you. And don't forget, the younger and fitter must help the weaker and older. Once we get into the snow, you will have to wear whites, so make sure you keep them handy.'

When we moved off, the night was getting much colder. Where the trail was not sheltered, the wind was strong, penetrating and icy. No one spoke, for we had to concentrate on the difficult track. The only noise came from the cracking of branches as they were trodden on, the occasional sounds and swearing of people stumbling or even falling over; for those like myself acquainted with forests there were also the noises of night wildlife. We were allowed to stop for a breather at about ten o'clock after a difficult stretch and then pushed on by the relentless guide. After a while, we ceased to climb, as the path wound round the side of the mountain; this made the going easier and kept us sheltered from the wind. Overhead, the almost full moon lit the sky, showing the speed at which the clouds were being driven across its face. Then, the first snowflakes began to fall.

We reached a large clearing where foresters had been at work some months before; here we were allowed an hour to rest and have some nourishment. We arranged logs for seats. Bohdan stood apart.

'Feeling all right, Bohdan?' asked Stan. 'You seem a bit quiet.'

'I'm all right. Just don't feel very sociable,' retorted Bohdan, finding himself a log and sitting nearby but separate from the others. His resentment at the question was apparent; Stan shrugged his shoulders, and turned to Kazio.

'And how do you feel, my boy?' he asked.

'Oh, I'm fine. I've a few butterflies inside,' Kazio admitted honestly. 'After all, this is a big thing. My biggest worry is that I'm always so terribly hungry. The more nervous I get, the hungrier I become.'

'Here, take these.' Stan fished in his pockets and produced a couple of large rolls. 'They only have butter on them, but they should keep the wolf from the door.'

'No, no... I couldn't, Stan,' protested Kazio, 'they are yours, and I have my own food with me.'

'Go on, take them. If I run out, I will come to you and

share your supplies. In the meantime, these get in the way in my pocket and will go stale, even staler than they are already.'

Overcoming his hesitation, Kazio took the rolls and consumed them with obvious relish.

'Be sure to tell me if you want any of mine,' he admonished, his mouth full of bread.

All too soon, we had to restack the logs and do what we could to obliterate any signs of our passage. Wasio changed the sequence of groups, and we set off again. It had become much darker, for the moon was now obscured by thickening cloud. The snow was falling. We climbed up slowly and then followed below the crest of a ridge for a kilometre or so. The snow was now knee-deep. The valley below stretched as far as the eye could see. Even in the dark, between the flurries of snow, the whiteness of the snow made it possible to distinguish the outline of the forest, stretching along the other side and about halfway up the opposite slope. It all looked so close!

Those of us who were used to the mountains knew that distances were not only deceiving in a straight line, but also meaningless. The slope below us was steep, very steep; in places, close to vertical. It would have been suicidal to attempt a direct descent. Wasio led us down in a traverse. Those unused to the hills, found it difficult to keep their balance. For a long time we did not seem to get any nearer to the forest which looked so close. When we eventually reached it, the trees suddenly towered high above us.

By this time, it was beginning to get light. It was seven o'clock in the morning when Wasio led us to a well-built refuge building inside the forest, a shepherds' hut used by woodsmen and tourists alike. Somehow we all managed to crowd in; I doubt if it usually housed more then ten at the most. Wasio gave us one of his little lectures.

'You will find provisions and firewood here. Please

make sure when you leave that everything is as you found it – in impeccable order. You may use the cooking utensils, light a fire and help yourself to tea and sugar, but do not touch the food. We shall stay here for at least three hours. If your boots are wet, take the opportunity to dry them out, and oil them. There is oil here for that purpose, and you can use it. This may well be the last opportunity for a hot meal or hot drink.'

A huge pot of water was soon boiling merrily away, producing large quantities of strong, very sweet tea. Some tried to heat up their food, others stuck to dry rations. The air was soon full of the smell of steaming boots and drying socks. So many bodies, so much heat created a real fug; sweaters and wind cheaters were peeled off. Within the hour the only sound to be heard was snoring.

Did Wasio sleep? He woke us up half an hour before he wanted us to leave, so that we could tidy the hut and get ourselves ready. I thought I was in good physical condition, but I ached from head to toe; apparently, I had muscles where I did not know they existed! Others were less fortunate. Looking around, I could see that some had to turn on their hands and knees to get up. From their groans, I realised how much worse off were many of my companions. And if I could see it, Wasio must also have noted this even if he never said a word.

Some boots and socks drying by the fire had become mixed up, with consequential argument and swearing as large men tried to struggle into small socks and boots which were not their own. By the time everything was sorted out, we could see the funny side of it!

Appreciating the condition of his charges, Wasio set out at a slow pace which he gradually increased as we worked ourselves in. This part of the forest was littered with fallen trees and branches, obstacles frequently concealed by the snow. Our progress was punctuated by a steady but liberal flow of curses from those who stumbled.

Wasio continued to grow in our estimation. He never wavered. He always knew exactly where to go. He was always aware of the difficulties of this disparate party facing unexpected physical exertion. He kept to the cover of woods and forests wherever possible. He seemed to know them like the back of his hand and marched on with absolute confidence while we followed like lost sheep. Sometimes, when confronted by a formidable obstacle, such as a number of big trees uprooted by the wind, he would stop us and cast about till he had found a good way round. We were at his mercy; how easy it would be to get lost in these ancient forests!

Despite this, some time that afternoon, taking advantage of a more open bit of forest, Bohdan approached Stan, put his hand lightly on his shoulder and said, in a voice which only those nearby could clearly hear:

'Stan, I think we are lost. I am losing confidence in our guide. I know the signs. I have a compass which I consult from time to time. Hungary is to the south, but we are moving west, sometimes even north.'

Stan looked at Bohdan over his shoulder. I could see there was no friendliness in his eyes. 'Wasio knows these mountains like the palm of his hand. He knows the way he wants us to go and I trust him completely. Just relax, and don't spread fear and despondency.'

'I know what I am saying,' persisted Bohdan. 'I am not happy.'

'Look here,' snapped Stan, angrily, 'you know that I agreed to take you with us because I was ordered to do so. You presented me with the instructions you had from Budapest. Otherwise, I would not have taken you, without first having you vetted by my people. If you don't like what is happening and the way this group is led, just get lost! Go alone; see if I care! I shan't try to stop you.'

Bohdan resumed his place sullenly behind Stan, in a tense atmosphere. Nonetheless, Stan did go forward to talk to Wasio at the next halt. From a distance, it looked like a very serious conversation, yet suddenly they burst into laughter. He returned to us clearly happy. In fact, everyone was still in high spirits with the sole exception of Bohdan. Stan sought him out.

'Bohdan,' he said, 'I may have sounded a little unfair earlier, but we must trust the guide. He is the best there is in these mountains. He has to get us to the right place on the frontier, not just any old place. As you must surely know, in the mountains the direct route is not always the quickest or the safest.'

Bohdan, who was sitting on a fallen tree looking at the ground, stayed silent for so long that it seemed he was not going to reply. He suddenly looked up sharply and said, 'All right, I have had my say. I have the right to speak my mind, after all I am probably the most senior person here…'

He did not finish. Stan reacted sharply, 'There is no seniority here as far as I am concerned. I am the leader and organiser of this expedition. Wasio is the guide. Our orders will be followed. Andrew and Jurek are my deputies, if anything should happen to me. Until I hand you over to the Polish authorities on the other side of the border, your seniority in whatever organisation you belong to counts for nothing. You are just one of the party. If you like, you can turn back, and turn back now. In that case, I want a written statement before you go. You can continue with us if you choose. I will then expect you to be supportive and constructive and not subversive.'

Stan turned on his heel and stalked away. The atmosphere, loaded before Stan tried reconciliation burst like bubble, it may have been loaded before; now it was positively explosive. Bohdan could scarcely control the fury which suffused his face.

Was Bohdan merely uncouth and unpopular, or was he becoming dangerous?

We pressed onwards. Late in the afternoon, when it was obvious that we needed to stop and have a decent rest, Wasio lead us into a forest clearing. Judging by the numerous tracks in the snow, some of which were very recent, animals had also found this well-sheltered resting place. Wasio must have been very sure of our safety here, he skilfully built up a small fire which gave not a wisp of smoke; it gave us plenty of assurance but was of little other benefit. It was to be a long halt. The groups were huddled together sharing their food and talking in hushed voices; some were drying out their boots and socks, many looked generally exhausted. The warmth of bodies huddled together generated enough warmth which allowed some to snatch a short sleep.

I was dozing off, wondering about Bohdan, when I was suddenly conscious that he was sitting next to me. He looked as if he wanted to talk, which did not appeal to me, so I concentrated on my food, which had slid off my lap to the ground when I dropped off. After a while, he addressed me in a very low voice.

'Are you happy with the way things are progressing?'

'Yes,' I replied. 'I have complete faith in Wasio. He is first-class.'

'I am still unhappy, but so be it,' he murmured and then changed the subject, 'What are you hoping to do when we get there?'

'I am not sure. I suppose I will do what I am told to do.' I was hedging.

'But what would you like to do?' he persisted. 'I know people. Maybe I can help.'

I wondered where this conversation was leading. I was sure I didn't want or need Bohdan's help. Help? What kind of help? After a short pause he went on, 'You know the mountains?'

'I know parts of the mountains. I don't know this part at all. I've only been to Worochta once.'

'But you know and understand the mountains. Surely it makes little difference where you are. With a map and compass you could find your way.'

'I don't understand what you are driving at,' I replied, uneasy at the direction this conversation was going. In order to break off, I started to pack my rucksack. Suddenly, I realised I understood what he was proposing.

'If you are suggesting something that could be linked with your earlier conversation with Stan, then you are being subversive, unconstructive and verging on danger-ous.' I made to stand up, but he gripped my arm. I was surprised how powerful was that grip.

'You are to say nothing of this conversation to anyone,' his eyes bore into mine. 'That's an order. Break it and you will take the consequences.'

I broke free of his grip.

'Go to hell! Get lost! You can't give me orders here. If I want to talk to the others, I shall.'

'You'll be sorry,' he threatened.

I got up and joined Stan and Jurek on the other side of the fire.

'I see you've made a new friend – congratulations!' laughed Stan, a twinkle in his eye. Then Kazio materialised from the darkness behind us.

'Hey,' he said quietly, 'that Bohdan has a nerve! I over-heard your conversation.' He repeated our exchange, word for word.

I was glad when the time came to move off. I was unset-tled by what had happened, and couldn't get warm.

'Are you all right?' inquired Stan, who must have no-ticed. I didn't bother to answer, but just looked at Bohdan, who was engaged in animated conversation with another member of the group.

'Is he trying to persuade someone else?' asked Stan, quietly.

Half an hour after we resumed walking, we stopped. Word came back for us to don our whites. There was a frantic search. Wasio's earlier advice had been forgotten by some, and many a rucksack had to be emptied and repacked. At last, we moved off again. We passed out of the tree line and the long snake of the party became a line of moving shadows. We had been marching like this for a good half hour when Bohdan shouted, 'My rucksack! I have lost my rucksack!'

Stan turned on him, 'How could you loose a bloody rucksack!' he shouted. I thought he was going to hit Bohdan. There was a general commotion, and Wasio came running back to see what it was all about.

'What is all this shouting? Don't you realise how sound carries up here? Shut up.'

'I have lost my rucksack,' wailed Bohdan, for Wasio's benefit, 'with all my belongings in it.'

'How can you have lost a rucksack?' demanded Wasio. 'Where did you have it last?'

'When I got my whites out,' Bohdan did not seem in the least repentant.

'At least it isn't too far back. I'll go back and get it. Jurek, you go up front, and lead. We want to get to the top and left of the peak ahead of us, traverse the slope gently.' He pointed it out with his stick. 'If you get to the top before I return, which isn't likely, stop below the top, and wait. Take it steady; no one is to go to the top without me.'

'I'll go back with you,' volunteered Bohdan.

'Nothing doing,' Wasio was quite firm. 'If you come with me, you will only slow me down. However, you can take my rucksack. It's not very heavy.'

'Then let me go alone.'

'You will get lost and we will have to come and look for you. Unless, of course, you are looking for an excuse to go back, in which case you are welcome to go. We certainly shan't wait for you.'

Bohdan took the rucksack reluctantly. Wasio walked back rapidly, soon to become a mere shadow against the snow. Jurek assumed the lead, and we started off again. Bohdan exploded once more, 'He won't come back, he will take my things and go. Mark my words.'

'Don't be such an old woman,' said Stan curtly, fed up with Bohdan.

'I tell you he will not come back. I didn't leave my rucksack by chance. I did it on purpose to prove to you that I was right not to trust Wasio.'

Stan, who could normally control himself, lost his temper. He turned on Bohdan.

'You dirty swine!' he shouted. 'You filthy, dirty bastard!' He hit Bohdan so hard that one could hear the crunch of jarring teeth. Bohdan fell back on to the ground. It looked as though Stan was going to kick him as he lay there. Kazio and I restrained him, murmuring, 'Steady on, Stan!'

Bohdan struggled up from the ground, spitting out blood.

'I'll get even with you for this, you upstart,' he snarled.

'You are lucky you got off so lightly,' retorted Stan, turning his back.

The incident upset the whole party, especially our group, who had heard most of it. The column moved off again, with a lot of murmuring. I was at the very back, walking with Kazio. We had developed a really close friendship through this shared experience, and were virtually inseparable. Such closeness happened with others, Stan and Jurek for example, but they had known each other for ages. Kazio told me that Bohdan had approached others, and he had made it his business to listen in to the conversations. He had interpreted Stan's instructions quite literally, and passed on all he heard.

Wasio returned far sooner than I had expected. He tapped Bohdan on the shoulder. 'Here is your rucksack.'

Bohdan seemed startled, and Stan said, very loudly, 'Bohdan thought you would not come back.'

'Oh, come off it,' protested Bohdan, 'I was only joking.' He then thanked Wasio very politely.

'You have a very heavy rucksack,' observed Wasio, 'I would rather carry mine then yours.'

Wasio resumed his lead of the column and sent Jurek back to rejoin us. He led us into a deep gully. Although snow lay everywhere, one side of this gully was clear of snow. This was to be our hide-out. To the east, the sun was beginning to lighten the clouds and to cast shadows. There were large boulders in the gully where we were to rest. We spread whatever we could find on the bare stones to minimise the cold and damp. Wasio set out to spy out the land, and when he came back, he gathered us together for a briefing. He spoke with authority and assurance.

'From the crest of the ridge, you will be able to see across one valley to the next one. That is the border. There may be patrols along the border. Once we cross this ridge, we are committed. Most of the journey will be in the open except for a belt of woodland at the bottom of the valley and then trees at the border. We will stop there. It will be our last halt on Polish soil. Patrols are generally on skis; occasionally they are in tracked vehicles. During the day, they might even be in the air. Every one of us must be on the alert and act as lookouts. If anyone sees any activity, you have to give the alarm. The warning word is *down*. If possible, give the direction of the danger. Use the clock system. Twelve o'clock is straight ahead in the direction we are going; *down* two o'clock means you have seen something forward right; nine o'clock is dead left, three o'clock dead right, and so on. The moment you hear *down*, drop down exactly where you are. Don't move. Don't lift your head to look. Try to keep out of sight and melt into the ground. Only two people are allowed to look – myself in the front and Stan at the back. You stay down till you hear the cancellation – *carry on*. Only Stan and I can give *carry on*.

'It is going to take us a good seven hours' walk to reach the frontier. The border is marked by marker stakes. They are tall, so that they can be seen in deep snow. Each marker is numbered. On the Polish side, they are painted in white and red stripes. I will know exactly where we are, from the number. The border line is tricky; it is easy to get into Hungary and back into Poland just by walking in a straight line and there are trees among which one can get lost! My aim is to cross into Hungary at dead of night.'

'This is your last chance to have second thoughts,' he looked straight at Bohdan, 'and return free and alive. From now on, I have to regard anyone who wants to go back as a traitor, because if they are seen or caught by a patrol, this escape route will be completely compromised.'

No one wanted to go back.

The snow-clad mountains glistened in the morning sun; ridge after ridge, mountain after mountain, carpeted with the dark blue green of the forest. It was as if Poland was mounting a spectacular display for our departure. My mind was flooded with memories; would, could life ever be the same again? Would I ever see those I loved, again?

Wasio did not give us time to be overwhelmed by our emotions. He set out at a cracking pace, approaching a run, so anxious was he that we should not remain, silhouetted against the sky line. It was not until we approached the woodland belt, well into the valley, that he allowed us to slow down. The broad valley was covered with fresh snow; it looked as if a small river ran through it. The going was also easier here and we became a bit more relaxed. Suddenly a voice called out, '*Down* nine o'clock.'

We dropped where we were, as if cut by a scythe. Stan was a little ahead of me, while Jurek and Kazio and I were behind, at the rear. I could just see his face buried in the snow.

'What have you seen?' came Stan's voice.

After a few seconds I heard Bohdan's voice reply, 'There was something moving dead left, just above the line of trees on the other side of the valley.'

'Oh, it was you then,' Stan cut in. 'Lift your head slowly and see if you can spot anything where you thought you saw movement.'

After a while, Bohdan said he could not see anything now, but that he had seen three shadowy figures, maybe three figures in white. Stan lifted his head to look and was joined by Wasio, who had crawled back from the head of the column.

'Who was it?' he asked.

'Bohdan reckons there were three shadows, he thinks people, over there, just above the trees.' Wasio and Stan produced binoculars to scan the spot.

'I can see no new tracks, of men or beast,' observed Wasio, 'although there are some old signs of animal tracks.' He stood up. '*Carry on!*'

The column got up out of the snow and moved off. We moved faster, for everyone longed for the cover of the trees. This had been a false alarm; the next one might not be. The snow was frozen hard on top. Walking became easier, although slippery and treacherous. Every so often, the crust broke and someone would find himself plunged waist-deep in snow, needing help to get out. With sighs of relief, we reached the trees, at last. A smooth and even animal track led on along the bottom of the valley. There was indeed a stream there, which showed signs of flooding. Nor were there many trees, for apart from the wetness of the ground, there were great outcrops of rock, out of which grew some ancient trees. We reached a crossing point, where large boulders in the stream formed stepping stones. Above the crossing were ledges which gave shelter from the elements and also provided dry seating surfaces.

Wasio gathered together a few willing hands to look for dry twigs and branches which, with practised ease he heaped for us to sit on in the dry. We dreamed of a warm fire!

Everyone was tensed up. We were by now almost down to our last bite of food, and shared what little we had left. The only thing most of us wanted was a hot drink. Wasio came over to speak to Stan. 'A quick word with you?'

The two wandered downstream, out of earshot, and were soon plunged in deep conversation. At one stage, it looked as if they were arguing. Then they walked out of view. When they came back, they seemed to have reached an understanding. Stan came over, beckoned Jurek and me to join him, and drew us away, as Wasio had done with him earlier. He was clearly concerned about something.

'I have to be honest with you,' he said. 'Wasio and I have been talking about Bohdan. When Wasio went back to get Bohdan's rucksack, he took the opportunity to look in it, to see what made it so heavy. He found a map of the area, a compass, a pair of strong binoculars, an automatic pistol with ammunition, and a couple of powerful torches, one of which was narrow beamed. None of them bore any identifying marks, and Wasio does not think they were of Polish origin. We've all grown suspicious of Bohdan's behaviour and don't know what to make of it. It could be that he's part of our own intelligence, and if so, these are just the tools of his trade. Wasio is very suspicious however.'

Stan paused for reactions, but not getting any, he resumed. 'Wasio is harsh in his conclusions. Frankly, he wants Bohdan eliminated. I told him there was insufficient evidence, and that it was I who would have to carry the can and I who would have to do the elimination. Remember, it was I who was ordered to bring him with us. I would prefer to hand him over to our people in Budapest. However, I have agreed with Wasio that if there is another incident which could endanger our party at this stage, he will be for the chop. I want you to watch him like hawks, and report any suspicious behaviour. I have to say I do not like the very idea of being a judge and the executioner.'

We returned to the party in time to attend Wasio's next conference.

'I want to reach the tree line in about an hour's time. From there, we will go as fast as we can. It will be dark when we emerge from the trees. Remember the *down* and *carry on* drill. The less we carry, the faster we can go, so get rid of anything you don't need – the Hungarians will feed us once we get there. Cache all uneaten food and whatever else you discard in that cave under the ledge; maybe the next party will find it useful.'

Then we set out on the final leg of our escape. The frozen crust of snow made the going fairly easy, even though we were climbing hard. The slope, which had looked so smooth from the other side, was cut by troughs and ridges running more or less parallel from the top of the ridge to the bottom, as if a giant plough had been run up and down. Some of the ridges were two metres above the troughs; as we traversed the slope, it was up and down the whole time. Overhead the moon appeared, to throw occasional shadows from the thin clouds. Our white-clad procession looked positively eerie. As we climbed higher and higher and our tiredness grew, the troughs seemed to be getting deeper and deeper. They slowed us down considerably, but on the positive side, they presented an insuperable obstacle to a ski or motorised patrol, and also offered excellent concealment.

In the valley below, a wolf howled, to be answered by another. Kazio grasped my elbow.

'Hey look over there,' he said and pointed. I expected to see a wolf. Instead, silhouetted against the skyline in the blue light of the moon were men. One, two, and behind them, a third. There was a quick flash of light from one of them.

'Down!'

We all dived into the troughs. 'Eleven o'clock!' whispered Kazio. But everyone must have seen the light. The three figures moved swiftly, and were joined by two more. They were clearly on skis.

From where I lay in the trough, Stan's boots were in line with my head, with Jurek's alongside, while next to me was Kazio. I was higher than he. Although my head was down, out of the corner of my eye I could still see the five skiers, several hundred yards ahead, standing out clearly against the night sky. Two of them scanned the slopes with very powerful torches. It was fortunate for us that the beams could only light up the ridges and we remained safely concealed in the troughs.

In front of Stan was Bohdan. He had worked himself up, almost to the ridge. 'Get off the ridge,' hissed Stan, 'they will spot you there.'

Bohdan slid a little way back. As he did so, I saw something gleam in the moonlight. So did Stan; Stan's whisper was louder and imperative, 'Whatever it is you have that reflects the light, keep it hidden.'

There was a confused movement ahead. Bohdan was suddenly on his feet. A beam of light flashed uphill for a split second but very wide of the patrol and then vanished in the trough as Stan leapt upon Bohdan.

'What the hell do you think you are doing?' he screeched as he tackled Bohdan. 'Lucky for us that they blinded themselves with their torches at the same time and hopefully did not see your light.'

Jurek and someone from the other side of Bohdan leapt at almost the same time, and the four of them tumbled struggling into the trough. There was a crunch of glass as Bohdan was overpowered.

The five skiers above us were now shining their torches exactly in our direction, maybe after all they did see something and now knew we were down there somewhere. It seemed ages before the searchers finally moved off, possibly realising that the terrain was unsuited for skiing. We all hoped they had not seen us. As they moved, the light from their torches could be seen flashing in the increasing distance.

Wasio crawled back from the head of the column.

'Good job someone spotted the bastards. I nearly walked right into them. Must have been blind,' he grunted. 'Wind is blowing towards us, so even if they have dogs they wouldn't pick up our scent.'

Stan interrupted him, his voice trembling with excitement, 'Wasio, look at this.' He pointed to the ground alongside his feet, to bits of a torch. 'This bastard was about to signal to the patrol above us.'

Wasio was startled. 'Had he used the torch?' he asked.

We all confirmed that it was so.

'Well, in that case, you know what we agreed.' After a moment's pause: 'You are the commander here,' and then he called, *'Carry on.'*

'They were not the enemy. They were not Germans,' pleaded Bohdan.

'Were they Polish?' Stan demanded.

Bohdan no more than shook his head.

Wasio sent Jurek forward to lead the group, whilst we, those close to Stan, formed a circle with Stan and Bohdan in the centre. Stan clearly recalled what happened whilst we all listened, watching the snake of the group slowly moving uphill and fading into the darkened snow.

Bohdan's voice was shaky as he defended himself. 'They were most unlikely to have been, but they certainly were not German.'

Wasio was impatient and wanted to press on. He said bluntly:

'We here,' he pointed at Stan, 'are in operational command of this expedition. We judge you guilty of an attempt to betray us to our enemy. You know the punishment for treason in the field?' He turned to us: 'Do you agree?' and before we could answer, he turned to Bohdan again: 'If you like I will call the group back, tell them what you tried to do – I don't envy you if they opt to show you their feeling. You know about mob rule…'

Even in the light of moon, Bohdan's face was drained of colour.

'You have no right.' He tried to protest. 'You can accuse me, but only my peers can sentence me, and then only after a court martial.'

'We have no time to play with conventions just now, and we cannot risk you remaining with us. I will report the event and our decision in Budapest and if I was wrong – so be it. We do not know who you are, the orders you presented to me to take you to Budapest may have been forged. However, I am a regular officer of the Polish army, we are all an active service; here—' he stopped himself as if thinking and formulating his move in the knowledge that none of us remaining with him, were officers. 'Here,' he continued, 'under the conditions we are all your peers.

'We will maintain formality of the occasion however…'

He turned to us looking solemn. And there, on Polish soil, so close to the border, and in such danger, Bohdan was tried by his peers, found guilty and sentenced to death.[3]

---

[3] This form of administration of justice and punishment, in cases of

His hands were tied together, his knapsack was taken, and Wasio left to rejoin the head of the column. It fell to Stan, to carry out the sentence; we knew he would not delegate the distasteful task to anyone else. We left him shaken, standing behind Bohdan, holding a large revolver fitted with a silencer ordering Bohdan to walk downhill whilst the rest of us followed fast to catch up with the group, by now vanishing in their white overalls. We expected to hear an explosion of a shot. After what seemed an interminable delay, there were two or three distinct plops. Shortly afterwards Stan caught up with us.

His head hung low. He looked at no one, and would not be comforted. The expression on his face said, 'Just leave me alone.'

We climbed on, in gloomy silence. Finally, we entered the trees again, and the going seemed suddenly easier, but I was worried about Stan, who was obviously greatly distressed. Suddenly Wasio called yet another halt.

'Gather round,' he said. When he had everyone's attention, he continued, 'We have reached the border, which passes through these trees. I want you to spread out in line abreast, and advance like that through the trees to the top. Keep in eye contact with your neighbours on either side. Look for the frontier markers. Whoever sees one, pass the word on but do not shout aloud!'

There was an immediate buzz of excitement. Even Stan snapped out of his sombre mood. We fanned out and moved on.

'Here! I've got one!' someone called excitedly.

Wasio ran to the spot and dug in the snow to find the number. It was a solemn moment. One step more...

---

treason and others of similar magnitude under field conditions of the Underground, was a few months later (April 1940) formalised and codified by our government in exile in Paris.

Someone intoned our national anthem and every one joined in, singing, 'What the alien force has taken away, we will regain with our might...'

We were revitalised. The belt of trees was narrow. As we emerged in Hungary, we could see lights in the distance.

'Somewhere there, towards these lights is the frontier post, our destination,' announced Wasio. 'Let's go.'

Hungarian Rhapsody

The emotional euphoria of our achievement had prompted us into the spontaneous singing of our national anthem. Stan was the first to break the silence which followed.

'Well, we have made it! Wasio has done a great job.'

Everybody cheered and clapped with their gloved hands. All at once, everyone was talking at the top of their voices. There was an excited high-pitched explosion as the restraints and fears of our adventure were released. It was brought to a halt by Wasio's powerful and dominating voice.

'We may have crossed the frontier, but we are not out of the woods yet. Not until we are a good distance into Hungary. Those bastards would think nothing of coming after us, even on this side if they saw or heard us. We need to reach the frontier control post and until we register there, we remain vulnerable. Come on, let's get going!'

As we struggled on, we were all but overwhelmed by our own fatigue. We seemed to have drained all the adrenaline from our systems. Our feeling of relative safety was expressed in previously unvoiced moans and complaints: blisters and rubbing boots, wet socks and aching muscles, upset stomachs and headaches, symptoms of a whole range of sicknesses, and the discomfort of heavy rucksacks. The discipline which had been kept up under the pressure of possible danger and the order of conduct, had suddenly gone. We had become just an untidy crowd. Pessimism began to creep in. How would the Hungarians receive us? Would the strong German influence affect our reception?

'How much further to the frontier post?' called a protesting voice.

'We'll soon be on a road, and then it's no further than two kilos,' answered Wasio. 'And there'll be no more rest 'till we get there.'

It sounded harsh, but Wasio knew that those who were at the end of their strength would never get up again once they were allowed to rest.

It was hardly surprising that at our slow pace it took something like an hour before a brightly lit cottage came into view.

'Here we are at last,' cried Wasio, laughing. This tireless man broke into a run and, reaching the cottage well ahead of anyone else, banged on the door to attract attention.

Outside the cottage, a small board, freshly painted and lit by a small reflector, proudly announced in Hungarian and Polish: 'Police and Frontier Guard Post with Customs Facilities'.

The door was opened by a tall, dark, powerfully built man in shirt sleeves, wearing knee boots, breeches and braces. Wasio greeted him as an old acquaintance.

'How many are there this time?' he asked, in passable Polish.'

'Thirty-nine.'

'Hmm.' The official scratched his head. 'I'll take you to the school house down the road.' He went back inside.

Through the open door, we could see him put on his uniform jacket and then make a telephone call. There were one or two groans at the prospect of having to walk yet further. Happily, the school was very near and took but a few minutes to reach. The building held three classrooms and a kitchen. It seemed to have been prepared in anticipation of multiple uses, as the school in the morning, and as a refuge by the likes of us at any time. The largest classroom had been cleared, except for long, narrow trestle tables with benches on either side, and a pile of blankets stacked in a corner.

Immediately, we started to shed our heavy clothing, and queues formed for the washroom. Jurek and I found the kitchen, intending to put on some water to boil, and found it already occupied by a man and two women busy preparing food. There were panniers of bread, jugs of coffee, saucepans of soup, a churn of milk, and hunks of *speck* (smoked bacon fat) liberally sprinkled with paprika. We could speak no Hungarian, they had no Polish, but they left us in no doubt that we were not wanted in their kitchen. We rejoined our party.

The tall dark man got everyone together and addressed us. He apologised for the limited facilities and welcomed us on behalf of the village. They were only a small village, their resources were not great and did not run to anything elaborate; 'But you are brave people,' he said, 'and we want you feel that you are welcome among us.'

We felt we were welcome, and said so. Soon we were gulping down the hot soup, and bread with chunks of speck, washing it down with coffee. Our hosts had even provided enamelled mugs, and plates and other eating utensils. We were famished and fell upon the fat *speck* with an abandon that was to prove disastrous for many, for it did not sit well on empty and unaccustomed stomachs.

The man in the kitchen had other talents. A local guide, he was a friend of Wasio's, of long standing, importantly for many of us, he was also a first-aider. His kitchen work finished, he was attending to the various blisters, frost bites and similar complaints which afflicted so many of us. After the food, and warmth of the room, on top of exhaustion, those who were not afflicted by sickness brought about by eating speck too rapidly and too greedily, were asleep within a few minutes, almost literally collapsing where they stood some not even bothering with a blanket. On the whole, it turned out to be however, a somewhat disturbed night, with much snoring and groaning, mad dashes to the loo by those who were suffering from the delayed effects of their intemperate consumption of food. At first annoyed, I thought of our reception at Bojarka where, in contrast, many were also sick, but for other reasons – such as poor food, and mental stress, on top of hunger – what a difference! I smiled, turned over on the floor and sank into oblivion.

That village did us proud. Next morning they fed us with black bread, coffee, and mountains of scrambled eggs and fried potatoes, and I was sorry for those who went green at the very sight or even smell of food; they walked out into fresh air.

Soon after, we were visited by officialdom. First arrived two military policemen complete with their feather-plumed hats, and accompanied by two civil policemen. They were followed by a customs officer. We were asked to give particulars, produce passports and make customs declarations. Needless to say, no one declared a thing, though most had something that was included on the list of prohibited articles, which they waved beneath our noses. Perhaps this was just a formality; they must have understood our predicament, for no attempt was made to search us. Everything seemed to have been designed to speed up the reception process. As far they were officially concerned, we were refugees and we would be dealt with elsewhere. The sooner we left, the easier it would be for them. Immediately the formalities were completed therefore, we were loaded into lorries, and taken to the local township.

We were accommodated overnight in army barracks, fed on army food and the following day, marched to the railway station en route for Budapest. Surprisingly, we found that we were not the only Polish party on the train, and were disappointed when we were politely, but firmly, told that we were not allowed to mix. We were put under guard in separated compartments, in different parts of the train.

Once aboard the train, Stan reasserted himself, shaking off the broody gloom under which he had laboured since his horrible experience. It was clear from what he said that he had made this trip before.

'They will either take us to the Citadel or to the old cavalry barracks. I hope it is the Citadel; it looks frightening, but the officers and guards there are decent chaps, and I know some of them. This doesn't mean that the barracks are worse, but I don't know them. If you want something from the guards outside of their normal line of duty, you may well have to pay for it. Don't be surprised if they refuse Polish zlotys. A paper dollar is a lot of money to them, a gold one is an untold fortune, and a Maria-Theresa dollar is just wealth they dream about. They will search us on arrival; most of us have nothing to hide, and they won't confiscate money.' For the three of us closest to him, he had extra advice. 'They are interested in arms and ammunition. Try to conceal yours if you can. If they do find them, they will confiscate them and, judging by previous experience, take it no further. If you don't want to risk it, hand them over, but I'd rather you didn't, so see if you can think up some suitable hiding place.'

He didn't tell us why he wanted us to hang on to our guns, and we did not ask. One did not ask Stan. He usually had his reasons. We had several hours to solve the problem. I discovered that my ski boots, if not laced up tight, would accommodate my pistol in one and the ammo in the other, under my heels if they were wedged with spare socks. I tried out the method in a walk to the toilet compartment. It was painful, uncomfortable, but possible. Jurek followed my example, whilst Kazio just smiled. He had an idea of his own which he was not sharing. Nor was Stan, who had two weapons to conceal his own and Bohdan's. Maybe he was relying on his friends in the Citadel not to search him.

It was only during Stan's conversation that I realised that Wasio was not with us. He had certainly come as far as the station.

Stan enlightened us. 'Wasio had all the necessary papers to satisfy the authorities and was released. He is not un-known in this part of Hungary, and is not unwelcome. For that matter, you will find a few others also no longer with us, they had their passports and were allowed to travel independently. Now however, there's another matter I need to talk about. Write out your report on the Bohdan episode as soon as you can. When you are interviewed at the embassy by our intelligence, which is probably the first interview you will have, hand over your report to the interviewing officer. I don't want to know, or see, what you have written.'

It was dark when we reached Budapest. The station was well lit, and full of people getting off the train. It was also drizzling, but the platform was well protected. We were not allowed to detrain till the normal passengers had cleared the platform, so we watched through the windows, remarking how different Hungarians looked from Poles. They had dark hair, dark complexions, and different features, not unlike our gypsies. When the platform had emptied, we could see two groups of civilians at either end. One was clearly composed of Poles, slightly shabby, wearing mainly old army trench coats and trilby hats, middle aged and haunted-looking. The other group in contrast, looked very German. They wore long black leather coats, wide brimmed hats and several had expensive cameras hanging from their necks. They were young, self-assured and cocky.

We now got the order to detrain and keep to our groups. As we did so, the Polish group on the platform tried to place themselves between us and the Germans, who were trying to take photographs. The civil police objected to the photographic activity and tried to move the photographers away, while the military police stood back and ignored what was happening, amusement showing on their faces.

'Bloody Germans!' complained Stan very loudly. 'Trying to get us on their records. Don't look in their direction.'

There were three Polish groups detraining; still in these groups, we were taken off the platform to waiting lorries. Jurek and I were limping so badly as a result of the contraband in our boots, that Stan and Kazio felt obliged to help us. One of the escorting civil policemen was sufficiently concerned to ask, in German, if we were all right, or whether he should find us wheelchairs.

We assured him we could manage, but were none the less not a little relieved once we were in the lorries and able to take the weight of our feet! Stan remained concerned, and wanted to know if we could manage at the other end. We told him not to worry. Stan did have other things on his mind.

'I didn't like those Germans at the station,' he said. 'Did you see that the military police were not interested, even if the civil police did not like it? I hope they haven't infiltrated the guard at the Citadel or the barracks.'

From the back of the lorry, we could see the gaily lit streets of Budapest, neon-lit advertisements everywhere. It looked so different from the wartime Lwow of only a few days ago. Suddenly Stan brightened up: he had recognised where we were.

'We're going to the Citadel. Here's the Danube. We'll be there in a few minutes.'

And there it was. We were crossing a bridge; on either side, we could see the Danube, wide and slow flowing. Brilliantly lit bars and restaurants, on shore and afloat, lined the banks, their lights reflected in the water. Their verandahs were empty, no doubt because of the seasonal weather, but inviting all the same. Over the bridge, the driver changed down to low gear and we began to climb a steep, cobbled incline. The lorry stopped, and we could hear the creaking of wooden gates being opened. As we drove through, we saw enormous ancient doors swing to behind us. We dismounted in a large courtyard before waiting guards, and were lined up, answered a roll call, and then were marched in single file to a large vaulted hall, where many an historic scene must have been enacted over the centuries. We were addressed by a very smart-looking officer.

'If you have any arms or ammunition, please declare them before we search you and your luggage.'

He looked up and down the line. No one said a thing. One by one we were called forward. Our rucksacks were quickly searched. The personal search was perfunctory and superficial. Nothing was found.

Fifteen of us, including Stan, Jurek, Kazio and I were taken down a corridor which seemed to go on for ever. Every step was hell. The relief when we were shown into a large vaulted cell, large enough to take double our number, was considerable. The four of us grabbed the four bunks nearest the door as we went in, leaving the others to sort themselves out.

Our guard spoke Polish.

'You will be locked up here,' he said. 'If you want to go to the lavatory, you will knock on the door.' He saw Stan, and added with a twinkle in his eye, 'Have I not seen you here before?'

'Yes, yes, you have,' answered Stan, 'I have been here before. I find it better here than under the Russians.'

The guard nodded and laughed.

'You will have your supper in about half an hour. I will be back to collect you.'

The well-oiled lock clicked behind him. At last Jurek and I were able to get our boots off and change into more comfortable footwear, leaving our treasure *in situ*. We exchanged looks, feeling highly pleased with ourselves. When Kazio, with a rather sly smile on his face, calmly took his pistol from the poacher's pocket in his jacket, we felt rather foolish.

The promised food, was good, substantial and welcome. The cell door was left open for some thirty minutes; a constant stream to and fro from the toilets and washroom was cheerfully tolerated by a good-natured guard, secure in the knowledge that escape from the citadel was not possible. But finally the cell door was locked and we were left to ourselves.

Stan unpacked his rucksack and re-arranged his things in it, suggesting we should do the same. He proposed that we hide our arms and ammunition between the blankets of a vacant bunk next to him, in case there was a sudden search. Then nothing would be found on our persons or in our rucksack. It seemed a brilliant idea. We did as he suggested, and having repacked and hidden the pistols, we turned in. I can remember Stan wishing us, 'Good night and good luck.' I was too tired to notice the 'Good luck' part at the time; I could not even remember whether the light was turned off. I must have gone straight into a deep sleep.

I woke up, on hearing the doors being unlocked. The lights were on. A guard was at the door. I looked at my watch – it was 6.30 a.m.

Next to my bunk, Stan's was empty and neatly made up as if it had never been used.

Jurek also awoke. On top of his rucksack he found a note on a scruffy piece of paper. It read:

Thanks to the three of you for all you have done. Good luck to you. I have taken what I may need and what would be an

*embarrassment to you. I hope you won't mind. We may meet
again somewhere, some time. Stan.*

We read and reread the note, scarcely able to believe it. The
space between the blankets of the next bunk was now
empty...

'I expected something like this,' said Jurek, 'but how did
he do it?' No one knew. No one had heard a thing during
the night. Stan must have known the occupants of the
Citadel better than he had acknowledged.

We were even more surprised when the roll was called.
Stan's name was no longer on it. We were all saddened by
Stan's departure, and felt subdued and lonely.

When we were marched back to our cell after breakfast,
a guard called out my name. I identified myself.

'There is a letter for you in the office,' he said.

I didn't believe it, and suggested there had been a mistake. He offered to go and check. While he was away, I
retrieved a couple of one-dollar bills from my belt. Remembering Stan's advice, I thought he would expect a
present, and who knows, I might need his help later. In a
few minutes he reappeared. There had been no mistake.
There was a letter addressed to me, and the handwriting
was undoubtedly that of Uncle Zygmunt.

I gave the guard a one-dollar. He looked at it and
thanked me. He then told me he would be on duty again at
lunch, clearly implying he was at my service, if required.

I sat on my bunk and tore the letter open, not knowing
what to expect. I read:

*I am writing this note on the off chance that you will come
this way after us. We left home two days after you, Nuna,
Ralph and your sister, Christine. We were under threat of
arrest and Mary [my mother] was anxious about Christine
so we brought her with us. Through the good offices of*

Nuna's distant cousin living in Budapest, who is a friend of the Admiral [Admiral Horthy, Hungarian head of state], we were released quickly. We are staying with Nuna's cousin. Christine is at the Sacré Coeur Convent in Budapest. If you get this note, try and telephone us: the name is Calderoszi. The guards may allow you to use the telephone and may help with getting through.
Zyg.

Below was an address and telephone number.

I showed the letter to Jurek, who remarked dryly, 'Well what do you know! I wonder which way they got out? So much for that high-powered organisation of Stan's – they left two days after us and got here sooner.'

On the way to lunch, I spoke to my friendly guard who had produced the letter, and asked if it would be possible to use the telephone to contact someone in Budapest, giving him the name and telephone number. On the way back from lunch, he said he was just going off duty, but if I liked to come with him, he would see if he could help. If the office was empty, and he expected everyone would be at lunch, he could try and get me the call. He was right.

When the number answered he handed over the phone. In German, I asked for my uncle. Aunt Nuna came to the phone. She called my uncle. Nuna's cousin could arrange my release within a day, he assured me, and as soon I was released, I was to come to the Calderoszi flat. Thinking of Jurek, I said I had a special friend and would be particularly grateful, if he, too, could be released. Uncle said he would try, but all had to be done through Nuna's cousin, so he couldn't promise.

By this time, the guard was getting restive. He was meant to be off duty, and the office staff could return at any minute. Reluctantly I put down the phone. On the way back, the guard revealed that he understood Polish. He had understood most of the conversation.

'Will they let you out?' he asked. I said I hoped so, and slipped him another dollar. He seemed delighted. He tested the note against the light, and then kissed it.

We were just about to go to supper, when an NCO whom we had only seen supervising the meals came into the cell and called Jurek and me.

'Please pack your things quickly and come with me,' he said.

'Where are you taking us?' I asked.

'Please hurry. I have little time,' was all he replied. We did as bidden, shook hands with a desolate Kazio, who looked completely abandoned, and followed our summoned. He took us back down the endless corridor and into an office, where the smart officer who received us was sitting behind a desk.

'Please sit down, gentlemen,' he greeted us, pushing a box of cigarettes towards us. 'It seems you have high connections here. I have orders from the Admiral's office to release you and send you to an address in Buda. Please sign these release papers.'

He handed us papers written in Hungarian, which were totally incomprehensible, except for our names. We signed, hoping that he was not tricking us.

'As you have no papers which allow you to stay in this country, not even Polish passports, here is a pass which you can use to get from your address in Buda to your Polish Embassy. It is unofficial. It may be accepted by the civilian police; it certainly won't be, by the military police.'

He stood up, terminating the interview, and wished us luck. We were conducted across the yard to a wicket set in the enormous main gate. Outside there was a car waiting. A uniformed driver took our rucksacks as we took our seats, and then drove off. Jurek looked at me and said, 'Unless there are some funny tricks, it would seem we are free.'

I just nodded my head. After a while, the car stopped outside a smart block of flats. There was a list of residents, among them 'Calderoszi'. I pressed the bell, and the door opened.

There were no funny tricks.

My uncle and aunt were waiting for us as we came up. We had a very emotional reunion. Then I introduced Jurek, who was profuse in his thanks. And then it was time to be introduced to the Calderoszis, with emotional scenes.

That evening, we heard how Uncle Zygmunt had escaped, at very considerable cost. More important was a stream of vital advice concerning the situation in Hungary. We learned of the infiltration by, and growing influence of, the Germans, particularly amongst the military police, who could be distinguished by the cock feathers in their hats. These men were frequently accompanied by men in civilian clothes, who were in fact the Gestapo. They were busy seeking out Polish refugees, who were immediately arrested if they did not have proper papers. Until we were issued with proper papers, we must travel only by a registered taxi, easy to distinguish by their illuminated TAXI sign.

Having thanked the Calderoszi for all their help, we set out next morning with Uncle Zygmunt, by taxi, for the embassy. The taxi drew up outside. There were military police hanging around the entrance; as the taxi drew up, its engine still running, Jurek and I grabbed our rucksacks and made a run for the door. Zygmunt himself was safe; he had his papers. He paid off the taxi and took his time. Safely inside, he went about his own business, after pressing me to ring him as soon as we had an address, and we joined a long queue of others in a similar position. Eventually we reached the reception desk, where we were given a number and told to go and have our photographs taken, while we waited for the number to be called. The photographer, who was set up by the back entrance, must have been doing a roaring trade, although his results were not very good. Nonetheless, he took and produced the photographs while we waited and we took them back with us.

When my turn came, I discovered that, although interviews were individual, they were conducted by three civilians operating in the same office. Stan had been right. This first interview was by an intelligence officer.

I handed over my written report on the Bohdan affair. We talked at length about my work with Stan, my arrest by the Russians and escape, about which he questioned me closely. If he didn't know Stan personally, he certainly knew about him, and said that if he wasn't already back in Lwow, he was on his way. At the end of the interview, I handed over my collection of negatives of the Red army in Lwow. He glanced at them as if this was nothing new, thanked me and said they would be studied. By the time he was finished with me, Jurek was already waiting in the next queue, and I had to take my place at the end.

Although the system was well organised, and waiting kept to a minimum, there were so many of us that it took most of the day. At the end of it, we were issued with provisional papers and provided with billets in a small pension in the centre of the city, not far from the embassy. We were advised to steer well clear of any military police patrols, and told to return next day to collect passports and proper refugee permits of temporary residence.

Feeling safer, we found our billets without difficulty. The owners were very sympathetic. Knowing from experience that our day at the embassy had been foodless, they rustled up a quick meal, and then we settled down in our room, where two other Poles were already ensconced. Before turning in, I telephoned Uncle Zygmunt to tell him where we were, and he asked whether the pension could also accommodate Ralph; it would do him good to be with people more of his own age and it would also relieve the pressure on the Calderoszis.

By mid-morning the following day, our passports were ready, and for the first time we began to feel reasonably safe. We met my uncle at the embassy at his suggestion. He warned us to be careful, for although the Hungarian papers were genuine enough, the passports were locally produced, and it could be argued by anyone choosing to create trouble, that they were thereby fakes. Suitably warned, Jurek set out on a sightseeing tour while Uncle and I went to visit my sister at the Sacré Coeur convent.

Christine, forewarned, was waiting with a warm greeting. She had settled in surprisingly quickly, helped by the influx of girls from all over Poland, while a good few adult Polish ladies were helping the nuns to cope. Christine was as worried as all of us were over the rest of the family, and no amount of persuasion could set her mind at rest. As for her, it had been decided that, at sixteen, she was too young to be issued with travel documents to go to France to join up. Uncle Zygmunt and Aunt Nuna were in not much better situation; it appeared that his political views were not acceptable to the Polish government in exile, and they did not want him. He had to stay in Budapest for the time being until he sorted out what to do with himself. While he was there however, he would keep an eye on Christine who was to continue her education at the convent. It was a relief to both of us that Christine was well cared for; we could only hope that she would be as happy as possible under the very testing circumstances.

As far as Ralph was concerned, it was hoped he would be able to travel to France with Jurek and me and join the Polish army there. In the meantime, the pension agreed to take him, and the embassy had authorised the allocation of a billet for him.

Back at the pension, Jurek, who had a good look round, suggested that we take a stroll down to the river and maybe have a drink at one of the houseboat restaurants. We met quite a few of our compatriots with the same idea, and swapped experiences. Our outing convinced us that our clothes made us conspicuous, to easy a target for the cock-feather brigade, so we decided we needed to go shopping.

When we set out the following morning, the first shop we went to refused to accept dollars, the only currency we had in adequate quantity. We thought that we had better look for a shop with a Jewish name, in the hope that they might be more willing to accept dollars. At length we found such a shop, a well-stocked outfitters in a back street not far from the embassy. Not only were the prices fair, but the proprietor was willing to exchange our dollars at a reasonable rate. By the time we had finished, we were well fitted out, had lost our refugee appearance – and had been presented with a tie each into the bargain – all for the price of a few dollars.

Two days later, we were summoned to the embassy to get our marching orders for France. We were walking along at a brisk pace when we were intercepted by two 'red cocks' and two civilians who suddenly stepped out of a side turning, only a few hundred yards from the embassy. They stopped us. One of the 'red cocks' spoke to us in Hungarian.

'Ich spreche kein Ungarisch,' I said to him in German. (I don't speak Hungarian.)

'Wer sind Sie?' demanded the civilian. *'Sind Sie Deutsch?'* (Who are you, are you German?)

I raised my hand surreptitiously. *'Naturlich – heil Hitler!'* (Of course – heil Hitler!)

'Heil Hitler!' responded one of the German civilians. *'Wass machen Sie dann in Ungaren?'* (Then what are you doing in Hungary?)

'Leutnant von Nahlik, Vierte Bureau,' (Lieutenant von Nahlik – Fourth Department), I said, clicking my heels.

'*Dann jetzt, lass uns gehen, wir sind in Eile.*' (So now let's go, we are in a hurry.)

'*Entschuldigung, Herr Leutnant,*' (Apologies, Lieutenant) apologised the German, stepping to one side to let us pass.

As we passed I muttered – '*Dummkopf*' (idiot) – loud enough to make sure they could hear. Jurek looked at me and said nothing for a while. We deliberately passed the embassy and turned down a side street in search of the back entrance. We did not want to be seen going in, by the German-Hungarian surveillance team.

'That was quick of you,' said Jurek, 'we wouldn't have got away with it in our Polish clothes.'

I had to agree with him. Clothes do make a difference.

We found the back entrance.

The first person we encountered was none other than Kazio. He had been released the day before. We told him where we were staying, suggested he changed his billet, and invited him to come and see us as soon as he could move about more freely.

Under the circumstances, Christmas was a non-event. Two days after it we were briefed and issued with papers for departure, having to say goodbye yet again to the family. Uncle Zygmunt and Aunt Nuna came in a taxi to collect Ralph and me from our lodgings, and took us to the convent to say our farewells to Christine. My poor sister looked very composed and calm but I could see from her red eyes that she had been crying, and that even now, she was close to tears. She said that she had prayed for us going to war and quickly ushered us out on the pretext that we needed time to settle down on the train, having first found good seats. She was mopping her eyes when we looked back from the taxi to see her waving from the window.

How grateful I was that she would have, at least for a time, the support of our uncle and aunt in the strange environment of an Hungarian convent, however friendly it may have been. My comment to that effect brought tears to Aunt Nuna's eyes, who after all was also saying goodbye to her one and only son.

We were in good time so Zygmunt took us to a bar and we had a large glass of very tasty *sliwowitz* to restore our nervous balance.

We were bound for the Polish air force in France. With luck, we would be there, belatedly, to see the New Year in.

Hopefully it would be a better year.

France and the Phoney War

I was glad when this first Christmas in exile was over, even though I was lucky. Not many of my compatriots had any of their family with them, as I had; my aunt's cousins were very kind and considerate, and I had friends. But like all of us, our minds were concentrated on our loved ones in Poland whence news was scanty, at best. On New Year's night, instead of the traditional revelries, we said our goodbyes. Jurek, Kazio, Ralph and I had a compartment to ourselves, in an almost deserted train; who would travel on the New Year's night? The engine had steam up, a whistle blew, someone shouted outside, the coach moved... Zygmunt and Nuna started walking along the platform by the window. They waved and we waved back. Soon they could not keep up and we just waved for the last time out of the open window.

Budapest was left behind. Shortly after, as the sun was setting, a big lake came into view and we rolled along its shores. The air above was thick with waterfowl on the wing. I remembered my father talking about the famous Hungarian waterfowl shooting places, hoping that one day we might be able to come together to have a few days' shooting.

All too soon it became too dark to look out and we prepared for the night. Stacking our baggage, such as it was, on the floor, we drew places for the dubious honour of sleeping in the luggage rack. I drew the rack, so up I went. These racks proved narrower than the ones we had in our railway carriages, where I had spent many nights during school and other outings. Additionally I was restless and as a result, I fell off two or three times – bouncing first on to Jurek who was below me, and then rolling off him on to the luggage and whoever slept on it, in the middle.

After a while, those on the 'ground floor' became both fed up and bruised and insisted we changed places. The change-over accomplished, the rest of the night passed peacefully, except for perfunctory passport and customs control visit. I suppose even officialdom would rather have been celebrating.

By mid morning we had reached Trieste. Changing trains gave us an opportunity to replenish our provisions at the station buffet, followed by a mad stampede to catch our next train – a slow one to Milan. Like all slow local trains, it was uncomfortable, dirty and crowded, mainly with local peasantry. Its smell however, was not that of sweaty and dirty bodies but of garlic, cheese, wine, all of which made our mouths water – all we could afford were cheap stale rolls filled with dry ham. We sat huddled together, talking quietly and anxiously watching out for uniformed officials. Our tickets were fine but we lived in fear of our passports being challenged. Maybe the collection of real, if only transit two-day, visas saved the day, for both police and other controls on the trained passed our papers, without as much as a raised eyebrow; or they may have become used to a steady trickle of refugee Poles.

I could not claim that Milan was a city of my young dreams. I had heard, and read, however about the splendour of its marble-halled central station recently opened by Mussolini, and of course who had not heard of La Scala! It was late afternoon when we rolled into Milan, with a night to waste before catching the next connection in the morning, and little cash in our pockets. What to do?

We arrived. Indeed the central station proved to be even

more spectacular than my imagination would conjure. The clever lighting picked up the marvellous Italian marble, adding emphasis to its vastness and colours.

We found an information office, where we learned that La Scala was staging the *Barber of Seville*, and that there were plenty expensive high-class hotels nearby, which we could not afford. Of cheaper hostelries, within our means, they could tell us nothing. While others were discussing what to do, I decided that I would go to the opera, find somewhere inexpensive to eat, and spend the night in the station waiting room, there was no one interested, so we arranged to meet on the train next day, unless they too, finished up in the station waiting room.

I got to the opera and bought a cheap ticket. The impression was overwhelming. From high up in the gallery, I took in the vast concourse of people below, many dressed up for the occasion in evening clothes and full dress uniforms, streaming in to take their seats, under the glittering lights and amidst a hubbub of voices and the tuning-in of the orchestra. It all combined to make a fairy tale effect. Why was I here, I asked myself? I was not even a lover of the opera. For years, I had been dragged to see visiting company in Lwow, I had been taken to the opera in Vienna and Wagnerian Berlin. But this was different. Here, as if by a miracle, I was transported into another world. And as the lights dimmed and the orchestra started up, it suddenly came to my mind that there was a war on, probably not many kilometres away, that I had left my family in a perilous situation and did not know what I was heading for. I sat through the performance but the thoughts running through my head made me feel subdued.

Afterward I found a small cheap restaurant, where I stuffed myself with a mountain of spaghetti dressed in sauce and topped with parmesan cheese, and washed it down with a cheap, sharp but marvellous red wine. I returned to the station with mental balance restored, to find my friends already fast asleep on the waiting-room benches.

It seemed to me that I had hardly fallen asleep when it was time to be on the move again. We snatched a breakfast of coffee and rolls and headed for the train. The number of our compatriots had swollen; Polish voices could be heard everywhere. As we did not encounter anyone we knew, we kept ourselves to ourselves.

Once we neared the mountains, we sat with our noses glued to the windows watching the snowy peaks. On the slopes could be seen happy skiers. How we wished we could join them! Jurek light-heartedly suggested that we should break the journey and have a couple of days fun. It was a pipe dream and he knew it.

The train rolled to a halt at the French frontier station of Modane, dead on time. While the 'ordinary' civilian passengers were being checked by frontier controls and customs, we were greeted by the heart-lifting sight of Poles, wearing the uniforms of dark blue of the air force, and lighter khaki than our of the French army, but proudly bearing Polish insignia and badges of rank. We were sorted into two groups, air force and army, and here we parted company with Kazio and Ralph, destined for the army.

Once our particulars were recorded, we took the waiting train for Lyon. Looking out of the window it was impossible not to draw comparisons with Poland at war. We could see happy smiling faces; people working, eating, drinking and enjoying themselves. And as the train continued its journey, there were no signs of panic, no sign of evacuation, no fleeing crowds, no tired, grimy, frightened faces. The war could be thousands of kilometres and as many years away. When would we have an opportunity to strike back?

It was not long before we found ourselves under the vast dome of Lyon railway station. The platform was swarming with the dark blue, air force uniforms, some with gold braid of the French, some with familiar silver shoulder stars, and hussar wings surrounding the Polish eagle on the caps. The Polish team walked up and down, instructing those destined for the air force to detrain. Friendly handshakes united old acquaintances and friends.

'Officers at this end of the platform, please!' shouted a captain. 'Other ranks over here!' bellowed a sergeant. One third were officers. Jurek and I joined the other ranks. We were taken by lorry to the base.

Again we marvelled at the peaceful scene as we drove through the wide tree-lined boulevards. Shops, cinemas and everywhere cafes, restaurants and bistros, with their pavement verandas, tables and chairs, full of people drinking their coffee, cognac or wine without a care in the world. At last we passed through a big gate bearing the gilt legend – BASE AERIENNE MIXTE DE BRON-LYON. Here was our new home, the nerve centre of the Polish air force in France.

Once off the lorry, the NCOs were separated out and the rest of us were addressed by a Polish sergeant. Having welcomed us, he told us:

'You will be housed in Block C, dormitories numbers 3 and 4. Block C is through the next gate, third block on your left. Leave your luggage there and go to the stores to collect your bedding and eating utensils. Take them back to your block and then go to the dining hall for supper at 5.30 p.m. The duty airman in the block will show you how to get to the stores and dining hall. Happy New Year!'

Suddenly, as I looked around me, I had the extraordinary feeling that I knew the place. I could see it in my mind.

'Jurek,' I said, little hesitantly, 'you will not believe it, but I have a feeling that I know this place as if I have been here before.'

'Don't be silly,' retorted my friend dismissively, 'how

can you possibly know this place.' I wasn't sure whether this was a statement or a question. He added, 'If you are so sure, you lead the way.'

So I did. I went straight to the block and the dormitory allocated to us. 'Maybe I dreamt about this place. I can't understand it either,' I said.

Was it to test me that Jurek decided he wanted to go to the toilet before doing anything else? I went with him an led him there without hesitation. When we returned, some of our companions were still unpacking, others ready to fetch their bedding. I suggested to Jurek we should now go and collect ours. He offered to go and find the duty airman.

'I know the way!' I announced.

Jurek and two others came with me. I ignored the main base road and took a shortcut, bypassing the airmen's dining hall, followed the path behind it and arrived at the door marked: 'Stores issued to Polish air force personnel 1500–1700 hours'. The time was 16.45.

When the rest arrived, led by the duty airman we had just about finished collecting our kit. 'How did you find your way?' asked the duty airman politely.

'He seems to have known the way,' replied Jurek before I could stop him.

The young airman looked at me incredulously, 'Been here before?' he asked.

I shook my head and began to blush.

'You haven't been here before and yet you know your way?' he said slowly; 'What else do you know about the base?' Suspicion ringing in his voice.

I told him that I knew where the airmen's dining hall was, and recognised it as we passed the back of it.

'That's not difficult,' he laughed, 'there is always a smell cooking that you can follow.'

I went back to the block hoping to be left alone, but Jurek told me I was making a fool of myself.

'Oh, belt up!' I snapped. 'I didn't say anything, you did; so you are making a fool of me, not I. I am just as uneasy about this sense of *déjà vu* as you are. I expected support not ridicule from you.'

Jurek shrugged his shoulders and continued making his bed saying nothing. For the first time in months there was a sign of discord in our relationship.

At supper we encountered other airmen, 'Hey fellows – welcome to France!' Among them I suddenly spotted the back of stocky figure with blondish hair, wobbly knees and a sailor's roll; I would have known him anywhere. It was Miet, my old gliding instructor.

'Miet, Miet!' I shouted. He looked round and saw me, then his face lit up with pleasure. I introduced him to Jurek, to find that he already knew Tad, as well as his other brother. Miet told us that we were not yet free to sit where we pleased; newcomers out of uniform remained segregated. We arranged to meet later in the canteen.

The mess tables were topped with sheet tin or some other metal, so thoroughly scrubbed that they looked like silver. The food provided, accompanied by mugs of red wine, was good and so plentiful that we were unable to finish it.

We returned to our dormitory, changed, took the opportunity to do a little laundering, and set out for the canteen.

Miet was already waiting for us. Nearby I recognised another acquaintance, who accepted a waved invitation to join us. This was Mat Ziebinski, whose mother had been at school with mine. He had arrived just before Christmas, having set out from Budapest two days after his eighteenth birthday, the minimum age at which volunteers were sent from Budapest to France. He too, was hooked on gliding and flying and had admired Miet in the air. Like all of us he was impatient to fly. Miet, speaking kindly and with authority, disillusioned us all.

'You will have to be very patient. It will be a long time before you, we,' he corrected himself, 'will be allowed to train. Even those who are qualified, but with full regular air force proficiency, will have to wait.'

Then, realising that none of us knew anything about the base he explained that there was a Polish squadron training on fighters, and two French squadrons. He told us about various types of aircraft employed, and went on, 'Even among the very experienced pilots there are only a few selected for the squadron. Once they have completed training, they will be moved to another airfield and a new squadron will be formed, again from very experienced pilots. The likes of us will have to wait very patiently. The only thing to do is make ourselves useful. Offer to work in offices – this will not only save you from boredom, but will get you known. You might even be able to persuade someone influential to get you at least the odd air experience flight or even, with luck, get you on a flying training course. I myself am working as a clerk at headquarters.'

With that he offered to buy us coffee knowing that we had no French francs.

On talking about mutual acquaintances we discovered that Captain Pawel was also there. Considered too old for squadron flying but too good to ignore, he had been appointed an instructor.

When the canteen closed, we walked back to the block. On the way, I told Miet and Mat about the unnerving sense of *déjà vu* I had experienced. My account was confirmed by Jurek. Miet, a well-educated and well-read man, said he had heard of such things and asked if there were any similar incidents in my family. So I told him of my great-grand-mother's strange prophecy that I would serve in a foreign army, and her plea that I should never forget that I was Polish.

'And here you are,' said Miet, 'about to don a French

uniform. Strange things happen – difficult to explain.'

Next morning we collected our uniforms, were paraded, and marched to a large hall for documentation. In charge was an elderly lieutenant, powerfully built, balding man with piercing blue eyes. He looked tough, an impression supported by a chestful of Polish and French medal ribbons, which included the Croix de Guerre which he won in the French Foreign Legion. A humorous twinkle in those penetrating eyes promised a pleasant personality, confirmed as soon as he started addressing us.

'You may not be fighting the war yet, so address your minds and energy to fight through the documentation before you. Make sure that all the sections are completed and all your answers are true. Those of you who have some flying experience and who hope to fly, don't add zeros at the end of your flying hours. We have a rough idea how much flying you have really done. Get cracking. I will leave you to get on with it for forty-five minutes.'

When he returned some were still struggling with the mountain of forms. When everyone had finished he gave us a lecture.

'My name is Ostrowski, Lieutenant Ostrowski. I am the Polish depot adjutant. The depot commander is Colonel Luzinski, on whose behalf I welcome you to the Polish air force in France. I spent six years in the Foreign Legion as you may have observed from my medal ribbons, I have also served not only in the Polish air force but also with the French so I know all the tricks of the trade, French as well as Polish, so don't ever think you might just fool me. You will be sorry if you do. I am not threatening, I am telling you. There are a number of things you need to know.'

'One. At present there are about a thousand of us here. We expect that by the end of January there will be over three thousand and we shall then open up a depot in the Lyon Foire – the market.

'Two. We are now training a selected bunch of pilots, all very experienced, to form a squadron.

'Three. We shall start training qualified ground-crew airframe and engine fitters, electricians, drivers and other personnel, on French equipment. It will be some time before we can offer any training to budding aircrew.

'Four. At the moment no one will be ordered to do anything. We rely on volunteers to meet all our needs, and that goes for everything from training to office chores. We can find work for a considerable number of volunteers in both Polish and French offices. We need people with languages, French, English and German.

'Five. Those who have nothing else to do *don't* create trouble. Our authorities and the French authorities will deal sternly with trouble-makers. We already have some fifteen airmen in a French military prison, locked up because they tried to make trouble. I promise you, French prison is not a joke!

'Six. Those of you who are not officers or NCOs have been allocated to Company B, your CO will be one Lieutenant Godlewski, who will be here in a few minutes. Those who wish to volunteer for office work will be moved to the headquarters company, which I command.'

His place was shortly taken by Lieutenant Godlewski, who said, 'Our company will soon be three hundred strong. Company B is merely an administrative unit. There will be a parade every morning after breakfast at which daily orders will be read out. There will then be drill, after which you will be left to your own devices. New arrivals who have had no pay as yet will be issued with two weeks' pay later this morning. You may leave base without a pass after 4.30 p.m. and must be back by 10 p.m. If you want to leave earlier or return later you must have a pass. Until you are mustered to a trade, your pay will be six francs per week, plus two packets of cigarettes, a bar of soap, and a choice of toothpaste, toothbrush or razor blades.

'Those of you applying for aircrew will be know as aircrew candidates. When you start training you will become under-training aircrew, and your ranks will be confirmed when your papers have been processed and verified.'

Having had our hopes of flying shattered twice within twenty-four hours, Jurek and I followed Miet's advice, volunteered as clerks and were transferred to the headquarters company. To say that we were disillusioned and frustrated would be an understatement. I saw myself as a half-trained pilot, only requiring a 'finishing course'. I wanted to fight. If the worst happened, and flying became quite impossible, I wanted to be near the flying operation that I loved.

For a while Jurek and I reminisced about the last three months, wondering if we ought not go back to Poland and act as couriers, like Stan.

Jurek had an uncle in Paris who was a senior air force officer. He got a pass and set off for Paris to visit his uncle and seek advice from him, or his connections. Our return to Poland was ruled out completely, but Jurek's uncle could arrange to have us transferred to the army. We decided against that and contemplated a future of inactivity and penury with malaise, impatience and misgiving.

Soon we discovered that the clerical volunteers of headquarters company formed a somewhat elite group. We comprised an extraordinary collection of barristers and lawyers, engineers and historians, vets and agriculturists. Almost all had degrees. Those of us who had not yet finished our studies, were good-humouredly referred to by our seniors as uneducated or uncultured simpletons. With the exception of the officers and senior NCOs who had overall departmental responsibilities and were Polish air force regulars, we volunteers tackled the never-ending flow of paperwork for new arrivals, the routine everyday interaction between us and the French and everything else connected with the mundane matters of efficient running of the base. We were good and did everything asked of us, no matter how simple. In return, we were cosseted by the ever-caring Ostrowski. He knew very well the inadequacy of our six francs a week; the minute additions earned by the few whom he was able to promote to aircraftmen first class were derisory. However Ostrowski had his ways. Whenever there was a chance of an outing, ticket to a cinema, theatre of circus, he always made sure that his 'boys' had the pick. He also found us tasks out of the ordinary, to add variety to our work.

The biggest perk that came our way was the courier run. There was a constant need to take all sorts of papers to Polish HQ in Paris, the seat of our government which was at Angers and other units of the Polish or French air force. These trips attracted an allowance of twenty-five francs – more than four weeks' pay, the more valuable since food and accommodation was almost always found 'for free' at the other end, usually through Ostrowski's influence. On top of this, he had a wide variety of contacts which he happily exploited for our benefit.

My turn, when it came, was a trip to Paris. It entailed an overnight trip there, two days in Paris and a night trip back. Apart from the papers to carry, Ostrowski gave me a note to deliver to a lady-friend, without saying what was in it. Having delivered my papers, I carried out Ostrowski's errand and enquired if there was a reply. She read the note and then asked me in.

Ostrowski asked her to provide me with tickets for a show and to find someone to keep me company if I had no one but myself. I knew no one. Within half an hour a good-looking girl of about twenty arrived; she was introduced as Monique. I was given two tickets to the Folies Bergères, and some spare cash.

The Folies were a revelation. I have never seen so many bare bottoms, so many bare tops –in public – and from very good seats at that. The show, the drinks, the excitement of being in Paris in spring with a pretty girl were heady and I ended up spending the night with Monique and learning a thing or two for good measure from her.

Monique had to work in the morning. We parted after breakfast and I was left to my own devices.

When I got back and tried to thank Lieutenant Ostrowski, he brushed aside my thanks and hoped that I had had a good time.

One day I was summoned by Ostrowski; he had a job he wanted me to do. He had a request from the French base HQ for someone to help at the archives of the French air force at Fort Bron, a fortification just outside the base which predated the First World War.

'By French law,' he explained, 'a combatant of the Great War can claim exemption from call-up, apart from having several other privileges. The archives have to verify these claims as valid or reject them. They have hundreds of applications every day and there is only a staff sergeant dealing with them, so they have asked if we can help. The staff sergeant is reputed to be a mean sort of bastard, but is well meaning. The archives are stored in the cellars of the Fort, dark with poor ventilation, so there is an entitlement for a special hardship allowance of several francs per day. As it is too far to walk, you will be fed in their mess and you will be issued with a bicycle.'

It was an offer I could not refuse. The staff sergeant turned out to be thin, small funny sort of a man who had served in the Great War, and who was a solicitor's clerk by profession. Perpetually hanging from the corner of his mouth was a generally unlit cigarette. Hundreds upon hundreds of applications for combatants' rights poured into the archives in large bags. Every one had to be checked, stamped 'granted' or 'refused' and signed on behalf of the *'Lieutenant Colonel, Chef des Archives'*. The staff sergeant showed me what to do. In the early days when the volume of pending work seemed to grow, he occasionally gave a hand. He would also sit down for the last half-hour or so and sign the papers. After a few days, he decided that my indecipherable signature and unusual name would not be queried and that no one would suspect that the signatory was a *soldat deuxième classe*, let alone a Polish one at that! Once I was used to the work, he left me to get on with it. The only time I saw him after that was first thing in the morning to let me in, and last thing in the evening, to shut up shop. The *'Lieutenant Colonel, Chef des Archives'* existed on paper only.

There was an interesting side to this work.

Much of my searching involved the records of the French air force squadron in the 1914–18 war. There were times when I became so engrossed in reading about the famous aces such a Renee Fonc and Guynemer, that I neglected the work I was supposed to be doing. No matter – there was no staff sergeant there to keep my nose to the grindstone, nobody knew, or cared, and single-handed I could not keep up any more than he could before I arrived. Occasionally I made fascinating discoveries, such as the records of Escadrille Lafayette, which included a few American volunteer pilots and which after 1918 was 'lent' to Poland and fought in the 1920 Russian war. I was sorely tempted to purloin it, but honesty prevailed; doubtlessly it still languishes, accumulating dust in the bowels of Fort Bron – unless someone else could not resist the temptation.

All good things come to an end, and so did my secondment to the archives. I missed my extra francs each week, but won the bicycle which I forgot to return and which was not missed.

Once in France, I endeavoured to make contact with as

many friends and acquaintances outside Poland as I could find. One of these was a cousin in the diplomatic service as the first secretary of our legation in Berne. Through him I tried to find Hala, the one person outside Poland, whom above all others I wanted to find; we found no trace of her. I wrote to her last known address in Belgium, but no reply came. I had alas forgotten the name of the family for whom she worked and with whom she lived. Hala had vanished into the unknown. I did however, receive through this cousin, the much needed news from my family which was a help.

The cousin gave me also the name of a friend of his, a senior member of the Polish consulate in Lyon, and through his kindness I made some useful contacts. It was as a result of these contacts I received an unexpected letter from Comtesse de Villon, of who I had never heard before. Nonetheless, I was invited to spend the last week of April at their villa on the Riviera at Cap d'Antibes, where they offered hospitality to allied servicemen. I accepted with alacrity, having sought and obtained the necessary leave. In her next letter, the comtesse said she was delighted, because her younger daughter was studying Polish history and Polish language and hoped she would have an opportunity to improve her knowledge of the language during my visit. Everything would be very informal – dress and language were immaterial, uniform would be acceptable, so were slacks and shirtsleeves, but, since they had a tennis court and a beach only a few meters away, I might find sports kit useful.

My finances did not stretch to anything beyond the basic minimum, but my colleagues who lived in uniform and had no need for 'civvies', helped as they could. By the time I set off I felt adequately equipped.

French Leave

There was a driver waiting at the railway station for me and for a fellow guest: Pilot Officer David Laing RAF. We introduced ourselves. David, who was surprised that I could speak English, did not know the family either; we passed the journey in idle speculation.

The villa was beautifully situated in idyllic surroundings. As the car drew up, a soldier servant opened the door for us and took our luggage. We were shown into the salon.

'Madame la Comtesse will be with you presently,' murmured the manservant respectfully, closing the door behind him as he went out. David and I continued our speculations in hushed whispers. Then the door opened and a young woman, who was simply but smartly dressed, walked in, taking off her gloves.

'I apologise for not being here to receive you when you arrived,' she told us. 'You are both very welcome.' She looked us over, as if sizing us up and turned to David, 'You are – Andre?'

'No Madame, I am David; David Laing,' he said, shaking the extended hand.

'Then you must be Andre,' she said turning to me. I kissed her hand, and she smiled. 'Ah, yes, I can see you are European. I am sorry the girls are not in at the moment; you will meet them later. The comte is at work, for he is in the army and we only see him morning and evenings. This horrible war, it keeps him so busy. But of course, you know more about the war than I do. You, especially, must know a lot more,' she turned to me as she spoke. 'Anyway, we have a house rule; we don't discuss the war as a topic of general conversation.'

We, of course were both profuse in our thanks. The lady before us was a picture of a well-to-do and well-born Frenchwoman. She looked as if she had been pottering around, perhaps in the garden. A few carefully arranged wisps her hair escaped from under a large colourful protective head scarf. She wore a pearl necklace, and a matching set of earrings. Her hands were well shaped and beautifully manicured; her face was carefully, but unobtrusively made-up. I might have been younger than she, but I liked and admired what I saw.

'Alois, the count's soldier-servant will show you to your rooms in a moment. We shall gather here for an aperitif about 6.15 if that suits you. The count should be back about that time, and we dress quite informally for dinner these days, just slacks and shirt, unless you prefer uniform. I am sorry if you find your bathroom a little feminine; it is normally the girls', but while you are with us, they will use ours. Alois will show you the layout upstairs. If you need anything, just ring.'

Alois must have been waiting outside, listening to his cue, for he walked in precisely as she finished.

'Shall I show the gentlemen upstairs, madam?'

We followed Alois to the upper floor. As we went, he pointed out what was where. My luggage had been un-packed, and some of the items had been taken away – presumably for cleaning, ironing or brushing. Alois said he would be back with slacks and shoes shortly. On the dressing table was a note written in passable Polish welcoming me to the house; it was signed Lucienne de V; it said she hoped to improve her Polish under my guidance.

I sorted myself out, my things were returned, shoes cleaned, shirts and trousers neatly ironed and I changed. It was time to go downstairs. There was knock on my door; it was David, come to collect me.

'I say, old boy, did I make a *faux-pas* not kissing the countess's hand?' he enquired anxiously.

'Doubt it very much. Most people know that the English are not given to kissing hands, so she was not expecting it of you. You can always make-up for it when you bid her good night, but I warn you, if you are not used to it, it will not come easily.'

Despite my efforts at assurance, David still remained upset at his possible gaffe at the very beginning of his visit. We went downstairs, and as we did so we could hear feminine voices from the salon. The comtesse was standing by the door, as if waiting for us. We were spot on time.

'Ah, there you are, then! Come and meet the girls. This is Lucienne, the younger – Andre and David – Lucienne hopes to improve her Polish while you are here – and this is Jean – David and Andre.'

The manner and order in which we were introduced seemed to indicate how we were to be paired off, at least initially. Having been told that dress was completely informal, we came in shirts and ties. The comtesse had changed into a white linen dress which complimented her splendid figure, while white high-heeled open-toed shoe accentuated a pair of very good slim legs. When we first met, on our arrival, I thought she was in her early thirties. She must have been a little older than that to have a daughter of nineteen or twenty, but she did not show her age at all.

Her two daughters were very much like her, although somewhat darker, both striking girls with dark, naturally curly hair and a dress sense to match that of their mother.

We went on to the veranda, where drinks of every kind awaited us, and from where one could see the extensive sandy beach and a little further out a yacht anchorage. We were invited to help ourselves to drink.

'If we hurry the dinner, *Maman*,' suggested Jean, 'we might be able to manage a game of tennis before dark.'

David looked a little doubtful, whereupon a concerned Jean asked, 'You do play tennis – don't you?'

'Yes I do, though not very well, rugger is my game,' replied David, 'but the truth is that I have no tennis gear with me.'

Relieved Jean was cheerful again. 'Ah – rugby!' Jean smiled, and added, 'No problem with gear, I'll tell Alois; he will find shorts and shoes for you both. There are lots about the place.'

She was about to organise this when she was stopped by the comtesse, 'In that case, dear, tell them that we will have dinner promptly and will not linger over it. That will give you time to play.' As her daughter disappeared she turned to us. 'The girls often play in the evening, you know, but how do you feel about it? Do you mind playing straight after a meal? After all, some people think it bad for their digestion, and my husband always says that it is a heathen habit which does not do justice to either good food or good wine.'

We reassured her. Tennis was inevitable if we intended to start on the right side of the girls. However, the arrival of the comte, earlier than expected, caused the plan to be revised. He wore a uniform of a colonel of the artillery, and his tunic bore the ribbons of the Légion d'Honneur and the Croix de Guerre as well as campaign ribbons of the Great War. He introduced himself, apologised for not having been home to greet us, and then, having poured himself a drink, hoped that nobody would be inconvenienced if he changed out of uniform and joined us for dinner. It was a statement requiring no answer.

After he left, Lucienne moaned, 'We will not be playing tennis after dinner after all. He will be hours changing and will not hurry his meals or drinks for anyone, ever.'

The comtesse gave her daughter a scathing look, which prompted Lucienne to defend herself.

'Well, *Maman*, it is so and well you know it.'

But *Maman* just shook her head and retorted, 'You can always play tomorrow. You must not be disrespectful to your father.'

Poor Lucienne blushed. We talked about this and that until the comte joined us, also in shirtsleeves and tie.

'I need another strong drink before we eat,' he announced. 'An awful day at the office. Will you join me, messieurs?' He looked at David and me as he poured himself a very large cognac. We refilled our glasses without reluctance. He took his time and we kept him company.

When he finished his drink, he turned to his wife, 'Now I am ready to eat.'

One of the girls jumped up and rang the bell vigorously, as if hoping there might yet be time for tennis. Some hope. Lucienne's forecast was accurate; it was almost dark before we finished and in any case, the wine was too good to gulp. Our host confirmed the house rule that talk of war was out, but he added, 'Maybe you would not mind joining me in the study after breakfast for a while. You can tell me about yourselves over a cup of coffee. I would like to hear your opinions on the war. I am particularly interested in the Polish situation.'

Our talk next morning went on for over an hour. Before he left for his office he proffered some domestic advice.

'You do whatever you like, don't let the girls tell you what they want to do. Feel quite free. If you want to go sightseeing, borrow the car, with or without the driver. Leave the womenfolk here if you prefer to go out alone. Take your meals here or out, as it suits you. Don't feel you have to act as escorts as a duty – and that goes for my wife, too. She likes to be surrounded by young dashing men. I mean what I say. You are free – not prisoners of the household.' With that he stood up to go, and we went in search of the ladies.

The girls were waiting, dressed for tennis, and told us our things were waiting for us in our rooms. So we changed and went to the court. After a quick knock-up, they suggested a game.

'All right,' agreed David, 'Jean and I against the two of you.'

'Oh no,' replied Jean. 'We hate playing against each other; we two girls will play you two men.'

Reluctantly, we agreed. Little did we know that the girls had been playing up and that we were about to be taken for a ride.

'Have a bet,' said Jean. 'If we win, you take us for a swim. If you win, you decide whatever you want to do.'

We soon discovered that the standard of the girls' tennis was better than ours. Try as we could, there was no way we could stop them from thrashing us. The match was nearly over when the comtesse appeared.

'Why are the girls playing against you men?' she demanded. 'Did they make bet before you started?'

We said that indeed we had, replying before we realised that the girls were shaking their heads vigorously, behind their mother's back, trying to warn us to say nothing.

'Whatever it is that you bet, I absolve you.' She looked at her daughters very sternly and went on, 'I told you not to do this.'

'Oh *Maman*,' pleaded Jean, 'it's nothing. They are going to take us for a swim if they lose, and they would choose what they want to do if they win. Nothing more serious.'

'Whatever it is, you do not have to meet your debt of honour,' she ruled, 'and I mean this very seriously. I will talk to the girls later.' She looked quite upset and the girls looked very uncomfortable as she stalked off.

'Sorry,' I apologised. 'I saw you shaking your heads too late, when your mother asked.'

Just then the comtesse returned. 'Bet or no bet, if you decide to go for a swim, let me know, I am tempted to join you.'

We did, and she did. We went down to their private beach. In their swimsuits they could have been three sisters, the mother looked only a few years the senior.

The comtesse returned early to arrange lunch on the veranda, and we stayed on. As in tennis, the girls were good and stylish swimmers, but they appeared to lack staying power. After ten minutes, Lucienne said she was getting cold and tired and wanted to swim back. I called out to the other two that we were returning, and thought I saw David give a thumbs up sign, so I swam back with her. Lucienne suddenly appeared to be struggling.

'I have a cramp in my leg,' she complained, signs of pain showing in her face.

'Where is the cramp?'

'It's high up in my thigh,' she gasped, spitting out water.

I was not sure what to do. Could one apply a massage in the water, and if so, how? Was massaging a girls thigh, whether in or out water the 'done' thing? I even wondered if she was leading me on.

'I can't swim,' she cried. 'Please, you must help me.'

My suspicions evaporated and I abandoned any idea of underwater massage. There was only one thing to do, to tow her back to the beach in the approved style as if she was drowning. I turned us both on to our backs, put my left arm under her armpits and started out. My hand brushed against her breasts and she held it there with one hand, trying to help the swimming with the other; inevitably we were in a very close bodily contact. I hoped that the others would see and come to our help, but was afraid to shout out in case Lucienne became frightened. I could see no one, and set about getting back unaided, hoping that my strength was adequate. By the time we reached shallow water, my knees all but buckled from exhaustion as I stood up. I could not lift her and had to drag her ashore on to dry sand. Her face was screwed up in pain as she collapsed on the beach. Then she sat up with one leg tucked under her body and I could see the knotted muscles of the thigh in the other leg.

'This is where the cramp is,' she lay her hand high up inside her leg, almost at her crotch. I knelt down in front of her, held her leg between my knees and started to massage.

Slowly relief began to show in her face. Either the cramp was receding or she found the rhythmic movement of my hands in that area of her thigh far from distasteful. To me it was proving a very intimate, if unnerving experience. She caught my eye, perhaps reading my thoughts. A red blush spread across her face.

'What is going on here?' I suddenly heard Jean's voice behind me, and turned to see her eyes on my hand. She looked at us disapprovingly. David watched impassively behind her.

'I had an awful cramp while we were swimming, right up here,' insisted Lucienne, 'but it is now slowly going.'

'You are fooling around again,' snapped Jean. Then seeing that there was still pain showing on her sister's face, she added, 'Maybe you are not fooling after all.' She offered to take over from me and I was greatly relieved.

After a while Lucienne was able to stand up. She turned to me, 'Thank you very much. You must be very tired, it was a long swim.' After a while she added in Polish, 'Thank you again, you saved my life.' With that she gave me a light kiss on the cheek.

Lucienne refused any further assistance, and limping, slowly made her way back to the villa.

'You did well, Andre,' said David and Jean added, 'We owe you a debt for saving her…'

'You owe me nothing,' I interrupted. 'Anyone else would have done the same. Furthermore, I should not have swum so far out without making sure…'

Upset by the incident, we decided to follow Lucienne back to the house. The comtesse was at the top of the cliff, inspecting the results of her gardening efforts.

'What's up with Lucienne?' she called, 'I saw her come back on her own just now looking very glum.'

Jean gave a brief account of what happened.

'I am very grateful to you,' said the comtesse. 'She sometimes gets cramps, but this one could have been nasty. We are very grateful.'

Drinks were waiting on the veranda, and lunch was being prepared. But Lucienne was nowhere to be seen and Jean went in search of her; she returned after a while to say that Lucienne was fine, but ashamed of her performance, and asked for lunch to be sent to her room.

In the afternoon the comtesse decided she needed to go shopping, and suggested that David and I went with her to have a look at Cannes. We readily agreed. Little did we know that we were taken along to carry the shopping; we had little time to see anything of Cannes except some splendidly expensive shops, while the comtesse appeared to enjoy being seen with an escort of two young men, and not her soldier driver!

When we got back, the girls were waiting, dressed for tennis. This time, mixed doubles and no bets, announced Jean.

We were just about to finish playing, when the comte marched briskly on to the court, his spurs jingling gaily. Without any greetings he walked up to me, thanked me profusely for rescuing Lucienne, and kissed me on both cheeks, as if he had been decorating me with a medal. Feeling very embarrassed I tried to brush the incident aside.

'Don't play down what you have done for us.' The

comte spoke incisively, in the manner of the colonel addressing his troops. 'You have done very well. The comtesse was very upset and telephoned me at the office, which is why I am back early.'

That evening he produced his best champagne to drink his thanks to me. It was also suggested, that the following evening David and I might like to take the girls dancing – a welcome change from swimming and tennis. A table was promptly reserved at the club to which the family belonged.

I was worried; my funds were very meagre, and the club at Cannes would be expensive. I confided to David who generously offered to help out and save any embarrassment.

David's generosity was discovered unnecessary, at breakfast next morning. 'I insist', stipulated the comte before leaving for work, 'that you are our guests. Don't dare pay for anything, the club has been instructed to put all on my account.' He refused all attempt on our part to pay at least our share; or maybe my attempts at persuasion were not adequately convincing!

It was a warm and balmy evening, with scarcely a breath of wind. We had a table by a large door which opened on to a balcony and the club gardens. The band was excellent, the food superb – and the girls proved to be marvellous dancers.

As I danced with Lucienne, I could not help remembering the 'rescue', when our bodies had been so close together. She pressed her body against mine, and the top of her head against my cheek.

'You dance very well,' said I, trying to make small talk, 'and you obviously enjoy it.'

'Especially with you,' she whispered, 'especially after yesterday, but isn't it hot.' She stopped herself, and added, 'Or is it just me?'

She was right. It was very hot, too hot to be pleasant, though we all enjoyed the evening. After a while Jean, having twice refused a dance because it was too hot, suggested that we go back and have a swim.

'If we go back now, and if we hurry we can have a mid-night swim,' suggested Lucienne her eyes shining brightly, and looking knowingly at her sister.

'What a good idea! The moon is full, it could be fun,' agreed Jean enthusiastically.

So off we went, Jean driving back very fast. We rushed upstairs to get ready. David and I slipped on our swimming trunks under the slacks and hurried down to join the girls who were waiting in light blue button-through dresses.

'Come on! – Hurry up! It's almost midnight.'

Lucienne and Jean ran towards the beach. We reached the bottom of the cliff steps to see them disappear into the changing hut, which was on the beach. David and I walked to the water's edge, dropped our slacks and started wading into the shallows under the cloudless moonlit sky. We turned and saw the girls run out of the hut; they seemed to be wearing pale swimsuits. They ran into the water and then started swimming towards us. After the hot and sticky atmosphere of the club, the cool, clean sea water was deliciously invigorating. After ten or fifteen minutes, Lucienne had enough, and the girls decided to go back. As they stood up in the shallow water, I was amazed to see that they were not wearing pale swimsuits – they were not wearing swimsuits at all! We were, and how they laughed!

'Didn't you know about midnight swimming? No, obvi-ously you didn't – and you can't take your trunks off now, it's gone midnight!'

I hoped they could not see us blushing in the moonlight. They ran back to the hut to change, leaving us speechless.

'Midnight bloody swimming,' growled David, clearly put out, while he pulled his slacks over his wet trunks.

Time flew. There were still two days to go when David received a telegram recalling him to his unit. We took him to Nice to catch a train. Feeling sad at his precipitate departure, the girls and I wondered aimlessly round the shops, and I collected more parcels to carry, getting hotter and hotter. Before we returned, I was introduced to a local speciality – a red wine ice cream. It was very good and very potent, and made us feel a lot better.

My last evening came. The comte started talking French politics as soon as he returned from the office and then switched to the affairs of Poland. It was hot and sultry, and the heavy conversation added to the oppression we all felt. The comte retired finally before midnight, and the comtesse suggested we went for a midnight swim. She gave us five minutes 'to put on more sensible clothes'. I slipped to my room wondering whether midnight swimming was different with *Maman* around. Had David been there we would have consulted and at least presented a united front. I felt lonely and unsure, so just in case, I slipped on my swimming trunks.

We walked down to the beach, once again I went to the water's edge still debating whether I should go in, with or without my trunks. Greatly daring, I decided no trunks and slowly walked into the water till I was waist deep, feeling somewhat worried. Then I looked towards the hut. The girls were walking fast towards the water and the comtesse was running directly towards me. For a moment I panicked. I could see a splash of brilliant white on her – surely a white swimming costume. What did one do? It was too late to dash for my trunks.

As she approached, she threw a large white ball towards me.

'I can't just swim aimlessly,' she called. 'We will play a sort of water polo.'

It became clear what the splash of white had been; she was wearing no white swimsuit. She threw herself into the water and swam towards the ball with a stylish water polo crawl. The ball was by me and I flicked it over my head backwards, as we collided, she put one arm round my neck, ostensibly to stop herself going under, and then she pushed me under. As I surfaced, one of my hands caressed the entire length of her body. She was laughing when I came up.

The girls arrived by then.

'Two a side. You and Jean against Lucienne and me,' she decided.

It soon became tough, rather aggressive fight for possession of the ball, with flailing arms and legs and repeated body contact. They neither minded nor cared, and made me much less self-conscious of my own nakedness. So much so that I began to enjoy myself. I even began to wonder if the comtesse's aggression had not been deliberately premeditated and suggestive. Lucienne strove to match her mother and there were frequent times when I thought they were deliberately mistaking me for the ball!

By this time, I was beginning to get out of control, and it was something of a relief, when the comtesse decided we had had enough. Maybe she knew.

We walked out to the white sand holding hands, the comtesse on one side of me Lucienne on the other. As we passed my bundle of clothes, with my trunks uppermost, she slipped one hand round my waist and bent down to pick up the bundle with the other, and gave me a sly amused little smile, perhaps to show she had noticed, or perhaps for another reason. It was hard to remain relaxed while she demonstrated her preference for a close contact once again.

All the same, I was thoroughly enjoying this first experience of nudism in the company of very beautiful women!

The ladies entered the hut to dress. I could hear them gabbling away with lots of laughter; they must have been using a local patois and therefore I could not understand a word. Not very polite, I thought, but maybe understandable. They emerged quickly, decorously dressed, their wet hair and wet bodies showing through their dresses.

One of the girls remarked, 'I don't know why one bothers. We go swimming and we walk together with nothing on, in this moonlight which is as bright as the electric lighting in the salon, and then we demurely go into a hut and dress behind shut doors, and walk back to our own house where there will be no one to see us by this time. All for the sake of silly appearances.'

'Tut, tut…' was all the comtesse could manage as a comment.

We walked to the verandah, the comtesse and Jean walked in. Lucienne turned to me.

'I am glad you learned something from us and I am sorry you will be leaving in a few hours,' she said. Then she turned to me, took both my hands in hers, stood on her toes her body against mine, and planted a long and lingering kiss on my lips.

'Goodnight, Andre. If it hadn't been for you, I would not have been here any more. Please come and see us again.'

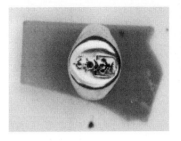

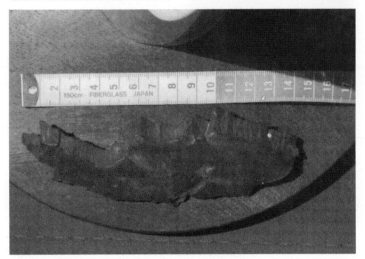

Top left: silver signet ring used to produce identification.
Middle left: pass to work at the archives of Bron.
Top right: the gorget – with Madonna of Czestochowa superimposed on
the eagle emblem of Poland.
Middle right: a sample of Konstanty's carving.
Bottom: the bomb splinter (now part of a table lamp).

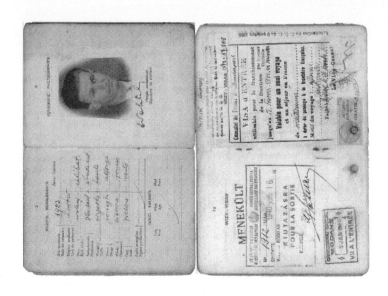

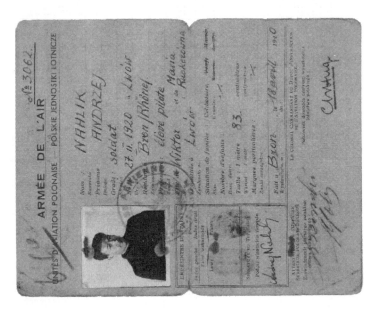

Top: Polish passport – issued in Budapest.
Bottom: Polish Air Force identity card – PAF in France.

Top left: Bezmiechowa – a high-performance sailplane on the start line.
Top right: tourist pamphlet cover – Bezmiechowa Gliding Centre with myself getting into the sailplane.
Bottom: Bezmiechowa hangar.

Top: 308 Squadron – dispersal in readiness.
Bottom left: Myself with Jurek, my companion of previous events, as my best man.
Bottom right: Myself – instructor on Tiger Moth aircraft.

Warming Up

During February and March a few of us 'aircrew candidates', by devious means and with friend's help, were given an opportunity to get flying instruction. Officially, there was no flying training for the likes of us, it was only for those with good operational experience. Opportunity came only through a combination of contacts for some, through volunteering for office work, for others, by getting to know influential officers and instructors, and having a fair amount of flying experience beyond basic training, and above all persuasiveness. Captain Pawel, one of the instructors, managed to get a few of his aeroclub boys not only airborne but instructed, on the side, and with a significant risk to himself. Some of us were even allowed to fly solo. I was very lucky. After a few flights, I was 'promoted' to a Devoitine fighter. It was no longer used in operational squadrons, but being an older model was 'demoted' to a training role. It was a low-wing monoplane with a fixed undercarriage and fitted with a fairly powerful Hispano engine. I had often sat on the perimeter of the airfield, usually with Mat, and drooled even at this old fighter flying about.

When I was told that I was to be allowed to fly it, I was over the moon and also slightly scared; it was a single seater so no dual instruction was possible. What impressed me most was the engine power and the fact that I had never before flown a low-wing monoplane. Captain Pawel gave me some preliminary instructions, explained the controls and the cockpit layout, emphasised the swing of the aircraft when opening and shutting the throttle and sent me off with the entreaty, 'For God's sake be careful.'

The roar of the engine sounded quite different in the cockpit than from the edge of the airfield. As soon as I opened the throttle to taxi, I felt the torque of the engine pulling the nose of the aircraft to one side, but this was nothing compared to the swing under full power on take-off. I had been warned, I should have been prepared, but all the same it took me by surprise. Maybe I opened the throttle too fast. The engine coughed and spluttered, and when it picked up its full 500 horse-power with a mighty roar, it pulled and pulled and I had to apply full rudder to keep it straight. But once in the air my heart was singing – and so was I. This, I thought to myself, was real flying.

My brief was to circle the airfield twice, and then land. From some 300 metres the speed of 250 kph with the engine nowhere near full power, seemed phenomenal. I was tempted to open up, but with Pawel watching from below, thought better of it. My only regret was I would not be able to tell Mat I had been flying a Devoitine; it was one of Pawel's conditions for flying.

Two circuits of the airfield was a matter of a few minutes, and passed like seconds. As instructed, I prepared for a long, powered approach. Knowing I was being watched, I determined to make a good job of it, if only to demonstrate my appreciation. Things did not go according to plan. I found myself too far off and too low, and had to use a lot of throttle to reach the airfield. As I applied power, the aircraft swung. Again, I was not prepared for it, had to make erratic corrections and came over the boundary low and fast. As soon as I throttled back, the wheels touched the ground and the aircraft started swinging in the opposite direction. I had to apply more corrections and before I knew what was happening, I bounced back in the air. The hangars were below my height, the nose was too high and the speed dropping sharply. I could feel the controls becoming sluggish and knew I was in trouble. I needed lots of throttle to stay airborne. Of course, as soon as I opened the throttle, the swing started again, I was once more late in applying correction and it was only by good luck and the Grace of God that I managed to recover sufficient control to make another circuit. I prayed very hard for a good landing and my prayers were answered. I hardly knew when the wheels touched the ground. What I did know was that I was in for a good and deserved telling off. I had hardly switched off before Pawel was at my side.

'That performance of yours reminded me of your first solo at the club,' pronounced Pawel, looking very angry. 'Bloody awful! I hope no one else saw it. Had you bent the machine, I would have been in the shit up to my neck. Now get out of the cockpit and out of my sight before I really lose my temper and forbid you to come back again.' With that, he turned on his heels and strode away.

I was crestfallen. I knew I had deserved this dressing down. I was mortified that I had done nothing but cause anxiety and anger in return for his kindness and understanding. I knew how exposed he would have been, had things gone wrong. Perhaps, after all, I was better suited for office work?

That evening, on the way to the canteen with Mat as was our custom, I started talking about the possible formation of a model aircraft club. We had been told that, if we could recruit sufficient members, some funds would be made available. Suddenly Mat changed the subject.

'I was free this morning. I couldn't find you, so I went to our usual spot on the perimeter to watch the flying. There was a guy in a Devoitine. He bounced so high on landing that he must have been well above the hangar height. I thought he had had it, for he had no speed and when he opened up to go round again, the machine swung and he really should have spun in. He was lucky, but he made a super landing when he came in the second time. I bet he was given a damn good ticking off when he got back. I wonder who it was.'

I was so glad I was not allowed to tell him!

At the beginning of May, when I had just returned from my holiday in Cannes, Captain Pawel came in for something from the office where I was working. Having concluded his business with Lieutenant Ostrowski, he came over and sat on my desk.

'I haven't seen you for a while,' he said. 'I think I had better give you some more dual, on long powered approaches to sort them out, You'd better come over first thing tomorrow morning. I've just cleared it with Ostrowski.'

No one could have been more delighted, or more grateful – and I said so.

Miet, Jurek, Mat and I were accustomed to breakfasting very early, as soon as the airmen's mess opened. At that time one could get as much coffee as one wanted, the bread was still fresh and warm, and one could often scrounge an additional portion of cheese. There was also time to have a quiet cigarette after breakfast and listen to the news on the radio. As the morning went on, the kitchen staff became edgy with the hustle and bustle of coping under pressure, and their tempers ran short.

It was just after six when we walked into the mess, laughing our heads off at one of Mat's early morning jokes. Those who were in the mess already shushed us to silence, with grave and critical expressions. The radio was on. No one was eating, every one was listening, as all faces were turned to the loudspeakers. Our laughter died, we stopped in our tracks, and listened.

'The German armies have entered Holland and Belgium

during the night. There are reports of military and government installations being occupied, shelled or bombed. Holland and Belgium have asked for urgent assistance from the French and British governments.'

I could feel a shiver running down my spine.

It took the edge off our appetites. We sipped coffee and chewed bread absent-mindedly, sitting quietly and listening.

Then the air raid siren went.

We left the uneaten and unwanted food, ran to our barrack block and then, to the emergency assembly area. Some were still getting out of bed; others were pulling on their clothes. When we got there, Lieutenant Ostrowski was waiting for us. His pyjama jacket could be seen protruding under his uniform, as if to prove he had not wasted time dressing.

When the last of the stragglers arrived, he vented his spleen.

'You can kiss my bloody arse. If I can get here from the officers quarters before you, you are a lot of bloody snails. You ought to have been here seconds after the sirens. It's just not good enough. You are all collectively confined to barracks, and I want some air raid trenches dug quickly. Get to it, sergeant, you are now in charge – take over. Get spades and whatever else is needed. I'll get the engineering officer to give you fuller instructions. Report to me when it's all finished. As for you lot,' he waved his hand airily in the direction of us, the office workers, 'if I want anyone in the office, I'll send for you. Now get bloody digging and don't complain of blisters, aches and pains. I would rather see you fall exhausted into the dug trenches than hear any excuses why you can't dig. If there are any shirkers, I will deal with them myself later.'

Ostrowski was livid. We had never seen him so mad. He had some justification. The assembly area was just outside our barrack block. His quarters were a kilometre away, and even if he had a bicycle, it should not have been possible for him to get there before us.

From time to time, one of us would be summoned to the office for a particular job. Apart from that, we applied ourselves to digging trenches. Ostrowski was back and forth inspecting progress. On one occasion he was accompanied by the base commander himself. Later that afternoon, Ostrowski arrived with a lorry, from which he distributed steel helmets, last-war vintage, and somewhat newer gas masks. We were ordered to wear steel helmets whenever the air raid sirens sounded and told there would be two gas mask drills a day. As if to underline the seriousness of it all, the French base commander issued an edict that anyone found not wearing a steel helmet during an air raid warning, would be put inside for seven days.

It took the best part of two days to dig trenches to the satisfaction of the Polish and French experts, who frequently contradicted each other. Finally, Ostrowski pronounced the trenches as 'adequate for you lot'. To compensate for the effort and blistered hands, he gave us an afternoon off, but no night passes. Nonetheless, there were still jobs to be done in the office; Jurek was among those so detailed.

Miet, Mat and I, scrubbed and cleaned, changed into our stiff serge uniforms, and set out for an afternoon in Lyon. We were stopped at the gate and given a warning by the duty NCO. The invasion of the Low Countries had sparked a wave of animosity against the armed forces amongst Lyon's population, and especially against the Poles, whom they considered to be the root cause of the war. We were warned to be on our best behaviour, and above all not to get involved in arguments and brawls.

We took a tram to the city centre. It was almost empty when we got on, but became fuller and fuller as we approached the shopping and business areas. As it filled up, the atmosphere became more and more charged. We were subjected to a barrage of unpleasant remarks, such as – 'You got the Boche on the move, now go and get them out!' or – 'Instead of chasing after our girls, why don't you go and chase the Boche?' It was galling enough to listen, even harder to ignore. We realised it would be impossible to relax under such harassment, so we changed our plan and decided to visit the Foire barracks.

Our visits to the Foire were fairly frequent. Apart from having many friends there who needed cheering up, we could walk along the banks of the Rhone bordered with picturesque tree-lined boulevards, visit the nearby bistros or buy snacks from street barrow vendors. There was also the zoo, with its excellent collection of animals, where the monkey house was a special attraction. We used to seek facial similarities between its denizens and politicians and the less popular among our officers, which gave rise to hours of innocent amusement. There was also less innocent amusement to be had in the neighbourhood and a dearth of the cash necessary to indulge in it. This afternoon, the Foire was less relaxed than usual, and a sense of antagonism was abroad. The war news was depressing; it filled everyone's thoughts and success seemed doubtful. And if there was any success, our participation as young and keen volunteers would be minimal. Morale at Bron was not high; here at the Foire, it was abysmal. Since attempts to cheer up our friends provided fruitless, we decided that, rather than risk becoming thus demoralised ourselves, we would revert to our original plan and go to the city centre.

While we were waiting for a tram, Miet remarked that we should have volunteered to join the RAF. 'I've had letters from many friends there,' he said, 'and they seem happy in England. By all accounts, our people in the RAF are being kept busy; everyone either has a job or is being trained for one – not like us, kept bored stiff doing nothing.'

The tram stopped and we climbed in, only to hear more snide comments. I took up where Miet had left off.

'I'm sure the British are not as openly hostile to our lads. They may be insular, but they are apparently better brought up, or something.'

Mat, quick off the mark and temper flaring, repeated what I had just said in fluent French, and very loudly so that everyone could hear. He added a disparaging remark of his own about the French attitude to us, their allies. Our fellow passengers erupted. For a few seconds I thought we were going to be torn apart and lynched. Fortunately, the tram stopped at some traffic lights, and we jumped out to safety, well before our intended destination.

'That wasn't a very clever thing to have done,' observed Miet, turning to Mat. 'You have a lot to learn, Mat boy, and one thing is, that when you are vastly outnumbered, like we were, and not wanting to fight for it, like we were, you keep your trap shut. We were warned about the attitude of the local population and have to be prepared for unpleasant comments. I learned that sort of wisdom when I was at university, where we had a lot of political activity. Much of it was opposed by the police and was highly unpopular with the locals. Mind you, I agree with your sentiments and feelings.'

I was surprised that Mat allowed Miet to finish without interrupting. He was red with anger, sparks metaphorically flying from his eyes.

'Belt up, don't preach, and bugger the locals!' he re-torted angrily. 'I can't stand this holier-than-thou attitude from you any more than from them.'

It was bad enough to endure taunting from the French. Among ourselves it was potential dynamite. I sought to pour oil on troubled waters.

'Before you start working up to a fight, let's decide what we are going to do. I don't imagine any of us fancy another tram ride. Bron is a fair way off, and if we are to foot it and get back before the gates close, we need to start back pretty soon. I could do with a drink. I've got enough francs to buy us all an *ordinaire*, if we can find a friendly bistro. How about it?'

'I, too, have a few francs,' offered Miet, 'if we are stuck. I don't have enough for a taxi back to Bron, but I also could do with a glass of wine.'

The situation seemed defused, but Mat remained silent and fuming. We walked slowly, talking loudly in Polish. As it happened, we were passing a taxi rank. The driver of the first cab made another derogatory remark.

'Snotty bastard,' said Mat, fortunately in Polish. An unexpected voice came from the third taxi. Heavily accented with the rolling French 'r', it was clear and grammatical Polish: 'What are you guys up to? Cheer up and take no notice of Alex here, he is always "anti" something or other.'

'You wouldn't know of a friendly bistro where we could be safe and not abused?' enquired Miet of the friendly voice, 'we don't seem to be very popular round here.'

'The only "safe" one, as you call it, is the one near Bron where your lads always go. Want a ride?'

We looked at each other in silent consultation.

'The trouble is', explained Mat civilly and honestly, 'that we only have a few francs between us. If we pay for the ride, there will be nothing left for a glass of wine, and we need a drink badly.'

'Tell you what, I'll take you to the bistro near Bron and join you for a glass of *ordinaire*. You buy the wine and I won't charge you too much for the ride.'

Mat looked hesitant.

'The way I feel just now, I think I would rather look up that vivacious mulatto in the knocking shop. I could just do with her, but she'll want twenty-five francs and I've only got few sous.'

'I'm willing to take you to Bron, even for free,' replied the Polish-speaking driver, 'but I will not treat you to a brothel!' He laughed a little and then added, 'I know the girl. She is famous. Twenty-five francs won't get you far with her. What is more she'll want a cognac or two, if not a bottle of champagne. I'll drop you on the way, if that's what you want.'

'Come with us and have a drink and cool down,' interposed Miet, 'then if you still want that girl and can afford her, I'm sure our friend here will drop you off on his way back to town.'

The cabby nodded his agreement and we climbed in. As we drove along, he told us that his parents, who were textile workers, had come from Lodz before the 1914 war, and that his wife was half-Polish. He understood both viewpoints, and tried to calm our feelings, especially Mat's.

We settled down at a table at the Bron bistro with a bottle of *ordinaire*. The clientele was predominantly Polish. There were a few local Frenchmen whom we knew by sight, and who usually accepted us as part of the scene. Just now, however, each side was keeping very much to themselves. One could hear fragments of their conversation, their *la guerre* and *les Boches* were just as frequent, as our *wojna*, *Niemcy* and *Francuzi* (*la guerre* = war; *les Boches* = the Germans; *wojna* – war; *Niemcy* – the Germans; *Francuzi* – the French; in the French and Polish languages respectively).

Suddenly Mat's face lit up.

'I just remembered. I've been offered flying tomorrow. I wonder if it's still on? We'd better get back in time. I have to check this offer and I don't want to be put in the cooler for being late. We haven't got passes. Even that girl couldn't keep me away from my trip, even if it is only a passenger flip with a friend who flies a Potez.'

That sounded more like Mat. He seemed to have calmed down. He even managed a polite apology for his outbreak. Our cabby downed his wine, handed over his card and got up to go.

'Come and look us up. My wife would enjoy meeting you. If you let me know when you can come, I'll ask my parents over and we can have a Polish evening. My mother is a splendid cook – but all kosher, you know.' He made for the door, calling out his best wishes.

'Nice guy,' said Mat, 'weren't we lucky! Hey!' he looked down at the card. 'Hey, M. Grabow, your fare...'

Monsieur Grabow looked back from the door, waved, *'Bonne chance!'* and went out with a smile on his face.

The proprietor could be heard grumbling about the war and the inability of the air force (theirs – or ours? he did not make that clear) to defend the country against the Luftwaffe. A voice suggested that our air force were up there patrolling, to make sure we were safe from attack.

'When the Boche decide to bomb us, they will bomb us. Our air force – pfui!'

The owner spat on his floor, 'They don't want to lift a finger! They are afraid that if they fight, the Boche will bomb us that much harder.' He was red in the face, seemingly the worse for wear. He turned towards the tables where we Poles were sitting and shouted, 'As for you! You do nothing!'

Someone – not Mat – shouted back, 'We do as much as your people allow us to do. If only we had more planes to fly, we would show you!'

'You've already lost one war,' raged the owner. 'Don't help us to lose ours.'

'Maybe you'd better go,' advised a large man at the bar. 'It must be close to gate-closing time at the Base. You don't want to get into an argument with him.'

We took his advice. Some thirty of us left together and walked back to the barracks, singing Polish songs.

It was so hot that night that sleep would not come, and everyone in our barrack room was restive, some even getting up for fresh air or to take a shower. I was awake when the first blush of dawn lit the window above my head. On one side of me, Jurek stirred restlessly. On the other, Mat seemed fast asleep. I thought I could hear aircraft flying, a long way away.

'Someone has been night flying,' muttered Jurek, half asleep. 'It wasn't from here.' He turned over and covered his head, as if to keep out the noise. But the drone got louder and soon it was apparent that there were several aircraft. The noise sounded vaguely familiar. I sat up listening intently, and suddenly realised why. It was the sound of bombers, of German bombers, and they were getting closer.

'German bombers!' I yelled, jumping to my feet. Jurek followed, and Mat began to stir. There came a shrill whistle outside, followed by explosions as the first stick made impact. My legs seemed to freeze to the floor by my bed. Everything shook; I felt something hit my bed; the glass shattered and fell in and there was dust everywhere, rubble coming from the walls.

'Bombs! Get up! Run for the trenches,' someone shouted. I remembered my helmet, and had began to run, when I also remembered my suitcase containing my few valuable possessions. I turned back, picked it up and scrambled for the trenches. Everyone was running, some in night clothes, others pulling up their trousers as they ran, some barefoot – which must have been painful through the broken glass and debris. I discovered I had my clothes under my arm, although I couldn't remember having picked them up. I looked up as I came out of the barracks and saw two formations of Heinkels overhead. I even thought I could see a shower of bombs dropping from them.

I am not sure whether I fell or jumped into the trenches. It is possible I was blown in by the blast from an explosion. I remember that I landed on others who were already there, and that they did not seem to mind. I also remember seeing a hangar explode in a cloud of smoke and dust.

In the trench, all faces showed a mixture of fear, hate and anger, and above all, of hopelessness and helplessness. For there was absolutely nothing we could do but wait. An air raid siren wailed somewhere, belatedly, in the distance, and a fire engine could be heard racing through the base. A slight wind blowing across the airfield brought with it a lazy tail of smoke smelling of cordite, burning fuel and rubber. Sporadic anti-aircraft fire could be heard. Looking up, we could see the puffs of shell bursts well behind and below the raiders. There was not enough of it, and what there was, was inaccurate. Just like Lwow, I thought!

Having discharged their load, the bombers went. A couple of fighters were starting up their engines at the far end of the airfield. They were far too late for a chance of interception. As soon as the all-clear sounded, a babble of voices rose from the trench, and we all clambered out to inspect the damage. There were several fires burning. The nearby hangar was blazing. On the near side of the airfield, some of the aircraft were damaged. There were also fires on the other side, where the squadrons, flying school and fuel tanks were located. The only damage in the domestic area as far as could be seen was the barrack block in which we were housed.

Lieutenant Ostrowski came riding up on his bicycle, 'Any casualties?' he shouted as he braked into a skidding stop.

The blast had caused considerable damage, but fortunately had not claimed any victims. A suggestion that we go to help the fire fighters having been turned down, on the grounds that we had no protective clothing and had received no training, so we were ordered us to set about clearing up the mess in and around the barrack block.

Of the beds in our barrack room, only Jurek's seemed to be in reasonable shape. Mine was littered with glass, bricks and other debris, and there was a gaping hole in the wall behind the bedhead. Mat, for whom this was the first direct experience of war, was rather excited. His reaction was unexpected.

'Bloody Huns! I was due to get some flying this morning. My friend who was to take me up promised he would let me handle the controls. Now it's all over!'

His apparently irrelevant outburst made us all feel better. Then suddenly he dashed out of the room as if the devil was behind him. I was worried in case it was a reaction – I need not have bothered. In next to no time he was back pushing a large wheelbarrow, full of shovels, brooms and rags.

'I thought these might help,' he announced, showing off his loot. 'I remembered seeing them behind the airmen's mess. That seems to have been damaged as well, but I didn't stay to find out – there was too much brass around.'

Mat's initiative earned merited praise from his hero Miet, which pleased him greatly.

Ostrowski returned with new instructions. As we had learned, the mess was damaged. There would be no meal as such; some kind of food would be rustled up, and rations issued for the rest of the day. Arrangements were made for exchanges of damaged clothes and bedding, but since stocks were low, it would be on a first-come, first-served basis. In the meantime, we were to sort out our block as quickly as possible and then report for duty.

Since Jurek's bed needed little attention, he gave me a hand with mine. He stripped off the top blanket, which was covered with glass and rubble and dropped it straight into the barrow. My pillow was under the second blanket; also, it was covered with dust. Jurek lifted it up and showed me a gaping hole in it. He plunged in his hand, pulled something out, and opened his fingers to show me. It was a large bomb splinter, five by fifteen centimetres, with a nasty jagged edge. It still smelled of cordite.

'It seems that this has been your lucky day,' he said slowly. 'This splinter moved your pillow half way down the bed. If your head had been on it...'

He threw the splinter on to the wheelbarrow. I felt somewhat sick, and my knees felt as if they were made of jelly as I realised how narrow an escape I had had. I remembered how my bed had been hit just as I sat up, at the beginning of the raid. It did not bear thinking about. I thought I would like to keep the splinter as a lucky charm, so I retrieved it from the barrow and put it in my suitcase.

Aborted Flight

The radio was full of news. The Germans had already occupied Belgium and Holland and crossed into northern France. The Maginot Line had proved ineffective, for it did not reach far enough north. The combined French and Belgian forces were resisting the German advance. The Allies were at this moment 'Consolidating in a tactical withdrawal to better defence positions'. This last statement rang many unhappy bells – how often had we heard the same about the Polish army, the previous September?

The office was full of news, gossip and rumours. The fighter squadron, which had nearly completed its training at Bron, was to be split up and sections of it were to be attached to the French air force. All the documentation had to be rushed through in a great hurry. There were rumours that the barracks at Foire had also been hit. This was proved wrong, but the French had decided that the Foire would be evacuated. No one knew where to, but we had to start preparing the documentation. In the course of the afternoon, we learned that they were to be moved to a nearby village, where a tented camp was being erected and the farm buildings, requisitioned.

While we were working away, Mat returned from the Archives, having taken that job over when I finished there.

'I am not wanted any more,' he told us, aggrieved, as if his personal integrity was at stake. 'They have suddenly gone all funny on me. Either they are about to evacuate, or not bothering any more. They say that the information in the archives has been declared secret, and I can no longer work there.'

There was a job waiting for him which removed his sense of affront. During the day, some Belgian and Dutch aircraft – Hawks and Koolhovens, both good fighters – had been flown into Bron to prevent them falling into German hands. The pilots had been ordered to report to their Embassies in Paris, and the planes were allocated to the Polish air force. The flying manuals were in French and Mat, being nearly trilingual, was set the task, jointly with a qualified aviation engineer also working as a clerk, of translating them into Polish as fast as they could. Mat was delighted and elated by this recognition.

'At last I have an interesting and worthwhile job to do,' he gloated.

Later that afternoon, we were told that the headquarters would remain at Bron, but we, all the volunteers and unemployed personnel would be evacuated to the nearby village, where the residents of the Foire barracks had been for the last three or four days. All our protests fell on deaf ears. We were to go, and that was that.

Although the evacuation was planned to take place the following day, there was a two-day delay. Then we were ordered to return the arms which had only been issued to us two days earlier, collect our bedding and be ready to move immediately after breakfast. We went to the new camp and joined our comrades from the Foire, feeling that our morale would soon be as low as theirs. There would be absolutely nothing for any of us to do – which we knew was the root cause of their depression.

Two days after the move, the entire group was assembled and addressed by the detachment commander. He had the reputation of being very demanding, but fair, a disciplinarian. When we were ready, a very long table was produced from the village bistro, large enough to provide an elevated platform for him, and his detachment commanders. Discarding all preliminaries, he began:

'This is only a short-term arrangement. We will soon be moved from here to…'

'The bloody Huns will soon see to it that we have to move,' shouted a voice.

'I will not be interrupted by any of you rabble,' retorted the detachment commander, making a show of loosening the flap of his revolver holster. 'Silence when I speak, and hold your tongue. I will have any one of you in the French military prison in Lyon for the slightest sign of indiscipline – and I might say that I would not wish it on my enemy to be locked up there. You have heard of its reputation, I hope.'

There was a murmur among those listening. He glared at us, visibly controlling his temper and went on, 'As I was saying, we will be moved to other locations, where I hope we shall be able to do something useful at last. Some will go into training so that they can take part in the struggle, others will go into supporting jobs, depending upon background and ability. Those for whom no suitable work can be found, will be attached to our army, given a short battle course and will back up the Allied armies in the land battle.' He stopped and looked around to assess the effect of his short harangue. There was little doubt that it had been effective, and, if nothing else, would check any incipient indiscipline.

More to the point, he had been accurate. Two days later, the first movement order came through. Some forty of us, including us four inseparables, were on the way to the signals centre at Base Aérienne Matha, near St Jean d'Angeli.

Matha was a large base providing training for both the French and Polish air forces. It offered courses for navigators, air and ground signallers in French air force radio communications and procedures. It was housed in a hotchpotch of converted, requisitioned buildings, ranging from racing stables to a distillers' warehouse, school and office building. All we knew about it was its location: the province of Cognac!

'Maybe we will find cheap cognac here,' observed Mat, as we got off the lorry on arrival. 'I was getting a bit tired of *vin ordinaire*. Good cheap cognac would be a welcome change!'

The centre was well organised. We were interviewed on arrival and allocated jobs. Miet, who was a qualified engineer with instructor experience, became a senior instructor on electric motors and generators. Mat and Jurek were appointed as interpreters. I had made up my mind to bluff my way to flying, although I came as a clerk. I knew that our papers would not arrive from Bron for some time, so during my interview I exaggerated my flying experience, including the unofficial flying instruction I had been given at Bron by Captain Pawel. Surprisingly I was believed and told that, although they had not expected aircrew, I would get familiarisation flying training, on the single-engined aircraft used for signaller training, at the nearby base.

My luck did not last for long. The documents arrived from Bron much sooner than I had anticipated. I was promptly put on a charge for stating a falsehood and endangering aircraft and their crews. It sounded serious.

I was wheeled in before my commanding officer, a pleasant, youngish captain.

He read out the charge and proceeded to give me an almighty dressing down, without giving me a chance to say a word in self-defence – and concluded by threatening to put me before the colonel because the charges were so serious. Although I had to admit to myself that the charges were correct, I really did not think that I deserved the apparently imminent firing squad. When he had finished, the captain dismissed the escort and told me in a more fatherly tone that while he understood my motives, they did not give me the right to make false statements. I came out of it better than I deserved, and joined Miet as an assistant instructor, employed in typing training manuals.

One very big advantage of the centre was the concentration of high-performance radio equipment. It was possible to listen in, not only to French broadcasts, but transmissions from the BBC, and even from Germany. The reports were varied and confusing. The French were always 'tactically withdrawing'; the British were forever 'engaged in hard fighting, bombing and leaflet-dropping raids' while the Germans were about to win the war, and announced with confidence that once they had disposed of France, the conquest of the British Isles would be a walk-over.

The good-humoured and witty Mat also had a flair for writing in a light-hearted fashion. His proposal to run a local newsletter was readily accepted, and he became chief editor and chief typist. Alas, the news he had to disseminate became progressively less happy and less encouraging. Poor Mat began to lose his sense of humour and grew more and more depressed.

'I feel as if I am working for bloody Goebbels,' he announced one evening, as we sampled the *ordinaire*, having soon discovered that even here, cognac was way above our means, except on pay days. 'There is nothing I can write about to give us even a ray of hope. I have tried funnies and humour, but they all fall flat, cold and untrue and out of bloody place.'

In the end he asked to be relieved of the duty. His request was refused, but a friendly young lieutenant was appointed to work with him as editor-in-chief. This young officer was awaiting his navigator retraining. His personality was complementary to that of Mat, and he was a linguist who could make full use of the BBC and German broadcasts. The two made a good team.

One day, an invitation was received from a local, well-known cognac distiller for a group of about forty to visit his plant and see the process of producing brandy. This invitation was passed to the 'editors' of the newsletter, who acted as unofficial PR men. Needless to say, Mat managed to get tickets for his three best friends. At the end of the tour, during which we sampled cognac at the various stages of its distillation, we were provided with refreshments. In what appeared to be the boardroom, a long table groaned under platters of delicious food. In front of the food stood a row of forty glasses filled with cognac. Behind the food stood a number of small thimble-sized, crystal glasses, which were being filled with a honey-like fluid by two or three well dressed ladies.

There was a general hum of conversation, some French, but mainly Polish. Food was passed round, which was just as well for we were already well tanked up on cognac as a result of the tour. I noticed the bottle from which the 'honey' was being poured; it was very dusty, very old and bore the barely legible handwritten date 1839.

Our attention was caught by the director, or perhaps it was the owner of the distillery: 'There are a few words I would like to say. First, we are delighted that you were able to come a spend a little time with us. The cognac that is now being offered out to you is one of our best, and some of you may have been lucky enough to have drunk it before.'

The first row of glasses was being handed round as he spoke. 'With this cognac, I would like to give you a toast – to our victory!'

We all responded. It was delicious, smooth and strong, with a delicate smell. Canapés were handed round at the same time. After a few minutes, our host resumed his speech, and while he spoke, the crystal, thimble-sized glasses were handed round.

'What you are now being given is quite unique. I will stake my reputation on the statement, that, not one of you have ever tasted anything similar to this. You simply cannot find it on the market. This cognac was distilled shortly after the time of Bonaparte. In fact, the hundredth anniversary of its distillation was last autumn, about the time of the tragic events in Poland last year. With this, I and my staff will drink to your health and success and a speedy return to your country.'

He raised his glass, put it to his lips and drank very slowly. We followed suit. The liquid had looked like honey; it had the consistency of honey. It clung to the sides of the glass. Its smoothness could be tasted and smelled and its taste was quite beyond any description.

'Don't be ashamed to lick out the glass,' called out our host. 'It is too thick just to drink.' He demonstrated.

It was an unique experience which we savoured to the full. A little speech of thanks and appreciation followed. Then our host said, 'As a memento of your visit, those of you who would like to keep your sampling glasses are welcome to do so. Now I have to leave. Please finish the food, and God speed.'

The euphoria of our visit lasted till we got back. The news brought us down to earth. Even the French now admitted that they could not hold the Germans. Power had been assumed by Marshal Pétain, the hero of Verdun, idol of the French and many others beside. It gave a fillip to morale, but not for long. Not only could Pétain not hold the Germans; it was rumoured that he was negotiating an accommodating surrender, which would allow the French to retain some independence. It seemed that nothing could stem the German tide. More and more people were fleeing west before their advance. It began to look like Poland all over again...

'We are suspending the news sheet,' announced Mat one evening on the way for supper. 'There is nothing that one can possibly say that people cannot hear on the radio, and the news is too depressing for words. There is a rumour that our Government are proposing to evacuate the non-fighting units to England if the British will agree and ships can be found. The French are opposing the idea.'

'I think that, if it comes to an evacuation, I will try to fly out in one of the signals aircraft,' I suggested, 'why should we leave these machines for the Hun?'

'Even assuming that, not being qualified as a pilot, you would be allowed to fly,' retorted Miet, always practical and unimpressed, 'which no one in their right mind would allow, where do you think you would go? Fly towards England, and the Hun would get you. They have complete air superiority along the northern coastline. You could not reach Africa without refuelling. A few miles west, to the coast, is hardly worth the bother and of little value.'

'It's a matter of principle and if need be I could steal an aircraft.' I tried to argue my case, but Miet just looked at me, disbelief and condescending compassion in his face. As far as he was concerned the case was dismissed. Miet's objections were fairly convincing but I believed I had a case.

Within days, the rumour was confirmed. Despite French objections, our government ordered evacuation to the western ports, whence it was hoped the British would pick us up. It was supposed to be secret but soon every one knew about it, even the intended routes to La Rochelle, Bordeaux and the more southern ports on the Atlantic for those in the west, and Marseilles for those in the central and southern districts. Because of this, I became more determined to try to fly out and started talking to one or two other enthusiasts who might be willing to participate in such a mad venture. I sought a personal interview with my company commander.

'There are some of us,' I told him, 'who are not officially registered as pilots by the French, who are nonetheless able to fly and who, have had unofficial flying retraining, even here in France.'

'I know all about that. You nearly took us for a ride when you first arrived here.'

'Well, yes. You know, sir, it was all well intentioned if poorly conceived. It couldn't have lasted. But that is not why I asked to talk to you. When the evacuation is ordered, the French would not suspect us since we are not officially registered with them as qualified pilots of taking their aircraft from the airfield, and flying out. But it would deny the Germans the use of the machines. Of course, in the meantime they may bomb them and burn them out any way. Why not allow some of us to fly out? I know that there are always at least three aircraft, on the line, in an easily accessible position, fuelled and ready to fly.'

'But where on earth would you go?' he asked after a few moments of thought. 'The Luftwaffe has complete command of the air in the north, you would not get past them. Africa is out of range, and if you flew to Spain they would intern you.' He looked at me, expecting some reaction and getting none, continued, 'It is a mad idea... You would be arrested if you landed on any military airfield; I suppose you could get some of the way to, say, Bordeaux, land in a field, burn the aircraft, and hope to get a lift to the port... but it is pointless.'

He had been thinking aloud. His arguments were the same as Miet's. It was hard to dispute them.

'It's a matter of principle more than anything else.' I was back with the same response I had made to Miet. 'A show of defiance, if you like. If you decide to forbid it, I shall obey. Nonetheless, I would be grateful if you would at least consider this request.'

He looked at me searchingly and finally made up his mind.

'All right. I have to applaud your eagerness even if I do not personally subscribe to your scheme. While I am in a position to forbid it, I am not in a position to allow it. The only person who might possibly agree is the colonel himself, and I doubt very much that he would. Do you want me to put it to him?'

Maybe he thought that the mention of the colonel would be sufficient to persuade me to drop the idea. It nearly did. But I said that I would be very grateful if he would raise the matter with the colonel, adding that I knew of one or two others, willing to participate in the venture.

In reply, he just shrugged his shoulders and turned to look out of the window. He did not even see my particularly smart salute as I left.

That same day the order came. We were to evacuate, the object being to leave France for Britain. As the orders were read out, pictures flashed through my mind of crowded roads and fleeing people. A few months ago it would have been ludicrous, unthinkable, that mighty France should succumb to the Germans.

The Polish army had fought on desperately to the end. The French seemed to have caved in, with virtually no resistance. The impact of the defeat of Poland had been delayed so far as I was concerned. But the realisation of what was happening now was immediate, the crumbling of civilisation before a ruthless giant. We were about to be squeezed right out of Europe. Where was there left to go? Spain was hardly on our side. If the Germans got to Portugal, the Portuguese were in no position to withstand them. Britain was the only hope. At least she seemed to be proposing to fight on. Would the Channel be enough, however, to stop the Germans? If not, the only escape would be drowning in the Atlantic. These were sobering thoughts…

In the meantime, we busied ourselves with executing the details of the evacuation order. While we were packing up our meagre belongings, I spoke to Miet.

'I have asked the company commander about my idea of flying out. His response was exactly the same as yours. However, he undertook to raise the matter with the colonel. If he agrees, which frankly I doubt, would you look after my things? If something goes wrong, do with them what you like. There isn't much of value, except for a few dollars which might help you, Jurek and Mat.'

Miet just looked at me. He said nothing, but there was disapproval in his eyes. I had just about finished packing when I was summoned by the company commander. His office was being packed up and there were a lot of burning papers.

'I have two things to say to you,' he said. 'You and two others, together with the platoon sergeant, will go to the flying centre to collect some papers which the colonel does not wish to leave behind. The sergeant knows what is needed and has full instructions. If the French challenge you, you are to abandon them and return here. We don't want any confrontation at this stage. The second thing is that, as promised, I have spoken to the colonel. He wanted to see you himself but has been summoned to a meeting of senior Polish commanders and has asked me to pass on his views. What you want to do is in direct contravention of French orders. They do not even recognise our government's right to order this evacuation. Officially, therefore,' and he emphasised the word 'officially', 'he cannot even consider your request. Like myself, however, he applauds the spirit in which it has been made.'

I thought that was the end, saluted and did an about-turn ready to walk out, when he continued, 'We will start moving from here at six thirty sharp tomorrow morning. If you and your accomplices are not here, no one will hold back for you. Having been left behind, you could be justified in stealing a car, or any other mode of transport, even an aircraft, to rejoin your unit. You must realise that if you are caught, you cannot expect any sympathy from either the French or the Germans, nor would you get any cover from us. The colonel would also be happier if there is an officer, a qualified pilot, but preferably not a regular, in charge of the escapade. You could follow the main route to Bordeaux or La Rochelle, or even further south, land somewhere in a field not far from a main road, and try for a lift. We know nothing of what you propose, and that's irrevocable.'

So it came about that three of us, including a lieutenant of the air force reserve, a trained pilot who had been an instructor in navigation at the centre, and was now unofficially in charge of the escapade, sneaked off to the airfield under cover of darkness. We hid in an air raid trench near the aircraft parking line and waited for daylight.

We worked out what we would do, down to the last detail. There would be no time to warm up the engines, once we had started them. We might be spotted and prevented from leaving. We would take off straight from the parking line. Fortunately there was hardly any wind so this would not present a problem. We would fly in visual contact both with each other and the main evacuation route, and maintain complete radio silence. We would fly low, not above one hundred metres, to avoid being spotted by German aircraft. If we were caught on the ground by the French, our story would be that we had been left behind by our unit, and wanted to catch up with them. We timed our departure for seven o'clock for this reason, and also because it was just before the French reported for work.

So at seven o'clock precisely, we jumped out of our

trench and ran to the aircraft. We threw off the engine and cockpit covers and climbed in. There was no one about.

All the engines started faultlessly and we were off, without delay. Once in the air, we turned south west, overflew the main evacuation route, and followed it some five hundred metres to one side, flying in an open formation, the Lieutenant leading. The road was full of traffic, all moving west. Cars, lorries, buses, horse-drawn carts, and people on foot. Memories of Poland came flooding back. And where were those happy, smiling, carefree faces we had seen when we first came to France? What had happened to those friendly people who had been so generous in their first welcome, so compassionate to us fugitives, so secure in their faith in the Maginot Line?

The frustration and the shock of the French, who had placed all their fate in Maginot Line, was understandable. The Germans ignored it and poured in their might through the Low Countries. Their superiority forced the Allies to retreat and the French population to flee west in panic and disarray, unprotected, and mindless of the unbridgeable barrier of Atlantic where all roads ended.

The only difference from the Polish exodus was that here motorised vehicles had taken the place of horses. Even that was changing before our eyes, as vehicles ran out of petrol and were abandoned along the roadside. Thousands of civilians were mixed with the military as they all headed westward along the roads that ended in the Atlantic. Hoping for ships to take them on?

These gloomy thoughts were mixed with the joy of flying, when I was jerked back into a sense of immediacy. I felt that I was losing power. Almost immediately, the engine started to cough and splutter, vibrating unpleasantly. The instruments showed that the oil pressure was low and engine temperature was climbing. I saw a puff of smoke come from the engine cowling, then another, bigger and darker, like oil smoke. I looked towards the others. They too were puffing smoke, especially the nearer one, the one flown by our leader. My engine became very rough, there was a sudden loud bang and it stopped altogether. My leader had begun to trail black smoke as well.

I concentrated on making a forced landing, and there was little time to choose a good landing strip. There were fields ahead, some cut by hedges and ditches. That flat-looking field ahead would have to do. I levelled out into a glide rather higher than I would have liked, managed to make a good three-point touch down, bounced once or twice and came to a halt. The leading aircraft came down barely four hundred metres ahead, and was just visible over the hedge of the neighbouring field. By now, clouds of smoke were pouring from under my cowling, and as I jumped out, I could see a steady drip of oil. It was too much of a coincidence; someone must have doctored all three aircraft.

The three of us, having landed so close together, ran towards each other. The lieutenant was holding a handkerchief to his face – it was red with blood. Just as he was finishing his landing, his wheels had gone into a drainage ditch. As his aircraft stood on its nose, he was thrown forward and hit his face on the dashboard. It didn't look too serious, even if painful and messy.

'Bastards – fifth column, or something at work. They must have tinkered with the aircraft to stop them being flown. We were lucky, others might have got killed.' He was stuttering slightly, spreading the bloody smear all over his face. His hands were shaking, possibly from a combination of anger and shock. We decided there was nothing to be gained from firing the aircraft. They were no longer flyable and setting them on fire could attract the attention of the Luftwaffe. We made for the road in search of a lift.

Going West

At first our attempts to thumb a lift evoked no response except an occasional friendly wave *en passant*. Eventually, a motorcyclist approached at speed, weaving in and out of the traffic. The rider wore the uniform of the French air force. Seeing us in the same uniform, he pulled in, eyeing our cap badges and the flying helmets in our hands, and asked us who we were.

'We were forced down just over there,' answered the lieutenant in good French, pointing towards the aircraft.

'Polish?' asked the motorcyclist.

'Yes, Polish,' we chorused in reply, expecting some disparaging remark.

'*Vive la Pologne!*' he shouted, to make himself heard over the noise of the traffic. 'Good luck to you. There's an English convoy not far behind; they'll probably give you a lift. Good luck again!' He waved and roared off.

Sure enough, a convoy of some five or six British lorries soon came along. We succeeded in flagging down the leading truck. I went to speak to the occupants. Next to the driver sat a captain.

'We are members of Polish air force,' I introduced myself. 'We were forced down in the field over there. You can see our planes. Can you please give us a lift west – Bordeaux, La Rochelle, anywhere near a port.'

'Don't waste time now,' answered the captain, 'jump in. There's room in the back.'

So we clambered in, helped up by the soldiers inside.

Within the truck was a sort of orderly chaos. Orderly, because the British were neat, well turned out and disciplined; chaotic because there were also three non-British aboard, one of them a stretcher case. By comparison, they looked dirty and unkempt. One of the English soldiers offered us cigarettes without saying a word. A corporal gave us a bar of chocolate. It made me realise that I was both hungry and thirsty. We had had nothing to eat or drink since the previous evening.

'What or who are you?' asked the corporal, speaking slowly and loudly since he knew we were foreigners, hoping that it would make it easier for us to understand.

'We are from the Polish air force.' I replied.

'Hoorah! It speaks our lingo! Them Frogs don't – all we know about them is that one is *français* and the others *belges*. We picked 'em up after they had a little accident early this morning. You speak English, then?'

'Yes. I know some English,' I replied, 'and what's more, I am very thirsty and would appreciate a drink of water.'

'You are a long way from your home,' he said, fumbling for his water bottle, 'much further than we are. We're both being chased by Jerry.' He handed me his water bottle, from which I took a long swig. 'You already lost one war.'

Nettled, I retorted hotly, 'I would prefer to think that we lost a battle, fighting against odds even worse than they are here. I hope that one day, together, we will win the war.'

'Well spoken, young Polish boyo,' came a voice from the back of the truck.

I asked the corporal if he had come far. He side-stepped the question, merely saying that they had been on the road since the previous evening. However, he said that they were going to La Rochelle to help with movement control at the embarkation point. After a little silence, he added: 'There is another convoy behind us, ten or twelve lorries, all air force. They aren't French air force, though, they have different badges. Maybe they're your lot.'

An hour or so later, we stopped. The road was passing through woodland, and the convoy was carefully manoeuvred under the canopy to hide them from the air, and to keep the road clear. The officer in the cab jumped out.

'All out for five minutes. Top up the fuel tanks.'

He walked back to find out more about us, and we told him what had happened. Someone offered us bread, a chunk of cheese and some lukewarm tea, which we accepted gratefully.

'I'm glad you are being looked after,' said the captain. 'We haven't got much left by now, but what we have, you are welcome to share.' He sounded a nice sort of person, and I thanked him for his help, adding that we thought ourselves very lucky. He repeated what the corporal had already told us, about the following convoy.

'What do you want to do, then?' he enquired, 'wait for them, or throw in your lot with us?' I translated. It didn't take long to make up our minds. The following convoy might not be ours, they might not even stop for us. We were better off where we were. I conveyed our feeling to the captain.

'All right. All on board! Let's get rolling!' he shouted.

We clambered aboard as the engines were started and tailboards lifted. Just then I could see another convoy with French number plates approaching. As they got nearer, I recognised Captain Bednarczyk, one of the company commanders from St Jean d'Angeli, in the cab of the leading vehicle. I waved to him, and he stopped, his cab almost abreast of our truck. I jumped out, ran to the front and spoke to the British captain.

'The other convoy is here. We are lucky, they are our own unit. I hope you will allow us to rejoin them.'

Captain Bednarczyk had dismounted and was standing by his cab.

'No time to talk now. I see you didn't get very far. Weren't those your aircraft in the fields some kilometres back?'

The convoy was blocking the road, and there was much hooting from behind. I nodded, and hastened to the back of his truck, where I and my companions climbed in as fast as we could. We started off, now in front of our British friends, to whom we waved goodbye and thanks.

The lorry was fairly full. I learned that Jurek, Mat and Miet were somewhere further back, but I would have to wait before we could be reunited. We were quizzed as to how we had come to be in the British convoy, ahead of ours. No one knew about our adventure until we told them.

We were followed by the British convoy until we came to the outskirts of Saintes. The road junction was tightly controlled by the French. Only the British were allowed to go to La Rochelle. The rest of us were routed further south to Bordeaux. There was a British sergeant standing alongside the French at the junction. I leaned out and called to him: 'Why are only the British allowed to go to La Rochelle?'

He seemed slightly taken by surprise, perhaps because I spoke in English.

'The truth is that there are not enough ships to evacuate everyone from La Rochelle. Maybe there will be some more at Bordeaux.' He stopped, as if realising that he had already said too much.

'How near are the Germans?'

'Too bloody near for my liking.' He turned away, to resume his work.

In the meantime, the convoy waited, while an argument

as to our destination continued. The tone of the traffic controllers soon made it clear that there was no choice in the matter.

While we were waiting impatiently to proceed, there were plenty of faces peering from the lorries behind us, all anxious to see what was afoot. Among them I suddenly saw Mat, who caught my eye, waved frantically, disappeared, and then was joined by Jurek and Miet.

As we approached Bordeaux, there was another halt. The lorries needed fuel. The men needed food. We gave our report to the captain, who found it difficult to believe what we told him.

'Cunning bastards!' was his only comment. 'Pity the colonel is not with us. Your story would have added more fuel to his fire.'

We were then allowed to rejoin our friends, and I was soon reunited with mine. The first thing Miet did was to hand me back my possessions, saying, 'I am glad I did not have to divide these between the three of us.'

My friends produced a couple of bottles of ordinaire from somewhere, and we celebrated our reunion as we drove on and I recounted my adventures.

The outskirts of Bordeaux seemed to be preparing for a siege. Military control points and military patrols abounded, stopping us every few minutes. On either side of the road, batteries of heavy and light artillery, anti-aircraft guns and machine guns had been dug in, all well-manned by the French and carefully camouflaged. It looked as if the French were expecting Bordeaux to be a major German target. We reached a main control point, manned by armed and business-like teams of French, British and Polish soldiers.

'Who are you and how many are you?' demanded a voice so loudly that we could hear it way back down the convoy. There followed a lengthy conversation between a

Polish army sergeant and our convoy commander, with a lot of pointing in different directions. After a while, we started to move off again. From our position, we could see convoys of different nationalities turning off down side streets marked with different coloured arrows.

After a while, we were again stopped, this time in a side street. There was a yellow board attached to a lamp post. We could hear our captain talking. Then, one after another, the engines were switched off. The second-in-command walked back down the line, telling us we could get out and stretch our legs, but to stay with our lorries until the captain returned with more instructions.

The street was more or less deserted. The few people about tried to ignore us, and only slowly did we begin to gather information, of dubious accuracy. The Germans had bombed the harbour, which had been mined by the French, it had been mined by the British, and by the Germans. The British had sunk a ship across the harbour entrance to block it, the British would only take out their own people, they had sold the French down the river, we were all going to be interned as deserters, and the Germans had announced that unless the forces left the city, they would bomb it. None the wiser, we were scarcely encouraged.

The captain returned, listened impassively to our stories, said he was sorry the colonel was not with us but gave no explanation, and ordered an issue of rations. Once this was done, he would talk to us all again.

The provisions sergeant was careful with the issue.

'Too much for one meal, and not enough for two,' grumbled Miet. Jurek agreed.

'Watch it, Miet. You are getting too fat,' teased Mat. I interrupted, to prevent the riposte which was about to come from Jurek.

'Jurek, do you remember poor Kazio? He, too, was always hungry when under strain.'

'Poor Kazio,' said Jurek, pensively. 'I wonder what happened to him.'

Dusk was falling when, food in hand, we gathered round the Captain's lorry.

'Pay attention. I will tell you as much as I can, as much as I am allowed to.'

He was interrupted, 'Come on, give us the truth. Don't hide it from us,' called a voice.

'I am not going to shout to shut you up. If you don't want to listen, go and get into your lorry. If you want to hear, shut up.' No one said another word. His quiet calmness commanded everyone's attention.

'First, look after your food. As the provisions sergeant told you, I hope, it has to last you through breakfast tomorrow. Earlier on, some arrivals at this dispersal point were taken off for embarkation. There was room in a British ship due to sail during the night. We don't know whether any more ships will arrive. If they do, there are two large convoys which got here before us, both British, and they have priority. There are also officials of both governments, and they also have priority. If the Germans do come, they are not expected for at least forty-eight hours, so there is that amount of time in hand, unless of course they bomb the harbour or the city. The city would like all troops to evacuate, for fear that their presence in the city might make Bordeaux a justified target for bombing.'

'Apart from the two British road convoys, there are several others who clocked in before us. On the principle of first come, first served, they have priority over us. I have been advised that the chances of us being evacuated from here are therefore very slim, and that we would be better off if we drove right down to the southernmost harbour on the Atlantic coast, beyond Biarritz – St Jean de Luz. It's a fishing port, shallow and very near the Spanish frontier.

The British may divert some ships there, and if they don't, crossing to Spain would be a possibility. There is no pressure on anyone. You have the following options. You can stay here and hope to be evacuated by the British. You can stay here and fade into the French environment, especially if you have friends or relatives, who can at least initially help you. Or, you can come with me to St Jean de Luz. You have until three o'clock in the morning to decide. I will move off with those who decide to leave, at three thirty sharp. We will divide the transport and supplies, when we know who goes where. The decision is yours!'

Towards the Light

Having become accustomed to being ordered around, it was somewhat bewildering and disconcerting to be confronted with the necessity of deciding our own future. Miet broke the silence.

'I think that staying on here on the off-chance that we might be taken off by one of the ships would be mad. We have very low priority, we have no means of changing that priority and in any case, I agree with the logic of allocation.'

'At least, there is a chance here,' countered Jurek. 'We could be cut off on the journey south by the advancing Germans, before we reach Biarritz or the St Jean place.'

'Or the Germans come here in two days' time and put us in the bag,' retorted Miet promptly.

'So what's the difference? Be caught by the Germans here or somewhere else?' argued Jurek.

'There is always Spain, from St Jean, as the captain was saying,' interposed Mat. 'But Spain means internment, and the Spanish are not very caring about their internees,' he added quickly. 'I have relatives in Portugal. Maybe I could get there?'

'Your geography is not very good,' I said, 'Portugal doesn't have a frontier with France.'

Miet remained adamant.

'Better get interned in Spain than be caught by the Germans here. They won't love us for getting out of Poland and then fighting them again here.'

Those were my sentiments as well, and I said so.

'One thing I will not do,' stated Jurek, 'is this fading into the French countryside. If you go south, I will obviously come too. I don't feel like making big decisions right now and being left alone is not appealing.'

Thus, we four made our decision jointly. Others were still arguing, this way and that. It was a long time before silence took over from the murmur of debate. There was no light in the streets; it was pitch dark. But '*luz*' is the Spanish for light and that was the direction we had decided to take.

Because of the prolonged debates, few had much sleep before we were awoken and reassembled. First light began to illuminate the sky from the east, where the Germans lurked. As we walked over to the captain's lorry, Jurek caught up with the second-in-command, who was a friend of his of long standing.

'What are you going to do?' he asked.

'I am staying put. The Brits will not let us down. They will come to pick us up. At any rate, someone has to look after those who decide to stay behind.' It sounded as though that decision had not been entirely of his own making. When all the lorries were reported empty, and it was presumed that everyone was present, the captain spoke to us once more.

'Right. Those of you who have decided to stay, join the second-in-command. Those who are coming with me, bring your gear up to my lorry so I can see how much stuff we have to carry. You have ten minutes.'

That didn't take long. None of us had much luggage. Those opting to go south outnumbered the rest by two to one. The quartermaster sergeant, who was standing next to me, grumbled, 'One bloody half of me wants to go with the captain and the other half wants to stay here. At worst, I have some family not too far from here, who would probably help me.' If he was thinking aloud, those thoughts were overheard by the captain, who interrupted them.

'In the meantime, sergeant, get the third bloody half of you back to the rations lorry and divide the supplies. Two-thirds to be put in my lorry, the rest to stay where they are.' A happy smile spread over the sergeant's face; he had got something to do which would stop him worrying. He could delay his final decision, and he got down to work.

'Now for the rest of you. Some of you go and help with the provisions. Driver-mechanics, select the best nine vehicles, and fuel them up. Leave a quarter-tankful in the vehicles which are being left behind; load all spare fuel into my lorry in drums and cans. Food is a little short, but I have enough funds to buy food when an opportunity presents itself. I will leave some funds with the 2-i-C, and anything left over at the end will be divided among you. Those coming with me, divide yourself into eight groups. There won't be space in the back of my lorry, except for the quartermaster sergeant and a couple of helpers.'

So the sergeant would have to agonise no more; his mind had been made up for him.

'I will appoint someone in charge of each vehicle. All arms will go south. Those staying won't need them, and we might. Officers and NCOs stay with me, the rest of you get on with it.'

We sorted ourselves out with a driver whom we knew and who had selected a newish-looking lorry, rolled up the side covers as instructed. Then we went to make our farewells to those who had opted to stay. It was, 'See you in England, if all goes well,' and then we were off.

At four o'clock in the morning, it was light enough to need no lights. As we drove out of the suburbs of Bordeaux, we could see the gun crews working on their weapons. Here and there, we encountered patrols, some on foot and others in vehicles. Perhaps they were watching for the Germans, for no one knew where they were, or how far away.

There were traffic controls at major road junctions, and these directed us out of the city, routing us in the direction of Biarritz. We left Bordeaux behind and drove along a rough road surrounded by farmland. We saw a large expanse of water. At first we thought it was the Atlantic, but it turned out not to be; we happened to be just landward of the great Arcachon Basin. We followed the road south-wards, and some three hours after we had set out, stopped. Resuming our drive, we at last came to the shores of the Atlantic proper, and long, seemingly endless beaches of golden sand. To our amazement, there were people to be seen sun bathing and swimming. We envied them, and wondered how they could be relaxing thus at such a critical time.

We turned eastwards to take the track which was said to lead between two large lakes to Biscarrosse, and thence to the main road south, to the Spanish border. We were at the edge of the second lake when a halt was ordered. There was a little pine wood, which gave cover for our vehicles, the lake was only a few hundred metres away, and just off the track was a large farm-cum-boarding house. This time, we stopped for a good rest and a wash in the lake. Two French speakers were sent off to the farm to see if we could buy food, or better still, if they could provide a meal. The emissaries came rushing back, smiles all over their faces.

'Food!' they shouted. 'They will cook us a meal of ome-lettes, potatoes and vegetables, soup and cheese. They will sell us cheese and cooked meat, milk and butter, but they are short of bread.'

It would not be cheap, but the captain decided it was worth it. Soon we were sitting on benches and bales of straw in the farm yard, guzzling from plates piled high with food. In broken French, our quartermaster sergeant negotiated for provisions to take with us.

We set off once again with hampers of food stored in the front lorry and well-filled stomachs. The beaming farmer counted the thick wad of notes which had been handed to him, whilst our departure was accompanied by shouts from the family – *'Vive la Pologne'* and *'Bonne chance'*.

We joined the main route to the south just after midday. Ahead of us we could see a tall column of blue-black smoke rising into the sky. Something was on fire, and we anxiously hoped it had not been caused by Germans. The large, prosperous farms which lined the sides of the roads, with peacefully grazing cattle and an occasional vineyard, gradually gave way to thick forest. It was then that we realised that the smoke came from a forest fire.

As we got closer, the smoke became denser and denser. Soon we saw the first flames shooting high into the sky. As we proceeded, we found trees alongside the road were aflame from the bottom of the tree trunks to the very tips. The noise of the crackling fire was supplemented by explosions caused by resin boiling under the bark, which split, sending spouts of fire and sparks sideways, and spreading the conflagration. Everything was as dry as tinder. I learnt what the expression 'spreading like wildfire' really meant. It was just that.

We came to a halt where the road cut across a large open field free of trees. The captain jumped out and issued clear and urgent orders.

'Cover up all the fuel with blankets. Stack your luggage on top of them. Roll down the side tarpaulins, otherwise you might get scorched. If the tarpaulins catch fire, you'll have to beat the fire out. We'll race through the fire at top speed and hope we can get through quickly. There will be smoke inside the lorries, so find whatever soft material you can and cover your mouths. If the need arises, use the water and milk in your bottles to put out any fires which take hold. You six, in the back of my lorry, make sure the fuel does not explode with a bang.'

The drivers raced through the blazing forest at the maximum speed they could coax out of their vehicles, without getting too close to the one in front. The smoke was dense, the visibility almost nil. The noise of the fire was deafening and very frightening. Flaming branches were falling on the tarpaulins and soon the vehicle behind ours was well alight, the flames fanned by the speed of the truck. We could see the crew inside, desperately seeking to douse the blaze. Inside our lorry, the heat was awful and the smoke choking. It must have been even more terrifying for the drivers.

Suddenly we were out of the belt of fire, with fields once more on either side. We stopped and jumped out. One of the vehicles ahead was blazing away, and there was frantic activity as we all sought to beat out the flames. The lorry behind us was burning fiercely, its wooden sides aflame.

Our captain was on the scene. 'Abandon that truck at the back, douse the flames on the middle one. Crew from the abandoned vehicle, get into the others,' he ordered.

We moved forward again as soon as we were ready. Ahead lay another fire which seemed less ferocious than the one we had just survived. We were about to start on our second race, when there was a colossal bang and the lorry we had left behind exploded.

It may have looked less, but the second fire seemed endless, and there was a time when I thought we would never get through it. The holed tarpaulins let in more heat and more smoke. We were choking, coughing and spluttering, and hoping that the drivers were better protected in their cabs. We seemed to be engulfed in that fire and smoke for an eternity. It may have only been two or three minutes, but those minutes were very long minutes indeed, before we emerged into a clear blue sky with no more fires to be seen ahead.

Our convoy drew to a halt. It was time to take stock. Surprisingly, this time not one of the lorries was on fire, although some tarpaulins were still smouldering. Men were spitting and retching. Some had burns, mainly on their hands where they had tried to put out fires. Being military lorries, they carried first-aid kits, and those with first aid training set about dressing the burns. The captain inspected each lorry in turn and supervised the final extinction of the smouldering tarpaulins. There was little water or milk left.

The lorries were also low on fuel as a result of the high speed dashes and a general refuelling was ordered. As the turn of the last lorry came, someone suggested that, since we had some spare space, we could save petrol by leaving one vehicle behind and crowding a bit in to the others. The captain looked at his map to calculate how far we had to go, and consulted with the quartermaster sergeant and the drivers. They concluded that we had a little fuel to spare with eight vehicles, quite a lot with seven.

'We will take all of them,' decided the captain. 'One may break down, or maybe we will meet someone needing help. It would be unfair to refuse to help because we have no space and too much fuel.'

So the last vehicle was filled up, and we were on the move again. There was little traffic on the road. Perhaps it was all moving in the same direction, at the same speed. Once or twice we passed other convoys resting under the trees, all showing the scars of fire.

The captain must have had a premonition that someone might be in need of help. We had not been driving for very long when we spotted some men marching across the fields, a hundred metres or so from the road. When they saw us they began to wave frantically.

They were in uniform. It was the wrong colour for Germans and they were wearing a funny kind of headgear, unlikely to have been German. Also, it did not seem to us that Germans would be on foot. The convoy was ordered to a stop, and the captain waved to them. They broke into a run and reached us very quickly.

There was little doubt that they were British. The detachment consisted of a lieutenant, who cannot have been any older than I, a sergeant, a corporal and five men. Our captain got out of the cab.

'Scots Guards,' announced the young officer, saluting smartly.

'Captain Bednarczyk, Polish air force,' replied our captain in Polish.

The young lieutenant looked blank. The captain tried French, and still got a blank look. The lieutenant tried very bad German, and got an even blanker look in return.

'Captain, sir,' I called out, 'may I help? I speak a little English.'

He beckoned me without a word. I jumped out of our lorry and joined him.

'You are a lieutenant, sir?' I asked.

'Yes. Lieutenant Campbell, Scots Guards.'

'I will try to help, if I may. This is Captain Bednarczyk, Polish air force.' I then told the captain the Scotsman's name and rank.

'Thank God someone speaks our language,' said Campbell, laughing. 'We tend to be a bit lazy about languages. Then, when it comes to a show like this, we have problems. We lost our transport in the forest fire back there. We were cut off from our unit, couldn't regain contact, so headed for the sea and evacuation. We thought the south-west corner would give us the best chance. We understood from the French that the Germans are overrunning the country rather fast.'

I continued to play the role of translator. The captain replied, 'We are making for St Jean de Luz, right on the Spanish border. We hope the British navy will pick us up there.'

The lieutenant had turned to his men and was talking to them fast, and in a low voice. The captain said, 'Tell him that I will give them a lift in our trucks. In return, we will expect him to put in a good word for us with the British when we get to St Jean de Luz, especially when it comes to negotiating the embarkation.'

That seemed to me to be close to blackmail, but I translated as instructed.

'In that case, I have to decline your offer,' came the laconic reply from the young Scotsman. 'I am not prepared to negotiate the terms on which you take us. Either you take us as an ally, or, if need be, we will take one of your vehicles by force. I am probably better trained for it than you are, and I hope you will not force me to do it.'

He spoke very politely, but he clearly meant what he said. They were better armed than we, even if there were a lot fewer of them. Somewhat ashamed, I translated once more. There was a tense moment. The captain went a little pink in the face, whether from shame or anger I do not know, but I translated his answer.

'I apologise. Of course you are welcome. Please come aboard. We are pleased to share whatever we have with you.'

The Scotsmen had little to offer except a few cigarettes and a bar or so of chocolate. However the lieutenant said, 'We are all qualified to drive heavy transport, so we can relieve your drivers for a spell. If you need guards or a forward patrol, we are better used to that than your airmen, and are at your service.'

'For the moment, I think we had better get going. My sergeant will give you and your lads some food. You can have a rest en route. This airman will go with you as interpreter.'

I asked, and received permission, for Miet, Jurek and Mat to join me, and we all piled into the second lorry, swapping places with those already in it, which suited them since they did not fancy being swamped with English conversation they could not follow.

The lieutenant faced his men. 'Fall in!'

They formed a single file.

'Right dress – eyes front – stand at ease.'

He reported that his men were ready to board. Old habits die hard, I thought, as I admired their sense of instant discipline. I noticed quite a few faces peering out of the lorries, impressed. I also noticed that two or three of them had bruised and slightly burned hands, and one was burned on the face. I collected a first aid kit while Mat went to collect my gear. We boarded, I introduced my friends and handed over the first-aid kit. The soldiers attended to their scars.

The convoy rolled forward. As soon as they had eaten, the Scotsmen set about cleaning up. Rifles first, then boots, then uniforms. By the time they had finished, their uniforms, although some showed signs of burns, were cleaner and more presentable than ours. I was particularly envious of their boots.

They didn't talk much, once they had explained what had happened to them. They had been sent forward to reconnoitre a holding position in the forest, in case their unit had to withdraw to the south-west. Having evaded any prowling Germans and reached the edge of the forest, they had been caught in the fires. This separated them from rest of their unit. They had driven along a forest ride when the wooden sides of their vehicle caught fire. Fearing that the truck might explode, they got out in the nick of time, for it exploded almost as soon as they abandoned it. They had been marching on foot since that morning.

Tired as they were, they attended to their equipment before falling fast asleep. I remembered our lorry with wooden sides, and was glad all the others had metal ones.

It was getting dark when we reached the outskirts of Bayonne. It was not much further to St Jean, but the captain ordered a halt, since driving at night without lights was dangerous, and driving with them might attract unwelcome attention from the Luftwaffe. Our convoy drew into a side road, and we debussed. The quartermaster sergeant distributed the remains of his provisions, which were not substantial. The captain ordered that guards be posted, and no fires be lit. He then set out in his lorry, with the quartermaster sergeant and two others for the centre of town, in search of information, food and drink. Guard duty was taken on by the Scots Guards, who were anxious to 'show their appreciation' – an offer none of us felt disposed to dispute.

The captain returned late, bringing water and some rather sharp wine, and the welcome news that he had found somewhere to buy provisions first thing in the morning. The news was that St Jean was already fairly full and that the Germans were at least two days away, if not further. The wine helped, even if it was on the acid side, and we soon turned in and fell asleep. The Guards, however, could be seen cleaning and polishing their equipment – to save time in the morning, one of them explained – before bedding down.

We were off at six next morning. All we had to do was to refuel the lorries and get in. We stopped for provisions, as expected – but all there was to be had was bread, cheese, mineral water and milk. It was soon distributed.

We also learned one shattering piece of news. Marshal Pétain was negotiating an armistice with the Germans. The French had given up, and France had fallen.

We soon reached the outskirts of St Jean de Luz, where we were stopped at a mixed control point. The giving of instructions seemed a lengthy process. Then we slowly rolled downhill into St Jean. We found the British Sector, where we dropped our passengers. Profuse in their thanks, they were clearly delighted to be back with their fellow countrymen. A British military policeman led us to the 'Polish Camp'.

We had reached our destination. We were now trapped. The Germans were behind us, Spain and internment lay to the south, and the Atlantic lay between us and freedom.

On Tenterhooks

There was little to cheer us up in the 'Polish Camp'. We were ordered to stay with our vehicles while Captain Bednarczyk went to Allied Command Headquarters for instructions and information. We garnered what news we could from other Poles there. It was rumoured that only the British were to be evacuated out of France and that the French, interpreting their armistice terms, would use force if necessary to prevent anyone else from leaving. What force was at the disposal of the local French authorities was unknown; but we did know that we, along with several thousand others of various nationalities in a similar plight, were but poorly armed. There was a sense of betrayal in the air, even among the French, and it created a strained atmosphere. The group next to us had been there for nearly two days and shared some useful local knowledge. They had found hotels which offered facilities for a bath, wash and shave, and advised us where we would be made welcome, and where not.

On his return, Captain Bednarczyk gave us the latest news.

'There is not much I can tell you. At the moment, there are no ships to take us out, nor do we know of any on their way. The French, especially the military, are unfriendly. They are sticking to their interpretation of the agreement with the Germans. You may use the town facilities, but under no circumstances must you get involved in arguments, brawls or the like. There are some friendly bistros and hotels, but many are openly hostile, do not allow entry to non-French military, and many of them have notices to that effect. We need to ensure that there is a good spirit fostered among the different nationalities here, so it is important that you maintain good discipline.

'We need to keep watch over our possessions and vehicles. You will be divided into three watches, one on duty with the convoy, one off-duty and resting but available to give any help that may be needed, and the third, free to go into town. No one may be away for more than two hours, without reporting back.

'All arms will be stored in the back of my lorry, and two of the duty watch are to remain inside, guarding them at all times.

'Food will be issued from the field kitchens, which are manned jointly by all services and nationalities stationed here. At the moment, supplies are fair but they will not last for ever and replenishment will be tricky. There is enough for about a week, unless there is a sudden influx of newcomers without their own supplies.

'I promised you I would divide what money I have left amongst you, and this will be done.

'The staff sergeant will arrange the watches and the duty roster. I will be back in about half an hour to distribute the money.'

We four friends were on the first watch, which suited us nicely. None of us had any French money left. Rumour had it that very few shops were accepting foreign currencies – so it was doubtful whether my remaining dollars would be of any use. However, the captain did us poor volunteers proud. Our weekly pay was but 6.50 francs. We each received the princely sum of nearly two hundred, the senior NCOs and officers somewhat more. To us it was a fortune, whilst they were quite put out.

As soon as we came off duty, we went into the town

proper and the harbour, which was small, mainly fishing in character. The harbour was full of trawlers and small boats, the town itself, geared to small holiday trade. There was no sign of fishing activity, and the only 'tourists' were the likes of us, in uniforms – a motley collection of diverse origins, unsure of the future!

We sought somewhere to have a hot bath and found a small and very friendly hotel. It had only two bathrooms, a rather inefficient hot water system, and a queue of six there before us. There was just time to manage, in our two hours. We filled in the interval with wine, cheese and a chunk of good fresh bread – there was nothing else on offer to eat.

Clean, refreshed and happy with the wine, we returned to the convoy just in time for a meal. It had been prepared by the British from British rations. We didn't know what it was, the taste was strange to our palates, but it was good to the hungry.

We were now on standby, and sought sleep in the back of a lorry. But sleep did not come easily. There was too much on our minds. The predominant question was – when would the Royal Navy arrive? No one openly questioned whether they would come at all. And when they came, would we be allowed to board? There were also a lot of French hoping for evacuation and it did not seem likely that they would readily submit to the terms of Pétain's agreement. Endless speculations based on the recent past, and dreams for the future were eventually replaced by the need for sleep.

Later that evening, we four decided to walk down to the harbour and look round. There was still plenty of light. The wind had whipped up the sea and large waves were breaking over the harbour wall. In the harbour itself, boats were bobbing up and down and rolling first to one side then the other. They were all unoccupied.

'If the worst happens,' observed Miet, 'we could nick

one of them and sail to Portugal. I've done a bit of sailing, and I reckon I could manage one, especially if it had a good motor.'

It might do, as a last resort. Others probably had similar ideas, for the harbour area was crowded. Every conceivable uniform could be seen. As for languages, it was a veritable tower of Babel. Every one wanted to know the same thing: was there any news of the British coming to pick us up? There were a few British about, but speaking to them, especially those in naval uniform, was like talking to a brick wall – not a word could we get out of them.

On our way back to the convoy, we indulged in window shopping. There was a photographic shop full of cameras. I was fascinated.

'Wouldn't it be fun to have a camera and take some pictures?' I mused. 'They could be of historic interest one day.'

'It would cost a lot of money,' replied the ever-practical Miet, 'and we haven't got much. You ought to keep what you have left, if you have any, for an emergency.'

I still had some of the dollars I had brought from Poland, and said so. Miet condemned the idea as stupid. Jurek supported him, adding that if we had to go to Spain, the money might be needed to bribe the guards. This closed the subject for the time being. Although we ceased to discuss the matter, the idea still persisted in my head.

We returned to the convoy and guard duty. There was no further official news, and we were confined to the vehicles for the night, 'for our own good'.

Early next morning, the detail despatched to collect our morning rations returned with the news that a couple of ships had been sighted on the horizon, but that they were not steaming towards the harbour. When we came off-duty at mid-morning, we walked down to the harbour to see for ourselves. Crowds lined the water's edge, watching two ships which were belching smoke from their stacks. They were sideways to the shore, and no one seemed to know whether they were British or German, or what. After a while, they turned about and steamed in the opposite direction.

The crowd speculated wildly. 'Maybe they are destroyers sweeping mines,' said one. This raised hopes. 'If they are sweeping mines, they must be ours,' said another. The resultant euphoria was rapidly dashed by a third who suggested that they might just as well be Germans patrolling the harbour or laying mines to make sure that nothing could get in or out of the harbour.

I left my friends watching the ships and walked slowly back to the camera shop. One half of me was obsessed by the idea of buying a camera, the other half wanted to keep the money. My worldly wealth consisted of some thirty dollars and two pounds sterling.

In the window, I saw a small French camera, similar to a Leica. There was no one inside but the shopkeeper. I could not resist going in.

'Would you sell a camera for American dollars?' I asked.

His eyes lit up.

'Of course. But what exchange rate do you have in mind?'

I was stumped. I had no idea of the value of an American dollar. He suggested a value, but a shifty look on his face indicated that he was hoping for too good a deal. We began to haggle.

'Which camera are you thinking of?' he enquired. I pointed to the one which had taken my fancy.

'A very wise choice, *monsieur*,' he continued, buttering me up, 'as good as a Leica but smaller and cheaper.'

'How much in dollars?'

'Sixty,' he came back without hesitation.

'Out of the question. I do not have that much money,' I

replied, turning for the door.

'Which country do you come from?'

'Poland,' I answered, opening the door.

'For the staunch ally of France, I will take fifty,' he offered.

I told him that I did not have even that much and left the shop. He came running after me.

'How much can you afford?' he shouted.

'Twenty,' I shouted back, and walked on, hearing him mumbling to himself.

My friends caught up with me, having realised that I had left them.

'You have been to that camera shop,' Miet reproved me; it was not a question.

'Yes I have. But he wants too much money for the camera I would like.'

Miet looked pleased, which made me want the camera even more. We went back to watching the ships. A third ship was coming, its smoke showing nearer. I tried to chat up the few British who were about. Two sailors refused to answer, the army swore they did not know. I bumped into the sergeant of the Scots Guards and even he was adamant that he knew nothing.

We had to return to our spell of duty. As we went past the camera shop, I stopped to point out the camera I coveted. The shopkeeper saw me and beckoned me in.

'Still interested?' he asked.

'Not really. I just can't afford your price,' I replied, smiling.

'Thirty-five?' he offered. I shook my head. As I reached the door he called out.

'At thirty I would be making no profit, but I will sell for thirty.'

He seemed very anxious to make a sale, so I turned back into the shop.

'Look, when the Germans are in control, your francs will be devalued like our currency was. It wasn't done officially, but you could buy next to nothing for zlotys, whilst marks or dollars kept their value and went up. My twenty dollars will keep their value, even with the Germans. So what about twenty dollars for the camera and two films?'

'Make it twenty-five.'

I fished out the dollars from the wallet – four five-dollar notes and five singles, knowing that there were a few more. His eyes brightened.

'I am not offering you all this,' I lied, 'this is all the fortune I have in this world, other than a few francs. You wouldn't expect me to part with all of it, my future unknown, just to buy a camera, would you?'

My little speech made a visible impression. He scratched his almost bald head and then said, '*Mon Dieu!* What does one do? I am so sorry for you.'

I was not sure whether he really meant this, or if it was just part of the show. I put all the money back in my wallet, feeling that he would go no further. I was wrong.

'All right. Twenty dollars.'

So the deal was clinched, he put the camera in its box with its case, and added a couple of films.

'*Bonne chance!*' he wished me as I left with my new acquisition.

I was delighted, despite Miet's unspoken disapproval of my extravagance. For all that, during our spell of duty, he joined in the task of finding out how the camera worked and trying to make sense of the instructions. These were written in French for Frenchmen, incomprehensible even to Mat, whose knowledge of French was excellent. We had to work it out for ourselves.

The captain came back with a detail carrying hampers of food which had been issued instead of a cooked meal, and a few bottles of wine, sent by the Scots Guards as a thank you present. The captain seemed to be in a good frame of mind and stayed joking with us for a while, before setting out to Headquarters to see if there was any more news.

He was back within half an hour.

'There are rumours, and no more than rumours, that the British might be on their way to pick us up. Two of their destroyers were patrolling out at sea earlier, and sweeping for mines. Behind them is a two-funnelled passenger ship. It is said that they have not yet had any instructions to come closer or embark, and without such an order they can do nothing. However, you had all better stay close to the convoy. Warn those who are off duty in the town when they come back. By the way, there are some very ugly stories circulating in the town and you must not believe them. I will keep you informed as the situation develops. If I am needed, I am at the Hotel Miranda, by the harbour.'

When the off-duty watch returned, they told us that the British navy were sweeping closer and closer to the harbour and that the liner was lying to, offshore. The weather was fine, but the winds were strong, the sea was rough and the waves were high. Disregarding the captain's instructions, we nipped down to the harbour at dusk to have a look. The destroyers were now close enough inshore for us to be able to see the crew at work. The liner still lay way out at sea behind them.

There was light enough to use the camera. I took a photo of my friends with the destroyers behind them. Then I had to be rescued by my friends from the crowds of people clamouring to be photographed as well. I could have made a small fortune as a photographer! It was just as well that the poor light made any further photography impossible, and we hurried back.

More rumours awaited us, reputedly of English origin

and therefore more reliable. It was said that the harbour was too shallow for the navy to use, and the sea was too rough to ferry anyone out. The navy were going to land a small team during the night and try to persuade local fishermen to undertake the ferrying. It was also rumoured that the French would prevent anyone other than the British from embarking; that they would use force if necessary, but that the British were on our side and would shoot it out if it came to the crunch. As usual, it was impossible to separate truth from fiction.

It was dark when Captain Bednarczyk arrived with positive news. We were to stand by, for embarkation from first light and no one was to leave the convoy.

This generated a great deal of excitement. At last, it seemed, we would be getting out. The dreadful possibility of internment in Spain for the duration, the fear at the back of everybody's mind the fear which was scarcely uttered it was so close, seemed at last to be receding. The lorries were humming with our conversation. What would happen when we got to England? How would we be treated by the RAF?

How long before we started flying? The ever cheerful Jurek was thinking much too clearly for my liking when he answered the last question.

'You, for one, can forget about flying when we get to England. You are one of the few among us who can speak English. You will be made an interpreter and we poor sods will be sent to school to learn the lingo, with its awful spelling. Many of our lads who went and joined the RAF had to spend the first two or three months learning the language before they could understand any instructions.'

'He's right, you know,' chipped in Miet. 'That's just what I have heard from my friends who went to England. They are much more thorough than the French have been.'

These were thoughts that had never entered my mind. I

was afraid that they might just be right. I was not cheered by the thought of working as an interpreter. What I wanted to do was to fly!

One by one we dozed off. We were roused at first light and joined by the captain, carrying his gear in a small grip. He addressed us.

'The British have just started embarking their own troops and various government officials. The sea is calm at the moment, but they say that the wind will rise during the day. We will march down to the harbour shortly – our vehicles, which have served us so well, will have to be abandoned here. You may take only the minimum of personal luggage, which must include tin hats and eating utensils. All arms and ammunition are to be taken with us. If everything goes according to plan, these will be dumped in the harbour. I want to see you march from here in a proper manner as a decent, well-organised unit and not like the rabble which can be seen round the harbour by the hundred. The better we look, the greater the chances. I shall leave my things here with you and go down there. When we are wanted, I will come back for you – there's no point in causing more congestion there than already exists. Get yourselves ready and wait for me.'

It was sad having to discard so much of what little remained to us. I wrapped my bit of the Bron bomb in a pair of socks, packed my documents and photographs from Poland with my diary notes and put them together with clean clothing and a few necessities in the small suitcase which had accompanied me all the way from Hungary. Jurek and I had worked out a joint scheme, sharing the distribution of our clothing to fit the space in our luggage. When this packing was done, I closed the case and looped my helmet strap to hang from the handle. I put my spare film in one pocket, money in the other and hung my camera round my neck. Then we polished off the remains of the food and wine.

We waited in a peculiar and eerie silence, which was only broken by an occasional exclamation when someone remembered he had forgotten to pack something. Space being at such a premium, those with some important valuable for which they had no room, searched for willing carriers.

It was well into the morning, by which time we were all growing increasingly tense, when the captain returned. He formed us up, put himself at the head of the column and marched us down to the harbour. To help keep us in step, he ordered us to sing a marching song. This lifted our spirits and released all the tension we had accumulated. It also drew attention to our passage, and our commander was delighted with the impression we made.

Underneath, we remained somewhat nervous. None of us was familiar with the sea, let alone sea warfare. Once aboard, we would be at the mercy of an unknown element.

Also there were the Germans; in the air, on the sea and under it, and they would be hunting us!

The Last Leg

The Royal Navy were in firm control of the harbour and embarkation. Unit after unit was called forward, and marshalled by armed and steel-helmeted officers and ratings. There was no sign of the French command who were supposedly meant to prevent this evacuation. Relays of rescue ships' lifeboats and launches, as well as local fishing boats, were ferrying out the evacuees; some of the fishing boats were manned by French fishermen who, it was said, had decided to go to England to join the French forces there.

To me, a non-sailor, the whole operation seemed fraught with hazard. Within the harbour, the water was reasonably calm and everything seemed simple enough. Outside the harbour wall, it was altogether different and it looked far from amusing. The waves were breaking over the harbour wall. With the exception of the larger fishing smacks, the sea tossed the small boats up and down. They rolled violently and every now and again were entirely lost from view behind the mounting waves, or were engulfed in spray. The wind grew in strength, gusting, and we expected the whole operation to be suspended if not cancelled. In the meantime, the ships anchored offshore looked a sitting target to threatened attack by the Luftwaffe.

'Maybe Spain would have been safer,' remarked a voice somewhere behind me, as we watched the spectacle with apprehension. It was worth recording, and I took some more pictures, using up half my first film.

After a seemingly interminable wait, our detachment was called for embarkation. The first few climbed into a half-filled boat, accompanied by two officers and two NCOs. Captain Bednarczyk decided he would supervise the embarkation, and be the last to leave.

Miet and Mat had already departed on one of the comparatively safe bigger fishing boats, when my turn came. Jurek and I climbed into one of the lifeboats from the liner. It was propelled by eight seamen at the oars, under the command of a coxswain at the tiller. They were all wearing black oilskins, life jackets, sou'westers and sea boots, and looked very tired and wet. There was a lot of water already in the bottom of the boat, which was being baled out while some twenty of us were scrambling in. I managed to take two more photographs as we pulled out into the harbour – one, of the town and the other, of the boats ahead, with the rescue ships in the background. It helped to take my mind off the fast approaching ordeal ahead, but Jurek jerked me back to reality.

'Better get your toy under your jacket,' he said, 'otherwise it will get wet with the spray.' He was right, as usual.

The coxswain issued his instructions while we were in the comparative quiet and shelter of the harbour. We would be taken as close to the bottom of the gangway as possible. We would jump two at a time, on his command. There would be seamen waiting on the platform ready to help us. I was able to translate and as I did so, I wondered what happened when no one could understand English.

Once we were into the open sea, things became hectic. The first large wave to hit us carried away someone's luggage with it. We could see it bobbing about on the water but the crew would not change course to pick it up. 'Too bad,' was the only response from the coxswain to impassioned pleas. Frightened, but not seasick, I saw the liner gently rolling in the swell while the boats discharging their human cargo bobbed up and down, sometimes well above the gangway platform, sometimes way below. The reception committee were being drenched and sometimes disappeared from view altogether. As we got nearer, the liner towered above us, and although her side gave some shelter from the roughness, we were still bobbing up and down like a yo-yo.

'I hope you're all good acrobats,' joked someone with a nervous giggle.

At last it was our turn, and we came alongside the platform. The first two stood on the seats amid ships awaiting the order to go, clutching their luggage and steadied by the rest of us. As our boat came to the platform with a downward heave, the coxswain yelled 'Jump'. They did, and were caught by the waiting sailors. The next two got ready. We were so close to the platform that I thought we would be smashed, but the order came as our boat rose upwards. The rowers used their oars to keep the boat at an exact distance, the next two jumped and were safely caught.

'Next two.'

It was my turn to stand on the seat. We were riding on a wave high above the platform, and as the boat descended, the coxswain bellowed 'Jump'. The man next to me jumped and I was a split second later. A gap appeared between the boat and the platform and it grew and grew while I was in the air and I knew I would not make it. I hoped they would catch me. Indeed I could feel hands grabbing at my clothes and sliding off. The boat was already below and I could see the faces of the occupants watching me as I fell between the boat and the side of the ship.

Around me was a lot of green water with millions of bubbles of air rising. Above me towered the monstrous side of the ship, below me its curve vanishing into the murky deep; it dwarfed the tiny bottom of the lifeboat above, with pin-like oars protruding from it, like legs from a water beetle. I still clutched my suitcase with one hand and struck upwards with the other. I could just make out the outline of the platform above and the boat almost on top of me. Hands grabbed my clothing and held it firmly, another hand grabbed and took away my suitcase. I felt a solid surface against my chest and the water pounding at my back helped to keep me pressed firm against it. Then I was lying down on the grating which formed the platform, spitting out water.

A voice yelled, 'Get the hell out of there and up the steps.'

I was pushed from the back and complied; a hand thrust my suitcase into my arms, and I found myself running up the companion steps, dripping water everywhere, while the boat was already disgorging the next pair.

My discomfiture was greeted with general merriment by the occupants of the same boat, having been enjoyed also by those who had already successfully completed the transfer.

'Who knew what to do and translated it for us, but couldn't do it himself?' jeered one, and 'Hope you managed to quench your thirst,' jested another.

The cabins were already full and the decks were filling up fast. Our detachment was allocated an area on the front deck just below the superstructure, and this was to be our 'home' for the voyage. It was well sheltered from the wind just then, and the sun was quite warm, but I shivered in my wet clothes. My own spare clothes, which were being unpacked by Jurek and Miet, also proved to be dripping wet. Dry clothes and a towel were produced by compassionate onlookers from their pathetically small stores. I found a cabin, but the bathroom was crowded with people and even the tub was being used as a bed. Hearing of my predicament, the occupant removed himself and his gear and let me in. I stripped, had a tepid wash, dried and changed, rinsed and wrung out all my wet clothes and having thanked the occupants for their hospitality, I returned to my friends.

Mat told me that he had rescued my wallet from my jacket, and also the spare film and both were now safely stored in his bag. Miet was holding my camera, water dripping from its case.

'Water may have got in,' he said. 'You'd better find a dark room somewhere and see if you can save the film. Then we can set about cleaning up the camera.'

I went exploring along the cabin corridor and found a linen locker, a perfect darkroom. As soon as I opened the camera I could hear the splash of water. My historic film was ruined, and probably the camera as well.

Back on deck, we inspected the inside of the camera. As it rapidly dried in the combination of breeze and sun, salt deposits could be seen forming everywhere. We watched the activity around us...

Two warships were positioned on either side of the liner during the embarkation, presumably giving protection both from the weather and the possibility of attack; one was flying the RN White Ensign, the other was Canadian. From time to time, they too, accepted a boatload of evacuees, whom we imagined must be persons of importance.

The stream of boats began to decrease. The lifeboats were hauled up the davits of their mother ships, and the ship's public address system announced: 'We will sail as soon as embarkation is completed. We are sailing for an undisclosed destination. Food will be issued once a day. We regret that food will be mainly in the form of tinned rations and biscuits. We will try to have a daily issue of tea and soup. Water will be rationed. Tap water in basins and bathrooms is not drinkable.' There then followed instructions for action drills, lifeboat procedures and other emergency arrangements, concluding with the message: 'Once we sail, the public address system will be used for emergency announcements only. That is all. Good luck to us all.'

Shortly thereafter, anchors were weighed. With no more sound than the gentle throb of the engines and a slight hiss as smoke escaped from the stacks, we steamed off into the Atlantic in a south-westerly direction. Our escorting destroyers were quartering the ocean, like pointers looking for game. Behind us, we left a motley collection of empty fishing boats bobbing up and down on the ocean, their crews somewhere in our little convoy on their way to join the Free French.

Miet and I began to work on the camera; there was little else to do and it helped to distract our minds from the present. We had found a corner protected from the wind, my clothes were drying nicely, but we were hungry and thirsty, no doubt the consequence of excitement. At Miet's suggestion, I descended into the bowels of the ship to see if I could borrow some instrument makers' tools and a little fine oil. In the crews quarters, which were as stuffy, smelly and overpopulated as everywhere else aboard, I found an engineer who had what I was looking for. He was reluctant to part with anything, until I left a silver cigarette case with him as a deposit.

Miet was delighted with my success, and we started to strip down the camera, Miet taking careful notes to make sure we could put it properly back together again. We extracted the last drops of fresh water from our water bottles to clean the parts before oiling them. An interested spectator produced a clean cotton vest for the purpose, a particularly generous gesture in view of the universal shortage of clothing.

We were well away from the French coast, which had faded from view and was obscured by a thin mist, and the dismantling operation was nearly complete when the alarm sounded Boat Stations. We wrapped the parts and the tools into the vest, put them safely in my case and ran to our designated station. As a result, Miet and I were late. Captain Bednarczyk had already finished calling the roll and we were given a sharp dressing down.

Nervously, we scanned the sea for signs of action. The two destroyers were belching heavy smoke as they quartered the sea ahead at greatly increased speed. There was a naval rating with a crew in charge of the boat station, and he gave clear instructions about boarding the lifeboat, about using the liferafts, and finished up by telling us that there were not enough life jackets for everyone and those with would have to support those without. Despite the clarity of what he said, his voice sounded a little excited, which made us feel that this might be more than just a practice.

Tension mounted as we waited and watched. It was all a new and strange experience. We saw the destroyers changing directions and speed, and felt our own ship doing the same, as if dodging some unseen obstacle. Our sense of hopelessness was relieved by the corny jokes of Mat.

'Weren't you the university swimming champion?' he asked Miet.

'Sure.'

'Then why don't you swim to England and take me on piggy back?'

'Only if you promise to have a piece of string with a bent pin, so you can fish on the way and feed me.'

Jurek put his oar in, 'Maybe we would have been safer in a Spanish internment camp. What's the difference? There you are eaten by lice and here you may be sunk by the Germans.'

'Ah, death from lice bites is slow,' came back Mat like a flash, 'drowning is fast, by comparison.'

I can remember these apparently puerile exchanges. They seemed funny at the time when we needed so badly to laugh. The destroyers' guns could be seen aimed in the same direction, as if at an invisible target. Our natural interest was spiced by the nagging realisation that we were helpless and passive participants. A long time passed before we were ordered back to our stations. The address system was not used. We never did find out whether it had been a practice or the real thing. At least with darkness nearly upon us, we should soon be out of sight and out of range of the Luftwaffe.

We used the remaining light to repack the camera parts, since it would no longer be possible to work on them, and to make sure that we had not damaged anything packing up in the panic.

At dusk, some ratings in naval overalls appeared bearing large boxes, from which they distributed food – two dry biscuits a head and a tin of sardines between four. They told us where to draw fresh water and ordered us not to throw anything overboard into the sea. We huddled down for the night. I was glad that my clothes had dried out and I was able to get back into my thick serge air force uniform, for it was becoming cold in the night wind. We longed for somewhere more comfortable to sleep, for the grooves in the deck planking made painful matching patterns on our behinds, and it was difficult to make the necessary shift in position without disturbing one's neighbours.

In this uncomfortable half sleep, I reflected on our predicament. First, of course, was the comforting thought that in a day or so we should be on terra firma in a friendly country, England or elsewhere. On the other hand, were the two unspoken fears – the fear of being attacked and sunk, and the fear of running into foul weather. As to the first, what would happen if we had to abandon ship? Even if discipline held, and it would be severely strained, some loss of life seemed to be inevitable. As to the second, what would happen to those of us on deck in an Atlantic storm? There was no room at all below decks, there were people sitting on the floor even in the washrooms and lavatories, and the smell was awful. And if we had to abandon ship, what would happen when all those battalions came crowding up to escape?

On the whole, however, hope predominated. In our minds and our conversations, the British had become glorified as our saviours. They had saved us from falling into the hands of the Germans and were offering us yet another chance, despite the precariousness of their own situation.

We scarcely dared to think of those German boasts that once France had fallen, the occupation of Britain would be a 'piece of cake'. If we had sometimes doubted that the British would get us to Britain, we also realised that if the Germans did take Britain, there would be no further escape. The dominions and colonies of the British Empire were far away across the sea. Of course, it was possible that we were being shipped to Canada, but that was a very long way away, not only from the Germans but also from fighting them.

We were all having similar thoughts. We speculated endlessly about our destination, our time of arrival, the reception we could expect, and what we would be allowed to do. On that score, we were more or less agreed that if we were being taken to England and if an invasion was expected, we would be directed to help defend the country and that, since there would be no time for flying training, we would all be drafted into the army.

We talked and thought into the night, till we were rescued by sleep from the morbidity of our thoughts.

The ship's galley started issuing rations. At first light, we had to take our place in the long queues which stretched from bow to stern. This time we collected a tin of fruit, a tin of bully beef – something we had never tasted before – a packet of biscuits, and drinking water to fill the water bottles. Our mugs, which we had brought with us in hope, were filled with strong, very sweet and lukewarm tea. Since all that had to last for twenty-four hours, we carefully divided it up and ate the portion we allocated for the morning. Then the four of us returned to the task of dealing with the camera. It was something to concentrate on; a task in which even Mat and Jurek joined.

Inside the camera, everything was caked with salt, and signs of rust were already beginning to appear, so each bit had to be cleaned and oiled again. Even so, we seemed to be fighting a losing battle; we completed the dismantling by midday and hoped that in the long term, it might just be possible to save the camera, provided it received profes-sional attention the moment we got ashore.

Miet was meticulous in his work. I had to admire the way he had kept notes and even more, the delicacy with which his, strong, short and stubby fingers held the tiny parts, and manipulated the equally minute tools and almost invisible screws, gear wheels and springs. It was a joy to watch. Two hours later, the camera was back together again. The only problem was that we were left with a tiny spring and a small screw!

'Where the hell do these belong?' he asked himself rather than us as he checked his notes. 'I could have sworn I recorded every bit and crossed it off as it went back.'

He operated the camera, the film advancing mechanism worked, the shutter worked, the aperture setting worked – and that had been the trickiest assembly of all – but the exposure time did not. It was apparently permanently stuck at one twenty-fifth of a second. However, so long as one remembered this limitation, the camera could be worked. So I loaded the second film in case there was anything interesting to record – there was at least a fifty-fifty chance of success.

Now that the job was done, I was the butt of some

good-natured leg pulling.

'You could have bought us a super meal for those twenty dollars,' ribbed Mat.

'And we would have had a good blow-out to remember,' added Jurek.

Miet, who had been so opposed to my buying the camera in the first place, came to my rescue: 'But you lot would have been the first to ask for pictures.'

They could only agree.

The borrowed instruments no longer required, I ventured to the crew deck. Luckily I found their owner and thanked him for the loan. He withdrew my cigarette case from his pocket. 'Better have this back,' he said, 'and good luck.'

Dusk fell as we began our second night at sea. The rigging sang in the wind, creating an eerie sound in the superstructure. From the distance came a cry, 'Cigarettes, chocolates, matches…'

It sounded like another poor joke. Then out of the darkness there loomed real figures distributing real cigarettes, real chocolates, real matches. Furthermore, our benefactors assured us that there would be hot soup for breakfast. Everyone collected their share, and general barter ensued between the smokers and non-smokers and the chocolate-eaters.

Our second morning on board was dry, warm and dull. We had not seen the stars the previous night; now we could not see the sun. We had completely lost all sense of direction. However, thanks to a suggestion from the crew, we devised a new distraction. If we all walked in the same direction, we could walk and stretch our legs. Who started it and who called a halt was a mystery, but we walked round and round the deck in a perpetual procession, all at the same pace, like a large flock of mindless sheep. It proved very popular.

Time dragged on, and all we could do was speculate. The fourth morning dawned to reveal a clearer sky and a visible sun, from which it was possible to deduce that we were now steaming east. Our escort had vanished. Then, over the horizon, we could distinguish columns of smoke rising from invisible ships. Afternoon came, and we spotted land ahead and to our right. Everyone tried to guess where it could be, and many tried to draw maps of possible coastlines from the dim recesses of remembered schoolboy geography. The general consensus of opinion was that we were approaching the west coast of Britain. Attempts to elicit information from the crew proved fruitless.

During the night, the sound of the engines indicated that we had reduced speed. There were those who fancied they could make out a faint coastline on our left, by the light of the stars. We eagerly awaited the morning.

The sea was calmer than it had been for the past few days, the wind had dropped but there was a new dampness in the air. Perhaps it was the mist which shrouded us. Then, through it, land could be seen on our left. It now seemed that we were steaming south parallel to the coast. Finally, well into the morning, a large city with a jutting harbour materialised out of the mist. Our ship edged forward. The water seemed full of ships, some already bearing the scars of war. We lined the rails, several deep, watching everything that was going on. Slowly we nosed our way into the harbour, while all around was the bustle of a busy port, ships being loaded and unloaded, people milling about on deck and ashore. Even at this stage, no one would tell us where we were.

Then Captain Bednarczyk turned up with the two officers and told us we were in Liverpool, and that we would be disembarking in an hour or two, and we were to wait. In the excitement I completely forgot about my camera, and no one reminded me.

We docked with the help of a tug, and hawsers were passed ashore and fixed to the winches. The dockside was crammed with people men and women in all sorts of uniforms, many completely unknown to us; cars, lorries, vans and barrows. Faces were upturned, scanning the rails as we berthed, as if they were seeking friends, or maybe just to see which nationalities were included in this latest collection of arrivals.

The ship finally stopped and was moored; gangways were slung out and connected us to land. When our turn at last came to land, our captain wanted us to march off down the gangway but this proved itself not practical so we joined in the general movement down the gangways. Finally, we stood on solid land once more but the slight heaving movement of the ship was still with us.

We gathered round Captain Bednarczyk, he formed us up to look like a disciplined unit with a mild suggestion that we should sing a marching song when we moved off, saying that it would make a good impression. So we marched a few hundred yards toward the harbour building, singing lustily in Polish, and every one around turning to look at us.

We had arrived in England, the Land of Hope and wondered whether it was also be the Land of Glory.

Part Two

England and Onwards

An Interpreter

Someone in broken Polish suggested that there was YMCA van with tea and sandwiches waiting round the corner. Immediately it was surrounded by a thick mob.

Did we expect a tea as we knew it, with sugar and lemon? And sandwiches – '*kanapki* or *zakaski*' as most of us understood the word? – Delicate small appetisers.

Out of a shiny urn came a brown liquid very hot disbursed in all manner of mugs and there were trays of sliced bread with something between the slices. Tea, in the English fashion with milk was a surprise to most, sandwiches were fairly soggy, a few with a leaf of lettuce or a tomato sliced up, from some, protruded slices of pinky grey meat – it was called 'spam'. Hungry and thirsty, with the ground still heaving as if on the sea, we were grateful, drank the tea and ate the sandwiches which, whilst not of high class and delicate, were well and gratefully appreciated.

Soon we were mustered, sized, formed in a column and having been ordered to sing, marched off to a nearby station with a fat, middle-aged English Military Policeman leading; we were to embark in the waiting train the policeman indicated in sign language. There was a tobacconist and a newspaper stall on the platform. I had my half-crown piece handy; it has been always with me, carried for months in a secure pocket. I crossed the platform and asked for a *Daily Mail* and packet of cigarettes. It is difficult to remember what they cost but I was given change, enough for another packet or maybe even more and was presented with a box of matches.

'Do you all speak our language?' enquired a surprised news vendor.

'No, but a few do,' I disabused him.

'Well, anyway – welcome and good luck,' he said, offering me one of his cigarettes and a light; I turned to rejoin my mates with the *Mail* sticking out of my pocket.

The cigarettes and matches were immediately popular, but many strangers in the open carriage looked suspiciously at the newspaper which I opened and ostentatiously put up to read.

'You read English?' several of them queried.

I nodded my head. It was all about the disasters of war, evacuation from France; Dunkirk was a name mentioned everywhere; the threat of the Germans bombing found its place in the paper. There was also a mention that the last of the few evacuation ships arrived from the French mainland at an unnamed port, brim-full of several Allied nations as well as few British, evacuated via France's Western coast. These snippets of news were being lapped up by my companions.

It was a short train journey, maybe an hour which we spent looking out of the windows, seeing Ack-Ack batteries manned and waiting; rather sad and serious-looking faces of the population. To my mind came the picture of my first glimpse of France only a few months back, how different: happy smiling faces, many skiers in the Alps as we crossed through Modane on the way to Lyon, and Jurek suggesting that we jump the train and join them.

A small station forecourt was full of large lorries waiting for us to climb on board.

An English soldier stood by the tailboard counting us as we climbed in. Thirty to a lorry and no arguing. A string of vehicles moved off and soon we were out of the small town and driving in the countryside. Where to? Everyone wanted to know.

The English soldier's mouth was twisted in a smile in a reply to many Polish questions but he uttered not a word other than 'wait'; I translated, '*Czekaj.*'

Indeed we waited helplessly and after a while we were driven through a large gate into a large nice looking park, with sparse old oak trees growing among a town of tents.

We stopped – one lorry to a tent.

'Your tent – unpack your luggage and wait,' a soldier said hoping that he would be understood.

I translated the words and thought of the humorous side of the word 'luggage' to describe what we had between us to unpack. We were delighted to find inside camp beds with clean blankets and pillows. Outside were arrowed directions Cookhouse, Toilets and Wash tents.

Our officers arrived after a few minutes.

'We march as a Company to the cookhouse to feed, then you are free – make yourself as comfortable as you can.'

To a question 'Where are we?' and 'What is to happen?' they said that they knew as much as we did.

A little later we were outside a field kitchen. There was a pile of metal dishes, mugs and eating utensils and we were invited to take a dish, mug, knife, fork and spoon and wait.

Food was served from large field kitchen containers, steaming hot – brown stew – potatoes and vegetables – wet overcooked cabbage and carrots, but it all smelled good and the black coffee was more than welcome.

We sat on the dry grass to eat in silence and afterwards were directed to long troughs of steaming water to rinse our plates and irons. All very strange.

Two or three days passed. We may have been told that we were in a park belonging to Lord something or other but were no better off for knowing where we were and what was to happen. There was no news from anywhere but we were each given a few shillings with which to visit the Salvation army tented canteen – dispensing tea, coffee and buns, cigarettes and a few newspapers.

On the second day, the newspapers of the previous day were given away free not having been sold; not many in this throng knew English.

It must have been about the fourth day when Captain Bednarczyk arrived, 'Nahlik – here you are wanted!' he shouted.

'You speak English and have an engineering education. You will be sent immediately to an RAF unit to interpret at an RAF commission which allocates our people to RAF trades.

'I understand that as *szeregowiec* [aircraftman second class] you will be paid two shillings and sixpence a day with a sixpence interpretership allowance. I will bring you your papers later, be ready to leave after breakfast tomorrow.'

It was thus that I was sent to my first job in England. I wanted to fly – instead I was to be 'an interpreter'.

I was put on a train, placed in the care of a train guard who told me after two or three hours that we were arriving. The train stopped and I got out. There was not even a board giving the name of the station.

There was an RAF man with two chevrons on his sleeve. 'You a new interpreter?' he asked, looking suspiciously at my French air force dark blue uniform, a blue beret and a striped dirty shirt – the only one I had.

'Follow me,' he said.

There was a small truck outside he got into a driver's seat and told me to sit at his side; we were off.

The RAF unit was called Insworth Lane – the board outside said No 6 School of Technical Training. There were rows upon rows of identical looking black wooden huts some small some large.

We stopped and left the truck. He made for a door and I

followed into a long corridor; he knocked on a door.

'The new interpreter, Sarge,' he said to a man sitting behind a table.

'Sit down,' said the sergeant, and taking out a large form started asking questions; name, place and date of birth, working right through all personal information including education, links with air force, flying, engineering etc.

He gave me a critical look, 'You can't walk about in this garb,' he said, 'no one will know what you are, they will arrest you for being a refugee or a spy on our air force property. I'll take you the stores they will give you proper uniform and things; you will then be shown to your hut and your bed; get organised there quickly. I will send someone to take you to tea in the airmen's dining hall. Tomorrow, after breakfast, you report here at 9 a.m. and I will take you to the board president. My name by the way is Sergeant Smythe and the unit we belong to is called Verification Board – this is the administration office and I am the NCO in charge.'

'What is NCO, sir?' I asked.

'NCO stands for a non-commissioned officer and that is what I am – you address me as sergeant not sir, keep sir for the officers.'

He took me to the stores. I was given riches of a new uniform, boots, shirts, socks, underpants, tie, pyjamas, cleaning utensils even towels, washing and shaving utensils. I noticed POLAND shoulder flashes tacked on the tunic. All this to be packed in a long round white bag which they referred to as kit-bag. In the days to come I learned how to pack it all inside and how to carry the handle-less piece of luggage.

A man from the stores took me to one of the huts.

'Make sure you remember the number – they all look the bloody same,' he remarked. 'The rows are marked by letters, the number indicate the hut in the row. And here is

338

your bed and some of your mates.'

The first bed was empty bed so I took it. There was only one other man perhaps a few years older than I sitting on his bed looking a bit forlorn. He was wearing an RAF blue uniform.

'Welcome,' he said in Polish. 'My name is Henio Milicer, what is yours?'

I gave him my name.

'The gliding man from Lwow and candidate for better things in gliding?' he inquired.

'The very same.'

We shook hands.

'You here to interpret?' he asked. 'There are three others who also arrived a few minutes ago who are being kitted out, so we will be five altogether,' he said.

He himself had arrived the previous day; we would all go to the verification board the following day for an interview with the president who had himself only just arrived.

*

We all walked into a large room and saluted.

There were four RAF officers sitting at small tables all old enough to have served in the previous war and the medal ribbons they wore must have been of that war. Two wore RAF wings – one pilot one observer, others had none. The first of them was a wing commander – Board President said a label in front of him with his name – it may have been Crawford or maybe Campbell.

'Come and sit,' the wing commander said. 'You are the first interpreters – welcome. Let me explain what is happening.

'We have your ground-crew people starting to arrive tomorrow and hope for more interpreters and board members. The board have to interview each ground crew; the interviewees have to satisfy us that the information they have given is true and accurate so that we can decide their trade allocation by our air force criteria – we call it mustering into trades. To do this we will question, virtually interrogate them and your job will be to interpret our questions to them and their answers to us.'

He explained that they were all engineering officers. Their air force and ours needed good ground crews to efficiently service complicated aircraft.

'They are all from France, recently arrived and in time, would be trained in servicing detail, but have to prove that they know the trade basics. The board and through them we have a serious responsibility to ensure that your countrymen are allocated to the right trades and given responsibility they are able to discharge. It will be hard going. The aim, for each member of the board, to interview fifteen to twenty ground crew a day and hopefully more as experience is gained. They hoped for more interpreters and a few more board members. They expected about 8,000, maybe 10,000 ground crew to be seen.'

We spent the rest of the day talking to the board members, all senior RAF officers, being briefed on the type of questions we would have to translate.

At the end of the day Henio asked for an English-Polish technical dictionary.

There was consternation. 'There isn't one available,' they said, 'you'll have to manage without.'

By the end of the day, three more interpreters arrived together with some clerical staff who were to complete the basic administrative detail on the verification forms. Some had been in England for several months having volunteered for service with the Polish RAF VR units being formed earlier since the end of 1939. Our little Polish colony grew and filled the hut, but we were not supposed, even allowed, to mix with those coming for the interview until after they have been interviewed, when usually they were sent on their way back to wherever they had come from.

We felt a little cut off from the Polish news but as the technical ground crew came and went we managed to collect snippets of information about a number of holding units and depots where our air force was trying to get organised the RAF way.

Our verification work was incessant; interesting for the first few days and calling for much concentration. Many were the occasion when we were addressing the RAF officers in Polish and our compatriots in English to the mutual consternation and sometimes laughter. Starting soon after 8 a.m. and working with a short break for lunch we were at it often until 6 p.m. As a compensation for our efforts we were issued with free tickets for the camp cinema, which had different film every other day. I found myself sleeping through the performances on more than one occasion. Sundays were free days, so we went into Gloucester where we tried to make contact with the locals whom we found very friendly. This is how I made my first contact with the First World War RFC pilot who lived a walking distance from our work, and worked in Gloucester.

The day came when one of the ground crew coming through was number 10,000; in the evening of that day the president of the board took the entire permanent contingent, RAF and Poles out to a local pub for a drink. I remember enjoying it hugely especially when it was announced on our return to camp that we were closing operations that week having accomplished our task.

Before our departure the president gave each of us interpreters a farewell interview, thanked us for the work we have done paid us a special 'bonus' of a nice new crisp five-pound note and promised to put in a word with his authorities to ease our way to the jobs we wanted. Most of us wanted to fly so he hinted that those who wanted to fly could go to RAF schools to learn to fly RAF aircraft; as we spoke English we should not have to wait for the formation of Polish units and schools. Our spirits were high...

And so Henio and I, at the end of our first RAF secondment, found ourselves in a train on our way to a place, meaningless to us, called Blackpool, to the Polish air force depot.

*

Blackpool did not boast of RAF facilities of any sort. The domestic and working accommodation was in hotels, and boarding houses, training took place in dance halls and larger places of entertainment. That was how we were to live; the smarter hotel, those on 'The Front' the Promenade, were for officers, we, the lesser beings, were in smaller hotels and boarding houses in the side streets. All this we learned at the billeting office at the railway station, on arrival where we were allocated accommodation in a hotel; ours was No 56 Lonsdale Rd, called the Lonsdale Hotel.

It was meal time when we arrived. We were shown to our allocated room, which we were to share with two others, by a young woman who, we learned later, was the daughter of the owners. We were then directed straight to the dining room filled to the brim with our countrymen. When they heard where we had spent the preceding weeks, they were anxious to know more about our work with the RAF and especially what the English were like to work with.

It was thus that we were introduced to the taste of fish and chips, the staple high tea diet of the seaside and to the smell of its deep frying, which we were to recognise forever after.

A few days passed in blissful adaptation to the new surroundings, to meetings with old friends and new friends,
exchanging gossips and news. We were not allowed too
much time to ourselves however, 'keep the troops busy'
was the motto of the hierarchy.

A few days after our arrival, Henio and I were ordered to
report to the office of the deputy commander of the Polish
depot.

'We had a note from the RAF officer for whom you and
some others worked on ground crew verification. Very
complimentary – well done.' After a few minutes of general
talk during which we were kept standing to attention he
came to business.

'Stand easy,' he ordered. Although there were some
chairs in his office we were not invited to sit, after all he
was lieutenant colonel in the Polish air force!

'You,' he turned to Henio, 'with a full engineering degree, will go to the ITW [Initial Training Wing] to interpret
at lectures conducted by the British. Mainly courses for
ground crew, the navigator and radio-operator training.'

'You,' he turned to me, 'will act as an interpreter at the
billeting office. As you know we live in hotels. The numbers are growing daily, our people do not speak the
language and so not surprisingly there are misunderstandings and problems. You will interpret between the hotel
management and our people – sort out misunderstandings.
You will need a bit of diplomacy, many of these are in the
officers' hotels. In addition you may be called to help
elsewhere at meetings and conferences as a back-up to
No. 1 interpreters who are officers. You cannot act as No. 1
on your own account because you are not officer rank.'
With that he handed us a piece of paper with the name of
persons to report to and address of the office and a tram
ticket to take us there.

To give some idea of what my job entailed I will try to

describe one of the more typical encounters.

I was sent to Hotel – let us call it Esplanade.

'Captain X is accused by the management of misbehaviour.' The standard forms of misbehaviour were either misunderstandings over food, insufficient, poor quality, badly cooked. The other 'misunderstanding' was over being caught taking a girl to the bedroom.

It takes little imagination to understand that living without work in a place like Blackpool with women, deprived by the wartime conditions of boyfriends, husbands etc., were delighted to accept the 'Polish traditional gallant hospitality' usually in a variety of forms.

Of course there were standard excuses – we were just going up, I was to give the young lady a present, a box of chocolates, (it could have been pair of stockings, show family photos etc.) leaving little to the imagination as to the innocent reason for such visit.

It could have been even worse; there were occasions where the discovery was made early in the morning with the lady sneaking out of a bedroom, or an officer and the friend still in a bed when someone entered to make up the bed! How does one pacify the offended parties? In the final analysis it had to come to an end by apologies, promises not to do it again or, with a terse management – an enforced immediate change of hotel.

Of course for an AC2 interpreter (like a private soldier-interpreter) it was not always an easy life to battle on behalf of one's 'seniors and betters'.

The redeeming feature were occasional, if rare, calls to London to the Polish HQ to help in their interpreter pool, usually attending meetings which could roam from administration, terms of service, to training, discipline – Polish Law versus King's Regulations for the RAF, even attending, as an interpreter, the visit by the top commanders of the Polish forces, often well-known colonels and generals. One such was with the colonel, commander of the Polish fighter force to a fighter base outside London, to witness and listen to a post-sortie debriefing by the squadron commander (at that time always an RAF officer). It so happened that on that occasion some Polish pilots broke the flying discipline by attacking an enemy aircraft against the squadron commanders order, who, during the debriefing, did not mince his words: 'When I order you to keep in formation I expect you to conform. You also know that chatting in Polish on the radio is prohibited – the reasons are clear. The fact that those of you who broke formation and shot down an enemy aircraft is not an excuse – I repeat not an excuse. Next time I will have you court marshalled for disobedience of operational orders.'

My commander understood enough of what was being said. 'Translate word for word and you can comment to enforce, I will then speak,' he ordered, puce in his face.

I did as instructed. 'Who was it broke the orders, step forward,' he instructed as soon as I finished.

Three stepped forward. He addressed them in his English so that the squadron commander could understand, 'I envy you and I congratulate you on your success. I deplore your lack of discipline and I suspend you from flying.' There was consternation.

The squadron commander asked to speak to the colonel but outside.

'Sir – thank you for backing me but I am short of good pilots, could you see your way of letting them off?'

'Most irregular but the war is on – I think it is a generous move on your part – but I will not hesitate to do it and will not be persuaded if it happens again, you will report to me directly if there is a repetition.'

We walked back to the dispersal hut where there was a babble of excited conversation. The colonel ordered silence.

'Your squadron commander pleaded with me on your

behalf; I am prepared at his request to withdraw the suspension this time. I repeat *this time* and no more, next similar incident, and whoever breaks the discipline will be sent somewhere to a non-flying job, maybe even to instruct.' He stormed out from the dispersal, jumped into our waiting car nearly forgetting that I was with him.

He uttered only one thing on the return journey. 'Undisciplined bandits,' he said with a smile.

To Gain RAF Wings and Polish Pilot's Eagle

Bad luck can't last for ever, mine also did not last.

After several months of the interpretership Purgatory, during which I attended the Initial Training Wing lectures sufficient in numbers to sit the exam as u/t (under training) pilot, I won my case. I was to be sent to the elementary flying training school at Carlisle for retraining first on basic Magisters then to advanced flying training at Montrose for real flying Masters and Hurricanes.

Elementary training nearly ended with a disaster.

My instructor, a middle-aged flight lieutenant, had a smirk on his face when he read my papers.

'So you are already an experienced pilot I see,' he started looking at me, 'you are an interpreter, you have been to university – a clever youngster, I see.'

I did not like his tone and had a feeling he did not take kindly to me.

'We will soon see,' he said. Was there a threat in his voice?

He had three other budding pilots, all three starting from scratch. He started with them giving each about thirty minutes.

After refuelling he beckoned to me.

'While the Maggi is refuelled,' he started, 'you know our throttles open and close opposite to yours, open – full throttle is forward, throttle always on the left side of the cockpit, next to is mixture control. Speed is in mph, altimeter is in feet and you set it to the level of the airfield at Zero. Yes I know you know it all, you have been through the ITW. Let's go.'

He supervised my getting the parachute on, then strapping myself in, not a word, just tested that the harness were tight to his liking.

The propeller was swung by a ground crew and the engine fired immediately.

He tested the earphones. 'Can you hear me?'

'Yes I can,' I answered. I was so excited that I spluttered the words.

'Didn't hear you – speak clearly – after all you are an interpreter.'

He taxied to the take off point and turned into wind.

'You have flown before – would you like to try a take-off?'

I said yes and showed him, 'Thumbs up'.

I opened the throttle, nothing happened before I realised that I opened the Polish way.

'It's meant to go forward,' – did he add 'idiot?' I was not sure because he opened the throttle.

At full throttle we were swinging – I tried to control – too much – the swing was in the opposite direction.

'I will take her,' he said and shook his head. When we were airborne he muttered, 'I thought you knew it all.'

I looked round we were turning left the airfield was below and at the end of wing tip. He was climbing on full throttle without a word.

Above 3,000 feet he came on the earphones. 'Do you like aerobatics?' he inquired.

'Yes, sir,' I answered.

He dived for a loop, lost direction in it, then made a half-slow-roll at the top, dropped his nose and tried a flick roll which finished in a spin.

He half closed the throttle and told me to take over and do a power glide towards the airfield. Once I gingerly lined up on the airfield and still at some height he came through again. 'Okay, I've got her.' I could feel his fairly firm hand on the stick. He landed and offered me to taxi to the dispersal.

When we were walking back to the Flight hut he made a few comments, 'You lost your head, forgot that throttle opens forward, you could not keep straight, I did not think you enjoyed my aerobatics, but the landing approach was not too bad. I could see you flew gliders.'

We never grew to like one another, he always referred to his twin-engine experience and did not think much of the 'Flash Fighter Boys' which I wanted to be. He held me back longer than I felt necessary, even the first solo which I expected to do after a few flights took a long time and lot of flying.

It was a relief when finally with 'Average' assessment I left Carlisle on a week's holiday before going to the service school at Montrose.

How different.

The Masters were the new Mark Two with radial engine Mercury 800 hp; more power than I have ever flown or handled, with modern constant speed propellers, complex cooling, retractable undercarriage, large flaps for landing, full instrumentation – a big machine. Our Polish P11 fighters had engines with about the same power in their Gnome-Rhones.

My instructor was 'Chipps', ex-fighter pilot, recently commissioned with a double DFM on Hurricanes. We immediately took to each other. In my eyes he could do no wrong. He had three of us, all Polish, as his pupils and his opening remarks were, 'I intend to teach you how to be fighter pilots, if you want to be anything else I will ask for you to be transferred to another instructor.'

Chipps was true to his word, he adored aerobatics and from the first flight gave me the feel of the possible combinations of figures. He also believed in instructing with 'hands-off'; it was rare, from the word go to feel his hands (or feet) on the controls. He talked his pupils through flying and probably showed only how things should be done if they were done badly by us.

An illustration of 'Chipps' method comes from the following experience.

We were flying at some 5,000 feet indulging in complex aerobatics and hugely enjoying ourselves. Chipps instructed me to do a climbing roll; as we went into it with the engine at full throttle complete silence enveloped us, there was a propeller blade firmly in front of me not even 'windmilling'.

'Engine's failed,' Chipps announced, 'we'd better look for a suitable field to land – too far from base. She is yours, you have practised forced landing now you can do it for real.'

By now we went out of the manoeuvre and were gliding losing height.

'Switches off?' he asked. 'Better let the flaps down to 15 degrees it will make our descent shallower – you will have to pump.'

I had switched off as soon as the engine failed and now selected flaps down and pumped, looking for a suitable field. There were several but mainly smallish ones and with typical Scottish stone walls surrounding them. One was a little bigger and seemed to be more or less 'into wind'. Just as I finished contemplating a voice came on the intercom.

'Have you selected a field for landing?'

I described the field.

'The one along the woodland edge?' he asked.

I confirmed that it was so.

'Good one,' he agreed 'she is all yours, just tell me what

you are doing if you can.'

I described my plan, 'Glide down wind, then turn and approach doing as many 'S' turns as needed to lose the height, if necessary side slip on the final approach.

'Just watch that you don't stall,' he said in a very matter-of-fact voice. 'Just one suggestion – land on the diagonal and if you find that the field is too short try to get the wing into the stone wall and not the engine – the wing will crumple gently, the engine may break back. Still all yours,' he confirmed.

We were at 1,000 feet on the approach doing 'S' turns. The field looked smaller and smaller as we got close: I must have murmured something like 'very small' which he heard.

'Yes, I agree but it is better than most,' he said encouragingly, 'I think you better sideslip to lose height and just get over the near wall, and leave your port wing slightly low, you will have to go into the wall at the end of the field. Still all yours – are you tightly strapped in?'

With that remarked we just cleared the wall in a gentle sideslip and touched the ground with the belly just like a sailplane.

'Good,' came over the intercom. 'Now the...'

I think he was going to say 'the wall' at the very moment that the port wing engaged the stone work. There was an enormous noise, a few stones flying, then the engine struck the wall with a heavy jerk and all went quiet except a slight ticking of the engine metals cooling off.

'You okay?' Chipps asked. 'Get out quickly just in case.'

We both unbuckled our seat harness and jumped out; there was no indication of fire anywhere.

'Well done and you did it all alone, I never touched the controls,' was all he said and smiled at me.

Two days after the accident I was called to the office of the chief flying instructor, a highly decorated wing commander.

'Chipps submitted his official report on your forced landing. The investigation shows that the engine seized up, there was a fault in the oil system. But that is not the reason why I called you in. Chipps says in his report that the forced landing was done from the beginning to end by you, that you talked him through what you were doing and he was happy to let you go on. He put your own life and his life on the line and that proves to me what an excellent instructor he is; importantly, how well you have performed and how cool and confident you were throughout; it does you credit.'

I thanked him for his kind words and confirmed that I thought that Chipps was a marvellous man and a splendid instructor.

Towards the end of the course we had been destined to fly a Hurricane. Two of these were on loan from the a squadron which had a detached flight at Montrose.

Chipps came with me to explain the cockpit layout and give me full pre-flight briefing. There were no two-seater Hurricanes so it had to be the first solo in the first flight.

I was exhilarated and frightened. A real Hurricane! And Chipps flew one in the Battle of Britain.

As always his briefing was careful and full. He helped me to strap in and stood on the wing as I started the engine.

'Off you go then,' he said before jumping off to the ground.

I taxied carefully to the taker-off point, looked round, turned into wind, made a sign of the Cross and opened the throttle. Soon I was airborne.

Flaps up, undercarriage up, propeller pitch, adjust boost to climbing, turn across the wind at 600 feet. I could not believe it – I was flying a real Hurricane. I was to fly two circuits around in visual contact with the airfield and come down.

It was the smoothest landing I ever managed. The aircraft came to a halt, I turned to the taxiway and taxied back to the dispersal where Chipps was waiting.

'Very good, good landing,' was all he said.

We walked back to our own dispersal. Everyone wanted to know how it was flying a real Hurricane. The words failed me.

At the end of the day Chipps asked if I would like to come to have a supper with him and his wife. He lived some way away so he offered to pick me up.

It was a jolly and happy evening but I was there with a heavy heart. I decided that in return for all that he has done for me I must share my colour perception problem with him. I did that when Mrs Chipps left us to wash up and we sat with coffee and drink.

I started with the painting, went through the ways of bluffing my ways through the medical and ending that sometimes, when I saw a colours signals flashed especially rocket signals, I was unsure of the colour.

'Why are you telling me all this?' He finally asked when I finished.

'I felt I had to be honest with you. You gave me a pair of new wings I would feel unworthy of your efforts if I had not told you the whole truth.'

He nodded his head, thinking. 'I wish I knew what to say,' he slowly muttered. 'My duty would be to go to the chief flying instructor and tell him. He would have to ground you, send you to medical board and this would be the end of your flying. It would be waste of your flying talent, you are a natural.'

I was moved by his words and he obviously said how he felt. His wife walked in and sensing something serious afoot excused herself with a headache and left us.

After a long while Chipps looked me in the eye.

'I value your honesty, and respect you even more for it,'

he started. 'I understand what flying means to you but you know that you will all be sent for a medical before the course ends. What will you do?'

'I will have to decide for myself, and can not involve you any further,' I answered. 'I will do my damnedest to find a solution, whether I cheat again the same way or find another way at the moment I don't know.'

'I will keep to my side of the bargain,' he said, 'and will tell no one unless my authorities ask me a direct question.'

We left it at that and he took me back to station for a disturbed nights sleep.

A few days later a few of us at a time were being sent for the medical board. I was in the last but one group, about two weeks away. I had a few friends among the budding pilots and two of these knew of my problem. One asked me a direct question, 'Will you get through?'

I had to be honest and said that if there was no change in the method of testing I would probably pass.

'I will go in your place,' he offered, 'it is not likely that the doctors will remember me from my own appearance at the medical.'

And so it was. I travelled with the group, but my friend went for the eye test.

Chipps was waiting for our return, saw me and his eyes asked the question. I said nothing just gave him a thumbs up signal to which he responded in a similar way.

Another two weeks and the course came to its end. We were awarded our RAF wings and returned the logbooks with certificate of assessment. Mine said EXCEPTIONAL with a star. One could do no better.

There was a final dinner party for new fledged pilots, instructors and wives. I sat with Chipps and his wife.

'Keep in touch,' he said before the party ended and Mrs Chipps gave me a kiss both cheeks, 'and look after yourself,' she added quietly.

★

We were all posted to various non-operational units as pilots before being sent to a fighter operational training unit (OTU) the aim was to give us at least fifty hours more flying experience. I was sent to Cleave in Cornwall mainly to tow targets for the anti-aircraft artillery in Henleys and Lysanders. Henley was a version of Hurricane built to be a low level bomber and we had to learn how to bomb in between the target towing sorties. On Lysanders we were towing also but were regarded also as reserve for ferrying underground agents to or from France.

It was dull flying with a red drogue on a 3,000 feet of steel hawser, flying always over the sea off shore, on a pre-set course at definite height. The crew was a drogue operator who let out and then wound in the drogue and released it before landing.

On one of the sorties our engine caught fire and smoke billowed from under the cowling.

'Cut drogue!' I shouted to the operator on intercom.

I called up the local flying controller and told him of our predicament.

'I will not make the airfield, it is too far,' I told him, 'I will do a belly landing inland of the artillery camp, please send fire team.'

'Good luck,' he confirmed. 'Fire on the way with ambulance.'

I told the operator to strap himself well in, tightened my own harness. By this time we were overland passing over the camp at about 1,000 feet with engine switched off and fire extinguishers hopefully operating. There was a strip of grass along the road with some large boulders; the best there was I decided, pumped down the flaps and we were down bouncing off the boulders with a nightmarish noise.

The machine stopped, smoke was choking.

'Get out!' I shouted to the operator – there was no answer.

I got out, unbuckled my parachute and returned to see what the operator was up to.

He was slumped over the winch barrel, probably knocked himself out during landing. Fortunately he was not a big man and I managed to drag him out hoping that he had no broken bones, for my dragging would not have helped him.

By the time I got him laid out on the grass an army ambulance was at our side and took over quickly, followed by the RAF fire truck and ambulance.

The engine was by now well alight but fortunately the fire did not reach the fuel tank.

After a local medic checked us both we were sent to Cleave in the army camp commander's staff car and with a bottle of whisky each.

After the formal inquiry I received a CinC's commendation and a posting to a fighter OTU.

The Squadron

The squadron was No. 308 Polish Squadron, on a rest in Hutton Cranswick in Yorkshire. It was equipped with mark Five Spitfires. I was allocated to 'A' Flight and after the long chat with the squadron commander and flight commander was introduced to the flight pilots and ground crew. As a newcomer I had to be introduced to what was called 'real flying'. My 'real flying' tutor was Flight Lieutenant Tad S., an old experienced hand as pilot but barely three years older than I. He came from the mountains, his father was a well-known brewer.

It was a nice spring day and Tad and I sat in two deck-chairs to chat. After a while he stopped.

'Enough of this social chat – now to work,' he said. 'We are short of aircraft, I have my own as one of the seniors, you will have to take anything that is allocated to you for each flight. We will go up shortly. Formation take-off we will climb to about 5,000 feet when we are at that height I will indicate to you that I am breaking off and I will play a Messerschmitt trying to get on your tail. When I am on your tail I will make machine-gun noise on the radio, when you hear it, waggle your wings, and will do the same again. All the time not only you have to shake me off, but try and get on my tail, if you succeed you make a machine-gun noise and I will waggle my wings. If you succeed, I owe you a drink.'

We collected our parachutes and walked to the two Spits, his was FZ-S, I was allocated FZ-K. Engines started, we taxied to take off. Tad stopped cross wind at the end of the runway then turned into wind giving me time to roll on to his wing, that done he opened the throttle and in no time we were airborne.

At 5,000 feet he indicated breaking off, and in a high speed diving turn vanished.

I saw him in my back-view mirror and turned so tightly that I blacked out.

'Well done,' he called. But within seconds I heard the machine gun call in the radio, there he was on my tail.

'Try again.' Again he broke off and I immediately started turning not to lose him, at one moment we were approaching each other head on at a high speed and I broke off to the left, he passed behind and I went after him in a half roll and vertically down.

I could not line up on him but only by a small margin, he turned and twisted and lost me – suddenly he was just not there.

'Got you!' he shouted. 'Now your turn.'

I broke off, dived and then pulled up almost vertically rapidly losing speed. My machine trembled at the stall and went into a spin. When I recovered from the spin I was barely at 2,000 feet.

'Return to base,' Tad called. I looked around and realised I was not sure where we were. In the distance I spotted Hull and the river and that gave me clue and made for our airfield.

We landed separately.

'It was a good getaway by sharp climb and allow the machine to spin. Were you lost?'

I had to admit that for a moment I was, until I found Hull on the horizon.

'Two lessons from this – one, never be lost, always know where you are and how to get back; two, you must try to turn as tightly as you can but without blacking out, often tight turn with a bit of side slip confuses your follower. For real if you spin to get away carry on spinning a bit longer, allow yourself just enough not to prang at recovery. But good for the first time.'

These lessons happened at least once, sometimes twice a day if there were spare machines to fly and different seniors took it turn to instruct.

Came the day when the flight commander called me.

'I am in the readiness section, you will be my number two. There may be a German weather recce flying in from Norway. We will probably be sent to intercept if he comes far enough towards us.'

It was only barely fifteen minutes later that we were at 25,000 feet off the Yorkshire coast. The flight commander leading, whilst I, a newcomer, was on my fifth operational flight as his wingman. We had been scrambled to look for the 'bandit', possibly a German weather reconnaissance from Norway, a frequent but irregular intruder over the British coastline. It was bit of operational flying for the squadron on a rest from the busy area of 11 Group around London and a good practice for the newcomers, like myself, when it happened. This was for real the aim was to at least chase him away, ideally to destroy him.

Below us the cloud, through which we had just climbed, was thick. At our altitude we were in sunshine, but flying in and out of the cloud-tops, steering East under the direction of a controller: 'Thrush control – this is Thrush red one, we are angels 25, vector 095 – over.' I heard the flight commander reporting that we have reached the altitude as directed and were still flying East.

'Loud and clear, Thrush red one, Steer 105, bandit 15 miles dead ahead – over and out.'

The flight commander looked at me over his shoulder; I could see his face in the perspex of the canopy. He gave me a thumbs up and I thought he smiled.

I tried to calculate. Fifteen miles we were flying at 250 mph; if the German was at similar airspeed, we were closing at 500 mph – we had barely two minutes!

'Bandit turning, Thrush red one, vector 180,' I heard the controller call.

The leading Spitfire seemed to slide sideways and I followed banking with him on to the new course.

'Thrush red one calling – vector 180,' confirmed my leader. We were now slipping into a higher bank of cloud and were almost entirely blanketed in a rain cloud. The windscreen, through which I peered with screwed up eyes, was covered with fast moving rivulets of water drops.

'Thrush red one – controller calling – bandit just below you a mile ahead, on vector 180 – over.'

'Red one acknowledged, bandit a mile ahead and below – over, out.'

'Thrush red one to red two – are you receiving me?' I was jerked back from my intense concentration; red two – that was me.

'Red two receiving loud and clear,' I confirmed. At the same time I noticed our airspeed increasing. In the clouds I had not realised that we were in a shallow dive causing the speed to rise.

'Stick with me, red two, whatever ha…' he broke in the middle of the word. 'Red one – tally-ho…'

I peered ahead; there, in the swirling grey cloud rushing past us, and no more than two hundred yards ahead was a deeper grey shadow like a silhouette of a Junkers 88. We were slowly closing in and getting below his tail level. I could see the target above my gunsight and somewhat to one side. Suddenly I realised that keeping station on the wing of my leader I had to open the throttle slightly; the silhouette was growing slowly as we closed in, still slightly above us.

I had my gunsight on and turned my safety ring on to

'fire', changed the propeller pitch to fine, all this was a standard drill. I glanced quickly at my leader rather than his aircraft, there he was crouched in his cockpit obviously his eyes glued to his gunsight. I realised that I was shivering with excitement? Or was it fright? Anticipation? I had seen a German aircraft before but usually as the hunted not the hunter.

We were about one hundred yards behind when I noticed the flight commander's aircraft shudder and I thought I could hear his canons or machine-guns firing. I had the starboard wing and engine in my sights and pressed the firing button. The Spitfire juddered. There was a puff of smoke from the Junkers' engine and his upper gunner was firing at us.

Then it all got enveloped in cloud. No Junkers, no flight commander and puffs of smoke from under my cowling.

I turned west, called the flight commander, 'Red two steering for home I have smoke from the engine; I am at 6,000 feet steering 270.'

'Controller to Red two you will see the coast as soon as you break cloud, steer 250 for base.'

'Red to controller – acknowledged.'

'Red one to red two,' came the flight commander. 'Are you okay?'

At this moment I broke the cloud and was just crossing the coast now at 1,500 feet.

'Red two okay but more smoke.'

Then silence on the radio.

There was a lot of juddering and rough engine noise, I called and reported.

I did not try to converse on the radio – there was no time. There was a long grass meadow straight ahead, almost good for wheels down but I dared not risk it.

Just before touch down I switched off all electrics and there we were sliding smoothly through a sea of muddy surface. It was only then that I noticed concrete poles dug in as obstacles to enemy aircraft landing. One of these did no good to my port wing, swung me sideways and brought me to a standstill.

It was not far from our airfield. A truck with the squadron engineer and ground crew found me and I was sent back. Much interrogation first about the reason for forced landing than debriefing from the operational flight.

'You failed to switch the radio to receive after your last call,' chided the flight commander, 'we will keep it quiet but do remember for the future.'

The aircraft check confirmed that aircraft ran out of oil! Operations gave us a 'shared damaged probable' and my error with the radio was never mentioned.

Even with the squadron 'resting' life was exciting for me. Every flight, every opportunity to gain experience was exhilarating.

About two months after joining we were sent for the air to air-firing practice in Norfolk.

I was not new to deflection shooting so shooting at a moving target, in our case a drogue towed by an other Spitfire, was only different to partridge shooting by speed and need to 'fly the gun platform' the aircraft to a deflection shot position and fire at a target moving at 200 mph or more and not 35. The reflection ring sight mounted in front of the cockpit was an enormous help. I managed to score maximum hits, a result which made me feel good and 'scored' me brownie points.

The growth of my confidence was very rudely interrupted soon after we moved to the front-line airfield at Heston as a part of the Northolt Wing.

We were on a sweep over northern France when I got an attack of appendicitis. I had to curl down in the cockpit to reduce pain. I was useless in the squadron and a liability.

I called my flight commander, 'Thrush leader, this is red

five; I have a very hard pain in my guts, could be appendix, am returning to base.'

'Thrush leader to five, okay Thrush, four will escort you – good luck.'

Curled in the cockpit I flew an uneasy trip home with my escort's help. We reached Heston and the escort reported to control for both of us. It was hard trying to see out which meant to straighten up in the cockpit to see over the aircraft nose.

Finally on the ground I turned towards the dispersal and as soon as I was away from the main field, switched off.

There was an ambulance and a doctor at the side and they helped me out.

Appendicitis was diagnosed but hopefully not a burst appendix. I was sent to hospital.

Little did I know at the time that this was the last day of my operational squadron flying.

Conflicts

The operation was successful even if its aftermath was to become a serious personal tragedy.

I was sent on convalescent leave which was of little interest, all I wanted to go back to the squadron. In fact with little else to do and short of ready cash, I spent most of it with my friends living in the mess and living the life of the squadron but without being allowed to fly for a month.

Just before my month was up I was called in to see the medical officer.

'Before you return to duties,' he said, 'you have to have a medical. I will do a preliminary but the medical will be in the hands of the medical board in London.' He gave me a good going over and pronounced me fit.

'You'll get your instructions in a few days,' he said on my departure.

A few days, true to his word I was given some papers, a warrant and a little money with instructions to report to the Central Medical Establishment, just off Regent's Park.

Those in the waiting room were all aircrew who, having been to hospital for any surgery, for health or wound, were in a need of consultant's clearance. Little did I know however, that it was also a practice to give the aircrew, at the same time, a full flying fitness medical board.

I remembered my colour test plates which were generally used so with little apprehension, towards the end of the process I finished with the ophthalmologist.

Out came his book, and not always seeing the coloured

dots which I was expected to see, I sang out what I learned by heart by reading the tiny page numbers.

'This looks fine,' said a young doctor, 'but we also have a new method, which we are still trying out.'

He drew the blinds on the windows, dimmed the lights. My heart was sinking fast.

'In front of you is a small screen, you will see lights of various density and in different places on the screen, tell me what colour you see.'

By now I was frightened.

Lights started flashing. 'Blue, red, green, blue again, yellow,' and so on I was singing not sure of what the colours were.

He switched on the lights. 'Just wait a minute,' he asked and left me.

He came back with a senior consultant with a four rings of a group captain.

'Polish air force pilot, sir,' he addressed his senior, 'would you like to take over?'

'The specialist tells me that your colour perception is suspect,' he opened, 'I will check you myself.' He repeated the briefing. The light went out. My heart was in my throat – I was feeling sick.

'Red, blue, green, red again, yellow, blue,' and so it went on.

He finished finally and was shaking his head with anxiety. 'I think we have a problem,' he said. 'Your colour perception is not up to the usual standard even if you seemingly can see the plates, the lights test is below standard for pilots. How much flying have you done?' he enquired.

I told him that I had flown since I was sixteen and gave him my flying hours. He enquired about my proficiency assessments and was obviously impressed with two 'exceptionals'.

'You should be grounded, he continued, but on account of your experience and proficiency I will allow you to carry on – Non-operational duties only – however. But it will have to be confirmed by the executive branches of our and your air force. Sorry, but these are the sad facts of life. Good luck.'

I tried to plead.

'It's no good, I understand your feelings, my rules are clear and I can not cheat them.'

No bombs were falling on London any more, but a bomb had dropped on me!

I went to the Polish headquarters where I had a few senior contacts. I shared the problem with them. They were all very sorry, promised to do what they could, but warned me that RAF rules were strict.

'Plenty of very essential flying you could do with your experience,' most of them would say, 'this is not the end. You are a budding engineer, maybe test pilots school, maybe Central Flying School and instructor's course.

They tried to encourage me but all of them knew that my heart was in operational flying with the squadron.

*

Everyone was very sorry. Those in authority said that they would do what they could and would fight for me.

A few days later I was posted to tow targets for the Ack-Ack in Wales. It was said that while my destiny was being finally decided, I better do something useful!

It was a grass airfield on the Welsh coast near the town of Towyn. The pilots were a mixed bunch of nationalities, ages and ambitions. We flew Hawker Henleys, exactly as I had done before and also did our low level bombing practices as we did in Cornwall.

One day I was given a different assignment.

'There is a new hush-hush radar being commissioned near Aberystwyth, it has to be calibrated. They need someone with operational flying experience – you will do the job. Take a machine, find the location – you can't mistake it they have three high radio masts, over-fly them, call them on the radio when you are ready to do what they want.'

If anything was dull, this was a dull job. I had to fly various courses, at different heights and speeds while the crew calibrated their equipment. I did not even know exactly what it was all about.

After a few days of this, I telephoned and invited myself for a briefing: they to tell me what they were doing, I to tell them what my limitations were.

In the perspective of time the detail of our meeting escapes me but what stuck in my mind was the presence of two good looking WAAF officers – radar supervisors. We were due to have a dance in the officers' mess so I asked if they would like to come.

They had to come by train, those with cars had no petrol and the use of air force cars was not allowed.

The dance was a success. One of the girls was a very good dancer. The band struck a Viennese waltz, my favourite; I asked her if she would like to waltz.

'My grandmother's favourite dance,' she said as she got up to join me.

It soon transpired that whilst she was good at the 'popular dances' waltzes were not her strong dance.

'You don't call whatever you are doing waltzing,' I said to her laughingly.

The smile dropped from her face, 'I am not used to your type of waltzing,' she answered sternly with blazing eyes. 'We better return to our table.'

We did as she suggested. I did not realise how hurt she was, nor did I know then that she would be reminding me of the occasion for fifty-odd years, for we were married about a year later...

Non-operational

The air forces suffered shortage of experienced pilots and not only in the squadrons.

The industry, now geared to wartime requirements and backed by the USA, were producing hundreds of aircraft which had to be flown to various destinations mainly in the UK. This was the job I was sent to, stationed at Croydon, the old airport serving the capital – London. It was amusing to see that in this highly industrialised country the municipal airport was not flat; it sloped down from the southeastern corner, and had no runway!

I was interviewed on arrival by the unit CO, a DFC squadron leader, Wally, who having served in a Hurricane squadron for a year was sent to a an air-sea rescue unit where he won his decoration 'fishing out' aircrew from the English Channel flying an amphibious pre-war machine the Walrus.

A short stocky individual with a sense of humour; his number two was also a fighter pilot Jackie, by name, one of the early MacIndoe's guinea pigs with a badly burned face and made famous many years later having been arrested and imprisoned in Lebanon where he then lived, released after nearly two years, I think in 1995, and died sadly a year or two later having been awarded a CBE for his strength and resistance to Arabs.

'How many hours' flying have you?' asked Wally, opening the interview.

I handed him my logbook.

He browsed through it. 'Two exceptional assessments I see, Masters, Hurricanes, Spits and Henleys,' he commented, 'total about 2,000 hours, since you started in Poland in '37. Are you on a squadron rest?' he asked.

'I am only non-operational flyer,' I answered blushing. 'The medics discovered I was colour-blind and downgraded my category, having threatened me with cheating at the initial medical board.'

'How interesting,' he said. 'How did you cheat them? They are not easy to cheat.'

I described how I learned by heart the coloured numbers which test the colour vision, each page in the test book had a tiny sequence number which I could read.

'Good on you,' he roared with laughter, 'but did it bother you at all?'

'Only sometimes when we were night flying looking for the Luftwaffe at night, but it helped when we were sent to spot the army camouflaged in the field, I could see what others could not, I was looking for shapes, not colours.'

Wally described the role of his unit.

'We fly anything within the flying training and fighter command, one or two engines. You have no twin experience, we will teach you how to fly twins. There is no time for a formal conversion course so you have to use your wits, relying on basic couple of hours on a twin-engined Oxford, in the army co-op unit here; after that Jackie will brief you about others like Baufighter and Mosquito and generally look after that end, if time and opportunity allow you may be given a couple of circuits and bumps with an experienced twin pilot.'

'We get our task daily from Fighter HQ and aircraft production, the admin corporal prepares the chits which authorise the collection of the aircraft and its destination, we fly pilots to their start of points, and try to collect them in the evening, but some times return is by train. You will always have a couple of spare open railway warrants, and you will be provided with a car from the airfield to the railhead if you ask for it.'

I was sent to collect a parachute, set of maps, allocated my lockup for flying clothing, shown how pilots planned their trips and sat chatting with the other pilots in the crew room mainly about the job; two Frenchmen, two Czechs, three Australians, a Rhodesian, a South-African, and US Eagle squadron on rest, and several RAF. Three with burned faces and hands in addition to Jackie.

After a while Jackie took me round to meet the ground crews and then to introduce me to the station commander, a Great War flyer.

Initially I was sent to fly Hurricanes and Spitfires, sometimes a smaller communication aircraft. I was given dual on a twin engines, first an Oxford in a local army co-operation unit then a D-H Dominie Rapide, ex Imperial Airways, used now for taking pilots round the country.

The day came when I was sent to collect and deliver a Typhoon from the factory to Duxford where the first Typhoon squadron was formed, rearming from Spitfires.

The factory pilot gave me a briefing:

'I suppose like the other buggers in your unit you have never flown a Typhoon,' he said.

'Never,' I confirmed, 'haven't even seen one that close to.'

'It flies like a Hurricane but has double the power and nearly double speed, pulls on take off and swings on landing, the large engine makes a forward visibility poor. Sit down, have a look at the pilots' notes, then I'll show you the starting procedure, cockpit layout and you have to be off within thirty minutes, they want you at Duxford before 3 p.m. Bad luck, no lunch but I will get you a sandwich to munch instead.

Later on he took me to the Typhoon just rolled out and

was fuelled outside. A nice looking if a little frightening machine with a bulbous nose of large cowling over the 2,000 hp engine.

The cockpit was more or less like a Hurricane. He explained the cooling which was controlled by a ring of radiator grilles. 'Watch the temperature when taxiing – gets a bit overheated.'

With that, while he helped me to strap myself in and start the engine he waved me good luck, and waved me off on my first Typhoon sortie.

The torque of the powerful engine pulled like mad on take off, but once in the air all became fine and I enjoyed the flight, setting course for Duxford.

Thirty minutes later Duxford was under my wing, Air Traffic flashed a green light and I came in to land. At the bottom of the grass runway was a truck waving me to follow, so I did as bid and taxied to the dispersal of the squadron. This was their second Typhoon – I was popular.

'How do you like Typhoons?' asked the squadron commander, who climbed on the wing to greet me.

'This is the first time I have flown one – seems okay,' I said.

There was sign of doubt in his face.

'Where were you retrained?' he asked as I was releasing myself from the parachute harness and packing the chute in its bag.

'At the factory before the take-off, by the test pilot,' I said innocently.

I heard the Dominie approaching spot on time – I was taken to the air traffic control tower where I was to be collected by our 'taxi'.

It was not always that easy going. We flew in radio silence and often got a bit lost, literally landing at an airfield asking where one was and taking off for the destination. Sometimes English weather played tricks and closed in when we expected good flying conditions. One of these ended for me with a Spit on its nose in the perimeter fence of a small army airfield, for which I was duly reprimanded.

I will never forget the excitement of the Russians joining the Allies in the war against Germany. We sat in the crew room when the announcement was made. I was very downhearted.

'This is the end of the Germans,' someone said very loudly. 'Don't look so gloomy, you'll be going home soon, the Ruskies will liberate Poland.'

'I think I would rather have the Germans for allies,' I said angrily, 'I don't trust the Russians.'

There was a hum of tense disbelief in the crew room, they looked at me as if I was a heretic.

The following day I was called to the station commander's office. As I was shown in by the adjutant I saw two civilians in black jackets and pinstriped trousers, wearing some club or Service ties.

I saluted on entry.

'Good morning,' said the station commander, 'let me introduce, Mr White and Mr Smith, they are interested in the comments you are alleged to have made in the crew room when you heard about the Russians coming into the war on our side as Allies.'

My very thin ring of a pilot officer on my sleeve looked very insignificant against the station commander's four wide rings. The civilians observed me with a grey, expressionless interest.

'I believe you speak English,' asked one of them.

'Yes I do,' I confirmed.

'Good,' said the other. 'Now about the alleged offence...'

'I do not understand what you are talking about,' I interrupted, 'in the first place I committed no offence, in the second place, who are you, gentlemen?

'Sir,' I turned to the station commander, 'who are these gentlemen, may I ask to see their identification? Mr Smith and Mr White, names which are not uncommon, who are they?'

The station commander turned to the visitors, 'Any comments, gentlemen?'

'As an opener I will say', started one of them, 'that if you did express the views about our Russians as they were reported, you committed an offence, it was subversive comment. In response to your question however I can say that you are right our names are not White and Smith, what they are your CO knows, and he also knows that we represent the intelligence security.'

'Now what do you say?' he demanded.

'Unlike any of you three gentlemen in this room, I can say that I have been a prisoner of war taken by the Russians during the 1939 Polish War; I escaped and made my way here via France. This proves I suppose that I am a true ally. None of you I guess have experienced the Russians. I have and I know the Germans too. I hate the Germans for starting the war, I hate the Russians for helping them and all I can say from my personal experience is that at least the Germans are, if nothing else, educated and have a recognised culture, the Russians are a wild mob.'

There was a consternation in the room.

'I think, Group Captain,' said one of the civilians, 'that we will forget this incident – if you are happy that is, but I have to warn the pilot officer here to be more careful in the future.'

'Thank you,' said the GC. 'I think I applaud your attitude. Let's close the case. Go back to your work,' he said turning to me. I saluted and left.

Towards Freedom?

The fortunes of war started turning in the Allied favour. The German attack on Russia and the US entering into the war after Pearl Harbour seemed the winners tipping the scales. The Allied might could not now be beaten. Slowly there was a chink of light suggesting that we would be returning to Free Poland. Not today, not tomorrow but the war could not now be lost.

However there was still a war raging, aircrew losses were tremendous and there was a need for training new crews. It perhaps came as no surprise that the 'net' caught me up. Without depleting the operational squadrons, there was I, with good flying experience of well over two thousand hours flying, on many types of British and American aircraft, with excellent flying assessments almost obvious choice for an instructor.

Wally was by now succeeded by a one legged fighter pilot, by name of Coward – not Noel Coward. One day he called me to his office, a rare event for usually he did all his work in the crew room.

'I have news,' he opened, 'I am not sure you will like it. You are to be posted for instructor training at Central Flying School, and then to a Polish flying training school. Your liaison officer at Command HQ telephoned and asked if you could be spared. I know you like this job but that is not a sufficient reason for me to screen you. I have only one argument in your favour, at the moment you are one of the three who have experience of all types of aircraft we have to fly. It will take me a little time to build up at least two others. On this ground I can block your posting for a month or two but no longer.'

I seem to have been doomed. I thanked him for understanding my preferences and paying me a great compliment. Compliment or no, four months later I had to pack up and get ready to go. I was given a good farewell party at which I was told that I had been recommended for an AFC, but the Poles apparently wanted to give me something else and the AFC was dropped.

By this time the Polish air force had its own instructor training flight; it was there that I had been put through my paces on Tiger Moth aircraft, which I grew to like and enjoyed flying. What I did not enjoy was the atmosphere. Among the instructors I was the youngest, with more current operational aircraft experience than any. Most were pre-war officers, not acceptable for operational flying on account of age or health. Some were almost openly resentful of my flying record.

Among them were two with whom I struck up a friendship. Both came from Lwow, my home city, one was a regular air force pilot, famous before the war for his skill in aerobatics, the other a fellow student from the university. Both older than I, both with some internal complaint which barred them from operational assignments. In a manner of speech they saved my life.

We were in the mess bar one evening, soon after I became a fully fledged instructor. They were 'filling me in' on tricks of the trade which were not a part of the instructor's course.

'Make sure, that as far as possible you have "your own" machine to fly,' said the aerobatics whiz-kid. 'You will be able to make small unofficial adjustments, look after your ground crew, they will keep your machine clean and polished and always on the top line. There is more: the stick is mounted in a socket and secured by nuts and bolts, take these out and replace them with wooden pegs with the original nuts to look normal, but tell no one about it; it will hold the stick secure. In an emergency, you will be able to yank the stick out.'

'Why should I need to yank – as you say – the stick out?' I queried.

'In case you want to beat the student on the head,' he answered in all seriousness and our other companion agreed. I felt he was joking but both my friends assured me that it was a wise precaution.

I bought them a round of drinks and we changed the subject. At closing time the aerobatics wizard said, 'Hey – that joy-stick lark, it can be done but it is simpler if you in fact have a hefty stick always with you in the cockpit, it will do just as well and is not a court-martial offence like tampering with the controls would be.'

I was due for a two weeks holiday during which I was to be married to my WAAF radar friend from Wales. A few days before my leave I was up with a fairly new student-pilot who owned up to disliking aerobatics. The very thing that I loved.

Aerobatics were essential for completion of the course and inability to complete the sequence was a quick way of getting grounded or being transferred to a navigator or air-gunner training. My student assured me that he wanted to complete the pilot training; would I help him? I readily agreed.

The next flight I had with him we went as high as the poor Tiger would climb, and started an aerobatics sequence, a loop.

'I feel fine,' he called on the intercom. A slow roll, 'I feel fine again,' a spin, 'not so good but I am okay,' he came again. A stalled turn…

After a long dive we went into a vertical climb position, I

told him to close the throttle: he nodded but the throttle did not move.

'Shut the throttle and apply rudder,' I called. No reaction, I tried to close the throttle, it was stuck solid, I tried to apply the rudder before we lost speed, solid, I tried to move the stick back, solid.

In the back view mirror his face was white and his eyes were glazed; I realised that he had frozen on the controls.

'Let go all controls, I'll take over!' I yelled into intercom and looked in the back view mirror. I saw his face nodding as if in agreement but no change in his or my ability to control the aircraft.

'You will be able to yank the stick out, and beat the student on the head.' Words hit me back through a thin by now frightened memory.

I pulled out my stick which I now carried, I turned in my seat and hit the student on the head. His hands came up in defence – the controls went limp. I chucked out my stick and regained control of the aircraft.

After a while he came to. 'What happened?' he asked on the intercom.

'I will tell you when we are down, now take over, the airfield on your left side, lose height and land.'

He made a meticulous circuit of the airfield at the prescribed height and made a perfect landing.

When we signed off in the flight log, we went for a little stroll along the boundary.

'How much do you remember?' I asked. He gave himself a few seconds. 'We looped, and rolled and spun – I didn't feel very happy; we then dived and started going up... then a blank. Something hit me, we must have collided with a bird or something, and then you called and told me to land... Now my head hurts as if I had bumped into something.'

I told him exactly what happened.

'So now I will be chucked out, I suppose,' he almost whispered, 'that's the end.'

'Do you want to try again? I asked hoping he would refuse.

'If you are prepared to risk it, I would be grateful.' I remembered Chipps!

Epilogue

Most of us like to think that we, by our own choices, play a determinate part in our own futures. In our thoughts and dreams we echo the lines of the poet Henley:

It matters not how straight the gate,
How charged with punishments the scroll,
I am the master of my fate,
I am the captain of my soul.

Our faith teaches us that we have a choice in the ultimate destination of our soul. We learn by experience that we have no mastery over the fate which determines our lives on this earth. Certainly, few of us who were caught up in the central European maelstrom thrust upon us by the ambitions of Hitler's Germany were presented with choices of our own initiation. We have no control over the fate which determines when we are born, how long we live and when we die. It is the Will of God, not ours, which determines whether the lives of those whom we love extend past our own, are terminated unexpectedly or are agonisingly prolonged. And it is that same Will, which some prefer to call Fate, which brings us together and makes friendships just as much as it sometimes cruelly breaks them up.

The reader who has persevered thus far will have been introduced to a whole range of characters, many of whom I would never have met had it not been for the invasion of Poland. That war is now long gone, and with it many of the contacts with those who, at that time, played so great a part in my life. At first we tried to keep contact, which lessened into the odd Christmas card, and then nothing. Now in my late seventies as I write this, I can only draw on an imperfect memory.

At the end of the war I was offered a regular commission in the Royal Air Force. This required a change of nationality which I found to be a significant and emotional step, for it also meant the automatic loss of the Polish one. I did not wish to make a decision hastily, without adequate and appropriate preparation and conviction as to the consequences and motives.

In the search for a decision which would involve inevitable long-term changes of mental approach to the situation I found a compromise; small and weak it may seem, but under the circumstances it appeared persuasive and acceptable.

Some time at the break of the eighteenth–nineteenth centuries, the family had altered its name, for some reason or other, by abandoning the prefix 'de'. Therefore, I decided that I could use this opportunity and, with a treble concurrent change, start my new life. Apart from the change of nationality, I also formally by deed poll reverted to the previous form of the surname and Anglicised my Christian names.

In fact, we were starting a new family line. The decision process was made easier by the fact that Poland was not free and under Communist rule, but my part of Poland, Lwow and the south-east, had become part of Russia itself, later of Ukraine. I was not allowed to fly in the RAF in peace time, because of my defective colour vision, but I spent twenty-three very happy years, making many friends and visiting many parts of the world. After that I spent some fifteen years in industry and now, in my old age, I have been able to revert to one of my original passions, and am deeply involved in the management of game and deer.

Lwow and the surrounding district were annexed by Russia at the end of the war, and I have no idea what became of the family property and possessions which were confiscated and nationalised by the Russians in 1939.

My father, whose wartime experiences remain a closed book as far as I am concerned, was not reunited with the family until the end of the war. His experience in food production engineering, especially in cold storage, resulted in his playing a leading role in the post-war reconstruction of Poland and by the time he died in 1963 in his eighties he had become a leading adviser on cold storage to the Ministry of Food. I corresponded with my father after the war, but never had the opportunity to see him.

Of the rest of my immediate family, my mother, younger brother and sister, fled before the Germans as they attacked Russia, and again before the Russian counter offensive, moving from one place to another. Their history would fill another book. Now they live in post-war Poland. My mother, mentally alert, but bedridden and almost blind, died in 1995 aged one hundred and three. My brother became the curator of the Museum of Textiles in Lodz; he died in the '70s from tumour on the brain following a skiing accident, and his twin sister a theatrical designer for the Polish National Theatre after the war, lived with my mother in Warsaw and still lives there. The other sister Christine, who was evacuated to Hungary in 1939, eventually joined the order of Sacré Coeur as a nun, and was teaching mostly in Vienna, and lately having retired, was moved to the convent in Warsaw.

My Uncle Zygmunt and his wife fled to Spain where they were interned. By 1942 they managed to get to the USA, where he established a meat import/export business with the help of some pre-war business connections. After the war he visited Poland from time to time, and also called on us in London. Both he and his wife are now dead.

His stepson Ralph joined the Polish army in France. He took part in the raid on Narvik, where he was wounded and captured. The Germans released him because of his health and he made his way to the Russian-occupied zone where he met up with my family. Shortly thereafter he was arrested by the Russians and deported. After the war he was one of the few released from captivity in Russia to Poland on account of his very poor physical and mental shape; he was quite unable to settle down. Eventually, at great expense, Uncle Zygmunt managed to get him and his wife out of Poland to join him in the USA; they are now both dead.

My air force aerobatic hero, he who recruited me into pseudo-intelligence in Lwow, also escaped to France where I met him fleetingly. Three years later we met again as flying instructors at the same Polish air force flying school in England, by which time he was suffering severely from some chronic internal complaint.

Jurek waited for pilot training on arrival in England, got fed up with waiting and volunteered as navigator/bomb aimer. By the time his turn came for pilot training he had completed an operational tour on Lancasters. By a quirk of fate, he was allocated to me as a pupil. With his agreement, I asked for him to be trained by someone else as I did not feel it appropriate to instruct such a close friend. Jurek was my best man when I married. After the war he obtained his professional qualifications in veterinary surgery in Edinburgh and set up in Scotland. Later he moved to South America, and very sadly I lost contact with him.

Stan and Wasio continued to operate as a team for some time. Wasio was ultimately caught by the Russians, allegedly not for guiding people to Hungary, but for some other offence. He, like many others, disappeared. Stan just vanished. Jurek, who was his pre-war friend of long standing, tried to find news of him through his uncle who was a colonel in the Polish air force HQ in Paris and later in London without success.

John Chmiel joined the Polish army and was killed in either North Africa or Italy. Tom also got to England, I do not know how or when, and was killed quite early in the war flying as a navigator.

Miet, Mat and Szleg formed a close-knit trio when we first arrived in England. Szleg was not fit enough for aircrew training. Miet was turned down for pilot training and went back into engineering, first as an engineering officer and subsequently in aircraft industry. Mat, who was so keen to fly, managed to wangle his way into pilot training soon after I did. He got his wings and was posted to a wireless operator and gunnery school in Northumberland to gain flying experience flying on the much unloved Botha aircraft, before joining a bomber squadron which was his great ambition. He was killed with his navigator and a team of trainees under inexplicable circumstances in Northumbrian hills.

The professor and his wife were deported by the Russians and never heard of again.

Captain Pawel, who so generously took me under his wing in France and found me the opportunity to fly was found too old and not fit enough to fly when he came to England. He spent his years in a sequence of staff jobs and died towards the end of the fifties.

And that leaves Hala. Alas, I have never found her or any trace of her. I have tried during and after the war to obtain news, all without success. Her parents lived in the part of Warsaw which was bombed from the first day of the war to the day when the Russians entered the city at the end of the Warsaw uprising. Their house and the whole area was flattened time and time again and I never found them.

Poland, who lost her freedom in 1939 the preservation

for which Britain and France went to war, and which was not regained after the war became a Soviet Communist satellite behind the Iron Curtain.

In the post-war days under the communist regime a slogan was coined: *'Zeby Polska byla Polska'*. It has two possible translations, both of them valid and appropriate: 'For Poland to be Polish' or 'For Poland to be Poland's.'

★

Voices of those born since the war questioned whether the war was worth fighting at all. Millions died as a result of it; there can be little doubt than many more millions would have died if it had not been fought. Since the collapse of the Communist state in Russia both forces of great evil were checked. The West has enjoyed the longest period of peace for generations, and the gradual evolvement of people power seems to be disposing of the last remnants of ideological oppression but not without bloodshed in Europe or elsewhere. Without the war the moves and movements for national freedom could not have happened, not all of these are peaceful and civilised in their attempts to achieve their not always fair and peaceful objectives, but the human race seemingly does not know how to survive without wars and skirmishes.

There cannot be so many left who trod the path to freedom that I followed, and I hope that this account will not only serve as a record but also be a reminder of the unquenchable spirit of many who have perished so that others can live…